THE RELIGION OF ART IN PROUST

BARBARA J. BUCKNALL

ILLINOIS STUDIES IN LANGUAGE AND LITERATURE

60

UNIVERSITY OF ILLINOIS PRESS   URBANA, CHICAGO, AND LONDON,   1969

ACKNOWLEDGMENTS

I should like to thank, first of all, Professor Erich Heller, who helped me to see the complexity of the task I had undertaken, and which I was inclined to view too superficially at first. If this study is still superficial, it is not his fault. My thanks also go to Professor Ranganavan Iyer, who first pointed out to me the oriental character of Proust's thought, Professor Charles Whiting, who, as my thesis director, watched over the formation of this work, and Professor Philip Kolb, who made a number of helpful criticisms. In addition, I should like to express my appreciation of the encouragement I received from Professor Renée Riese Hubert, Professor Judd Hubert and Professor Stanley Gray.

Quotations from *A la Recherche du temps perdu, Pastiches et mélanges, Jean Santeuil, Chroniques* and *Hommages à Marcel Proust* are reprinted with the permission of the publishers, Gallimard, acting on behalf of Mme Mante-Proust. The Mercure de France publishing company has kindly granted me permission to quote from Proust's translations of Ruskin, *La Bible d'Amiens* and *Sésame et les lys*. I should like to thank E. P. Dutton and Co., Inc. for permission to quote from Evelyn Underhill's *Mysticism*. My thanks are also due to Princeton University Press for permission to quote two passages from Heinrich Zimmer's *Philosophies of India,* edited by Joseph Campbell, Bollingen Series XXVI (Copyright 1951 by Bollingen Foundation Inc., published by Princeton University Press, 1967). I should also like to thank Penguin Books Ltd. for permission to quote passages from Christmas Humphrey's *Buddhism* and a passage from K. M. Sen's *Hinduism.* Two passages are reprinted from *Proust* by J. M. Cocking, with the permission of Bowes & Bowes Publishers Ltd., London, and Humanities Press, Inc., New York. George Allen and Unwin Ltd. has given me permission to quote one passage from John Ruskin's *The Art of England and the Pleasures of England.* Finally, Routledge and Kegan Paul Ltd., the publishers of *The World as Will and Idea* by Schopenhauer, translated by R. B. Haldane and J. Kemp, have given me permission to quote from this work. My thanks are due to all these publishers.

CONTENTS

Chapter Eight

CHAPTER ONE

MEMORY, CONTEMPLATION, AND THE ARTISTIC VOCATION

As we follow the narrator of *A la Recherche du temps perdu* through the mazes of his search for truth and happiness, we find that there are only two things in life which bring him real satisfaction. These are, on the one hand, flashes of involuntary memory which restore the past to life in hallucinatory detail and, on the other, moments of aesthetic enjoyment, whether of works of art or of the beauties of nature, which bring him a feeling of intensely living reality, far surpassing any other moment of present experience. Unfortunately, as he reaches middle life, he loses contact with these two sources of joy. He first becomes aware of this while on a visit to his old friend, Gilberte, at Tansonville. There he plunges into a mood of acute depression because of his failure to respond as he used to when a child to the countryside around Combray. The Vivonne, for instance, seems narrow and ugly instead of being a beautiful river. He is saddened by thinking that his capacity for feeling and imagining must have diminished for him not to derive more pleasure from his walks around Combray. But, in his eagerness to let us know the importance of memory in his emotional experiences, Proust adds a word of explanation to warn us that the narrator is mistaken in supposing that his lack of response is really due to nothing but a failure in emotional capacity:

Non pas que je relevasse d'inexactitudes matérielles bien grandes dans ce que je me rappelais. Mais, séparé des lieux qu'il m'arrivait de retraverser par toute une vie différente, il n'y avait pas entre eux et moi cette contiguïté d'où naît, avant même qu'on s'en soit aperçu, l'immédiate, délicieuse et totale déflagration du souvenir. Ne comprenant pas bien sans

1

doute quelle était sa nature, je m'attristais de penser que ma faculté de sentir et d'imaginer avait dû diminuer pour que je n'éprouvasse pas plus de plaisir dans ces promenades.[1]

However, Proust's word of warning, since the reader has not yet reached the descriptions of involuntary memory which will explain what he means by "contiguity," remains obscure, and the tone of this episode is determined by the narrator's despondency. To add to this state of gloom, the narrator receives another emotional setback, on the same visit, when he reads what purports to be an unpublished extract from the Goncourts' diary, describing a visit to the Verdurins. Portrayed in a work of literature, the Verdurins appear so much more interesting than in his own experience of them that the narrator hardly knows whether to blame himself or literature. Is he lacking in the emotional responsiveness which enables a man to find the Verdurins interesting, or is literature deceitful in its power to endow boring individuals with a charm which they never possess in reality? But Proust is unwilling to allow us to entertain either of these doubts for very long. Swiftly, he slips in an indication that what is lacking in the narrator is simply the specific talent of a Goncourt, the talent which allows a writer to see and describe the surface of things. Looking over the narrator's shoulder, Proust gives us to understand that his talent is of a much more profound nature than that of the Goncourts: "Aussi le charme apparent, copiable, des êtres m'échappait parce que je n'avais pas la faculté de m'arrêter à lui, comme un chirurgien qui, sous le poli d'un ventre de femme, verrait le mal interne qui le ronge. J'avais beau dîner en ville, je ne voyais pas les convives, parce que, quand je croyais les regarder, je les radiographiais" (III, 718–719). But the narrator's self-confidence is to sink yet lower, as we follow him through "Le Temps retrouvé." Seated in the train which is carrying him back to Paris, the narrator finds himself acknowledging the beauty of the scene around him in a purely cerebral manner, with no accompanying emotional response: "Arbres, pensai-je, vous n'avez plus rien à me dire, mon cœur refroidi ne vous entend plus. Je suis pourtant ici en pleine nature, eh bien, c'est avec froideur, avec ennui que mes yeux constatent la ligne qui sépare votre front lumineux de votre tronc d'ombre. Si j'ai jamais pu me croire poète, je sais maintenant

---

[1] Proust, *A la Recherche du temps perdu*, texte établi et présenté par Pierre Clarac et André Ferré, 3 vols. (Paris: Gallimard, 1954), III, 692. All subsequent references to *A la Recherche du temps perdu* will be made by volume number and page only.

que je ne le suis pas . . ." (III, 855). This lack of response to a scene which ought to excite his admiration make him fall once more a prey to the gloomy belief that he is devoid of literary gifts and that literature, in any case, is a vain and lying art. This may seem an unexpected conclusion to draw. After all Sartre, in *La Nausée*, found a positive source of literary inspiration in a very negative reaction to a tree. But Proust is sufficiently in accord with the spirit of the nineteenth-century idealists to feel that a writer, no matter how many scenes of gloom and depravity he may depict, must, in the last resort, bring his readers a message of joy. If he does not do so, then, for Proust, he is no true writer. And, at this point, Proust offers his readers no reassurance that his hero's doubts are without foundation. He wishes to keep us in suspense, so that the moments of involuntary memory which are to flash upon the narrator may come with all the impact of a totally unexpected revelation.

The narrator's despondency, for the time being, is such that he makes up his mind to live only for frivolities, since he believes himself to be capable of nothing more worthwhile: "Ce n'est vraiment pas la peine de me priver de mener la vie de l'homme du monde, m'étais-je dit, puisque le fameux 'travail' auquel depuis si longtemps j'espère chaque jour me mettre le lendemain, je ne suis pas, ou plus, fait pour lui, et que peut-être même il ne correspond à aucune réalité" (III, 856). Consequently, he decides to accept an invitation to a reception at the Princesse de Guermantes's, largely because the name of Guermantes retains a certain magic charm for him. He no longer believes, as he once did, in the superiority of the aristocracy, but Guermantes is associated, for him, with childhood memories: "J'avais eu envie d'aller chez les Guermantes comme si cela avait dû me rapprocher de mon enfance et des profondeurs de ma mémoire où je l'apercevais" (III, 857). Memory and imagination appear to have deserted him, and yet, in spite of everything, he retains a real, though only partly conscious, faith in both. In spite of all his moments of disappointment and discouragement, he is still dimly aware that if he can regain contact with the enchanted world of his childhood his numbed faculties of awareness and creativity may somehow return to life. This faith is rewarded, for his visit to the town house of the Prince and Princesse de Guermantes is to release a flood of involuntary memories which will bring him overwhelming joy, restore his faith, by means of that joy, in his capacity for artistic creation, and inspire him with a subject and a method for the book he longs to write. Memory smooths the ill-paved roads leading to the Champs-Elysées, causing the movement of the carriage down the familiar route to be received in pre-assimilated, dematerialized form by the narrator's mind. All exterior obstacles are suppressed because he does not have to pay attention to them. His familiarity with them causes them no longer to exist, and so he is able to rise above them in that airplane-like movement which, for Proust, is typical of the creative writer. Did he not say of Bergotte that the mental vehicle which he was destined to use was no Rolls-Royce but that it was superior to a Rolls-Royce in that it was able to get off the ground? "Le sol de lui-même savait où il devait aller; sa résistance était vaincue. Et, comme un aviateur qui a jusque-là péniblement roulé à terre, 'décollant' brusquement, je m'élevais lentement vers les hauteurs silencieuses du souvenir" (III, 858). The narrator's memory has been set in motion; now one involuntary memory after the other will crowd in upon him, in almost incredible profusion.

The first occurs in the courtyard of the Hôtel de Guermantes when, stumbling on some uneven paving stones, the narrator is invaded by a feeling of inexplicable delight, a feeling which is the complete denial of his previous despair. However, he is not content to enjoy the feeling merely; he forces himself to identify and analyze it. In his introspective effort he recognizes that this sensation has several aspects. He is confronted with the same felicity which he had felt on several previous occasions, occasions which had differed in nature but which had all had the common property of resolving his anxiety and doubts. One occasion had been his view of three trees near Balbec, one the sight of the steeples of Martinville, and one the taste of a *madeleine* soaked in tea. So two visual experiences and one gustatory one are linked in the effect they had on him, an effect which has been repeated by the sensation of the uneven paving stones beneath his feet. Strangely, these are linked with an artistic experience, that of hearing the last works of Vinteuil. Although music has nothing to do with taste or sight, nor yet with touch, the music of Vinteuil had seemed to synthesize all these other sensations. This is a curious circumstance which Proust does not, as yet, see fit to explain. Even more strangely, the sensation of the uneven paving stones is enough to make him feel completely reassured about the reality of his literary gifts and the reality of literature:

Comme au moment où je goûtais la madeleine, toute inquiétude sur l'avenir, tout doute intellectuel étaient dissipés. Ceux qui m'assaillaient tout à l'heure au sujet de la réalité de mes dons littéraires, et même de la réalité de la littérature, se trouvaient levés comme par enchantement. Sans que j'eusse fait aucun raisonnement nouveau, trouvé aucun argument décisif, les difficultés, insolubles tout à l'heure, avaient perdu toute importance. Mais, cette fois, j'étais bien décidé à ne pas me résigner à ignorer pourquoi, comme je l'avais fait le jour où j'avais goûté d'une madeleine trempée dans une infusion [III, 866–867].

As he searches after the cause of his joy, he discovers that Venice has been restored to him, in a kind of risen body, more glorious than the earthly, limited body which had clothed it for the narrator during his actual visit.

After this, the chinking of a spoon against a saucer recalls, this time with pleasure, the view which he had watched so drearily from the window of his train. Then the sensation of a starched napkin touching his lips brings back a vision of the sea at Balbec, as much more glorious than the real sea he had then observed as his remembered Venice is more glorious than the Venice he had visited in actual fact: "Et je ne jouissais pas que de ces couleurs, mais de tout un instant de ma vie qui les soulevait, qui avait été sans doute aspiration vers elles, dont quelque sentiment de fatigue ou de tristesse m'avait peut-être empêché de jouir à Balbec, et qui maintenant, débarrassé de ce qu'il y a d'imparfait dans la perception extérieure, pur et désincarné, me gonflait d'allégresse" (III, 869). Spirituality and joy are the hallmarks of these experiences. This continues to hold true even when the memory aroused is one of a solemn, not to say distressing, experience. Thus, the sight of *François le Champi* in the library of the Prince de Guermantes brings back memories at once sad and blissful, since they are associated with the night on which his mother had first given way to his unreasonable demands, and also with a period in his life when literature had seemed like the initiation to a mystery.

The narrator speaks as if he believed these memories to be supplied by a kind of artistic providence, to justify the validity of creative art, in general, and to inspire him to creative endeavor, in particular. This has already been indicated in the passage describing his evocation of Venice. In case the reader had overlooked this expression of faith, it is repeated: "Alors on eût dit que les signes qui devaient, ce jour-là, me tirer de mon découragement et me rendre la foi dans les lettres, avaient à cœur de se multiplier . . ." (III, 868). This requires some explanation: on the face of it, there is no absolutely necessary connection between involuntary memory and artistic production. The connection lies, for the narrator, in the rather special nature of his experience of reality. Since leaving the enchanted world of his childhood, the narrator has been continually distressed by a feeling of discontinuity in time and of fragmentation in his sensory and emotional experiences. He feels as if each moment in his life, as it slipped from the present into the past, had been bottled (so to speak), causing its emotional content to be preserved unaltered but, by the same token, rendered inaccessible:

Le geste, l'acte le plus simple reste enfermé comme dans mille vases clos dont chacun serait rempli de choses d'une couleur, d'une odeur, d'une température absolument différentes; sans compter que ces vases, disposés sur toute la hauteur de nos années pendant lesquelles nous n'avons cessé de changer, fût-ce seulement de rêve et de pensée, sont situés à des altitudes bien diverses, et nous donnent la sensation d'atmosphères singulièrement variées [III, 870].

Voluntary memory can do no more than measure the vases and transcribe the labels; an act providing information without joy. But involuntary memory breaks the seal and even allows the contents of the vases to be decanted into one another:

Oui, si le souvenir, grâce à l'oubli, n'a pu contracter aucun lien, jeter aucun chaînon entre lui et la minute présente, s'il est resté à sa place, à sa date, s'il a gardé ses distances, son isolement dans le creux d'une vallée ou à la pointe d'un sommet, il nous fait tout à coup respirer un air nouveau, précisément parce que c'est un air qu'on a respiré autrefois, cet air plus pur que les poètes ont vainement essayé de faire régner dans le Paradis et qui ne pourrait donner cette sensation profonde de renouvellement que s'il avait été respiré déjà, car les vrais paradis sont les paradis qu'on a perdus [III, 870].

The present is permeated by the past, in the influx of involuntary memory, releasing the rememberer as well as his memories. No longer bound to the moment, he realizes that his existence is not limited to the infinitesimal point of the moment. Beneath his superficial self there lies a real continuing, essential self. Not only is this self essential; it is extratemporal, since it belongs neither to the past nor to the present:

L'être qui alors goûtait en moi cette impression la goûtait en ce qu'elle avait de commun dans un jour ancien et maintenant, dans ce qu'elle avait d'extratemporel, un être qui n'apparaissait que quand, par une de ces identités entre le présent et le passé, il pouvait se trouver dans le seul milieu où il pût vivre, jouir de l'essence des choses, c'est-à-dire en dehors du temps [III, 871].

It is the coming to life of this extratemporal self which explains his feeling of overwhelming joy, and it is on this creative spirit that the narrator will rely for the composition of his book.

Another effect of involuntary memory is to free the narrator from the fear of death — a fear which, at a subconscious level, may have been partly responsible for his gloom — by transporting him temporarily to a sphere where death appears irrelevant: "Cela expliquait que mes inquiétudes au sujet de ma mort eussent cessé au moment où j'avais reconnu inconsciemment le goût de la petite madeleine, puisqu'à ce moment-là l'être que j'avais été était un être extra-temporel, par conséquent insoucieux des vicissitudes de l'avenir" (III, 871). There is no question of freedom from physical death, or from the realization of its inevitability, since the narrator is to go straight from the room where his revelations were received into the salon where the Guermantes's guests unwittingly perform a masque of old age, folly, mutability, and approaching death before his astonished eyes. The years have touched him too, he is made to realize, although the time he had spent in two sanatoriums had concealed the fact from his knowledge. But he becomes aware of it through the laughter of some of the guests when he refers to himself as a young man. Immediately after this reception he receives warning that death, as well as age, has gained ground within him. While descending a staircase, he comes close to falling, three times in succession. He returns home in a state of complete exhaustion, and from then on is unable to shake off the idea of his approaching death.

The question of personal immortality is often raised in *A la Recherche du temps perdu*, but hardly ever in a way which suggests that Proust regards it as more than a pleasing illusion. Only two kinds of resurrection are seriously envisaged by him: resurrection of the past, through memory, in one's own mind, and the resurrection of the artist's vision, by means of his work, in the minds of others. This resurrection of the artist's vision is expressed with great eloquence in a passage on the last illness of Bergotte, in "La Prisonnière": "Il allait ainsi se refroidissant progressivement, petite planète qui offrait une image anticipée de la grande quand, peu à peu, la chaleur se retirera de la terre, puis la vie. Alors la résurrection aura pris fin, car, si avant dans les générations futures que brillent les oeuvres des hommes, encore faut-il qu'il y ait des hommes" (III, 184). Again, in the same volume, Vinteuil appears to the narrator to live on in his work: "Vinteuil était mort depuis nombre d'années; mais, au milieu des ces instruments qu'il avait aimés, il lui avait été donné de poursuivre, pour un temps illimité, une part au moins de sa vie" (III, 254–255). Art, therefore, offers to the artist the only probable immortality. At the same time, approaching death urges the artist to make haste with his creative endeavor. And yet, in an irrational way, the step to one side of time, by means of involuntary memory, seems to be felt by the narrator as offering some kind of refuge from time and death. This step is mental, not physical; but the emotional effect upon him is such that it might almost as well be physical.

Certainly, even if it offers no escape from physical death, involuntary memory brings increased life in the present. This is a very real gift, and one of incalculable value to the narrator. From the time of his entry into adult life, he has been cursed with an incapacity for enjoying the present. This is not only because of the fragmentary, discontinuous nature of his experience of time. It is also because of his preference for the spiritual over the material, a preference indicated by his pleasure in the pure, discarnate nature of his memory of Balbec, combined with his rather Romantic taste for strong sensations. Only involuntary memory can provide him with an experience immaterial enough to satisfy his mind and vivid enough to please his senses and emotions. Moreover, when preserved within a book, his memories will continue to live, outside time in that time will no longer have power to alter or destroy them, and yet in the perspective of time, which will allow each moment in turn to derive density, color, and richness from the rest. Thus, involuntary memory is justified as an aesthetic subject and an aesthetic method.

But not only memory is involved in Proust's aesthetic method. Spatial perspective also plays a part. We have seen that, in the passage describing the sudden joy he feels when stumbling in the courtyard, the narrator associates with the delight he derives from involuntary memory certain experiences which, at the time when they occurred, had little or nothing to do with memory, being primarily spatial in character. He says that, as his involuntary memory of Venice began to dawn, he was filled with the same felicity which he had previously experienced on viewing some trees near Balbec, on seeing the spires of Martinville, and on tasting a *madeleine* dipped in tea. The last of these instances provided the occasion for an involuntary memory — that which heralds the complete evocation of Combray, at the beginning of "Du Côté de chez Swann" — but in the other two cases it is a question of seeing a group of three objects from a moving vehicle. In the sequence of the narrative, as well as that of the narrator's experience, the episode of the spires precedes that of the trees. The young narrator, who is riding in Dr.

Percepied's carriage, feels a special pleasure on catching sight of the three spires of two villages, not far from Combray:

Au tournant d'un chemin j'éprouvai tout à coup ce plaisir spécial qui ne ressemblait à aucun autre, à apercevoir les deux clochers de Martinville, sur lesquels donnait le soleil couchant et que le mouvement de notre voiture et les lacets du chemin avaient l'air de faire changer de place, puis celui de Vieuxicq qui, séparé d'eux par une colline et une vallée, et situé sur un plateau plus élevé dans le lointain, semblait pourtant tout voisin d'eux.

En constatant, en notant la forme de leur flèche, le déplacement de leurs lignes, l'ensoleillement de leur surface, je sentais que je n'allais pas au bout de mon impression, que quelque chose était derrière ce mouvement, derrière cette clarté, quelque chose qu'ils semblaient contenir et dérober à la fois [I, 180].

He is fascinated by the way in which the spires appear to change position as the carriage moves. He comes close to taking note of his pleasure without analyzing it, but, because the coachman is not inclined to talk, he is forced for entertainment to concentrate on discovering the precise nature of the pleasure which the changing perspective of the three spires had given him, now that they are behind him and almost out of sight. This pleasure forms itself in words in his head and he is inspired to write them down, thus producing his first disinterested literary composition.

The three trees which he saw near Balbec were also viewed from a moving carriage, that of the Marquise de Villeparisis:

Nous descendîmes sur Hudimesnil; tout d'un coup je fus rempli de ce bonheur profond que je n'avais pas souvent ressenti depuis Combray, un bonheur analogue à celui que m'avaient donné, entre autres, les clochers de Martinville: Mais, cette fois, il resta incomplet. Je venais d'apercevoir, en retrait de la route en dos d'âne que nous suivions, trois arbres qui devaient servir d' entrée à une allée couverte et formaient un dessin que je ne voyais pas pour la première fois, je ne pouvais arriver à reconnaître le lieu dont ils étaient comme détachés, mais je sentais qu'il m'avait été familier autrefois; de sorte que, mon esprit ayant trébuché entre quelque année lointaine et le moment présent, les environs de Balbec vacillèrent et je me demandai si toute cette promenade n'était pas une fiction, Balbec, un endroit où je n'etais jamais allé que par l'imagination, Mme de Villeparisis, un personnage de roman et les trois vieux arbres, la réalité qu'on retrouve en levant les yeux de dessus le livre qu'on était en train de lire et qui vous décrivait un milieu dans lequel on avait fini par se croire effectivement transporté.

Je regardais les trois arbres, je les voyais bien, mais mon esprit sentait qu'ils recouvraient quelque chose sur quoi il n'avait pas prise, comme sur ces objets placés trop loin dont nos doigts, allongés au bout de notre bras tendu, effleurent seulement par instant l'enveloppe sans arriver à rien saisir. Alors on se repose un moment pour jeter le bras en avant d'un élan plus fort et tâcher d'atteindre plus loin. Mais pour que mon esprit pût ainsi se rassembler, prendre son élan, il m'eût fallu être seul [I, 717].

Here, the problem at the back of his pleasure is a complex one, since he is not certain whether the experience is spatial, temporal, or both at once. On the whole, he inclines to the last supposition. In the end, because his social duty to his hostess does not allow him to plunge into completely concentrated introspection, the nature of his impression resists analysis. He is left with a sense of frustration and failure, in spite of the joy with which the experience had begun.

In both instances, whatever memories may be associated with the group of objects in question, the narrator is bringing his analytical powers to bear on a part of visible, external reality, not on an inner vision. Consequently, the tool of his creative awareness is, in these cases, not memory but contemplation: that is, the sinking of one's cognitive faculties in a visible object, as an aid to introspection. As we shall see later in this study, contemplation is extremely important to Proust as a means of approaching both life and nature, and this attitude has led several critics to consider him as a mystic, since contemplation is a technique which leads directly to the mystic vision. But, for the moment, we are concerned with his treatment of spatial perspective rather than his tendencies to mysticism.

It is interesting to notice that, for Proust, spatial perspective, contemplated rather than remembered, is subordinate to the perspective of time. The carriage, moving in time as well as in space, provides, as Georges Poulet remarks,[2] the means of uniting, through time, the separate parts of space, the separate parts of time being united, in their turn, through memory. Whether Proust is dealing with space or with time, his concern is for spiritual integration. Time provides the means of integrating space, and memory that of integrating time. So physical perception is finally subordinated to a mental process, and thus spiritualized or, as Proust might prefer to say, unbodied.

Other means of gathering up the scattered fragments of experience and, at the same time, escaping from the normal limitations of reality, are offered by drunkenness and dreams, both of which appeal to the narrator, at certain moments, as interesting stimuli to artistic creation. But both are rejected as inferior stimuli, especially the first. Drunkenness is a treacherous source of inspiration, since it eliminates the desire to perpetuate the moment of joy in a work of art, and even destroys normal concern for the preservation of one's

---

[2] Georges Poulet, *Études sur le temps humain* (Paris: Plon, 1950), pp. 400–401.

life. Dreams are considered more seriously. They have always interested the narrator, because of the tricks they play with time and imagination, but they do not really provide a reliable means of recovering lost time. Escape from the limitations of physical, fragmented space and time must be conscious and sober to be creative. The escape must be made in such a way that its nature may be made accessible to the intellect, and expressed in terms accessible to other minds as a result.

The literary expression of this escape, of this jailbreak from the prisonhouse of matter, is provided by the metaphor which, by its nature, breaks through all conceptual restrictions, binding the most disparate elements together. For Poulet, memory itself is metaphorical.[3] Involuntary memory brings together widely separated experiences; therefore, since a metaphor brings together widely separated facts and concepts, it is appropriate to call involuntary memory metaphorical. The metaphor is thus a suitable means of expressing the experience of involuntary memory and the ideas to which it gives rise. Hence the importance of metaphors in the book which the narrator plans to write:

On peut faire se succéder indéfiniment dans une description les objets qui figuraient dans le lieu décrit, la vérité ne commencera qu'au moment où l'écrivain prendra deux objets différents, posera leur rapport, analogue dans le monde de l'art à celui qu'est le rapport unique de la loi causale dans le monde de la science, et les enfermera dans les anneaux nécessaires d'un beau style; même, ainsi que la vie, quand, en rapprochant une qualité commune à deux sensations, il dégagera leur essence commune en les réunissant l'une et l'autre pour les soustraire aux contingences du temps, dans une métaphore [III, 889].

The metaphor, in other words, becomes both a substitute for the normal modes of causation and an escape from them, since it places the object or idea enshrined within it beyond the reach of all forms of limitation, destruction, and change. A work of literature celebrating a sense of intellectual and emotional release through an experiential metaphor fittingly relies on metaphor to express that release.

The prominence, in "Le Temps retrouvé," of aesthetic and metaphysical ideas naturally leads one to assume that Proust must be relying on some philosophical system. But this system proves oddly elusive. Bergson is frequently named in connection with Proust. In a letter written in 1910 to Georges de Lauris, Proust expressed his

[3] Ibid., p. 401.

admiration of Bergson, an admiration which, however, is somewhat modified by Proust's avowal of his lack of familiarity with Bergson's most recent publication:

Je suis content que vous ayez lu du Bergson et l'ayez aimé. C'est comme si nous avions été ensemble sur une altitude. Je ne connais pas l'*Évolution Créatrice* (et à cause du grand prix que j'attache à votre opinion, je vais le lire immédiatement). Mais j'ai assez lu de Bergson et la parabole de sa pensée étant déjà assez décrivable apres une seule génération pour que quelque *Évolution Créatrice* qui ait suivi, je ne puisse, quand vous dites Bergson, savoir ce que vous voulez dire.[4]

In the same letter, a little further on, he described how he had reacted with instant contempt to his psychotherapist's contention that Bergson was "un esprit confus et borné."[5] In spite of his avowed admiration for Bergson, Proust was surprised, although certainly not disagreeably so, when some of his contemporaries suggested that he had been influenced by Bergson. He wrote, in this connection, the following statement to Camille Vettard:

J'ai tâché . . . de faire apparaître à la connaissance des phénomènes inconscients qui, complètement oubliés, sont quelquefois situés très loin dans le passé. (C'est peut-être, à la réflexion, ce sens spécial qui m'a fait quelquefois rencontrer — puisqu'on le dit — Bergson, car il n'y a pas eu, pour autant que je peux m'en rendre compte, suggestion directe.[6]

This letter, while denying conscious influence, leaves the door open to Proust's critics to find an unconscious influence of Bergson upon Proust. F. C. Green, in particular, finds numerous parallels between Proust and Bergson. However, in his analysis, these parallels turn out, again and again, to be similar turns of phrase (which may or may not be verbal borrowings) used by Proust to express an attitude which differs significantly from that of Bergson. So, in discussing the distinction which Proust makes between the deeper self, preoccupied with the essence of things, which is reached by the involuntary memory, and the superficial self, which is served by the voluntary memory, Green lays stress on the fact that Proust says that the voluntary memory merely combines or arranges homo-

---

[4] Marcel Proust, *A un ami* (Paris: Amiot-Dumont, 1948), p. 205.

[5] Ibid., pp. 205–206.

[6] Marcel Proust, *Correspondance générale de Marcel Proust*, publiée par Robert Proust et Paul Brach, 6 vols. (Paris: Plon, 1930–36), III, 194–195. A stronger denial of Bergsonian influence is to be found in an interview which Proust granted to Élie-Joseph Bois in 1913. In this interview, Proust insisted that his own distinction between voluntary and involuntary memory is not to be found in Bergson and that his novel therefore cannot be considered Bergsonian. Proust, *Choix de lettres*, présentées et datées par Philip Kolb (Paris: Plon, 1965), p. 287.

genous elements. In this expression, Green finds "a distorted echo or Proustian variant" [7] of a passage in Bergson's article, "L'Effort intellectuel." [8] In this passage, Bergson says that when we use our memory in an idle and dreamy way we call up images which are homogenous in nature although representative of different objects. Thus the word "homogenous" is used to characterize the representations both of Bergson's day-dreaming memory and of Proust's voluntary memory. But, having established this parallel, Green goes on to point out that, for Bergson, the voluntary memory can also descend deeply and intensively through the planes of consciousness, a feat which, in Proust's opinion, is reserved for the involuntary memory alone. Again, while discussing Proust's description of the invasion of the present by sensations from the past, Green suggests that this is "a typically Proustian rearrangement of Bergson's idea" of *le déjà vu*.[9] His strongest claim for Bergsonian influence in "Le Temps retrouvé" is founded upon Proust's use of the idea of duration.[10] But another Proust critic, Poulet, insists that there is nothing more erroneous than to compare Proust's and Bergson's ideas of duration, for the former saw duration as fragmented and the latter saw it as continuous.[11] A third opinion is put forward by J. M. Cocking, who maintains that, while Proust borrowed ideas and expressions from Bergson, Bergson was by no means the only, or even the most important, influence on Proust.[12] In view of this variety of opinions and Proust's own disclaimer, it seems reasonable to look for some other philosopher who may have influenced Proust.

In his *The Proustian Vision* Milton Hindus makes a strong claim for the influence which Schopenhauer exerted on Proust. It is true that Mme de Noailles has left us an account of the "indifférence presque discourtoise" [13] with which Proust opposed her recital of some pages of Schopenhauer, but she does add that Proust had revered

---

[7] Frederick Charles Green, *The Mind of Proust: A Detailed Interpretation of "A la Recherche du temps perdu"* (Cambridge: Cambridge University Press, 1949), p. 502.

[8] This article, which first appeared in the *Revue philosophique* of January, 1902, and was later republished in the collection *L'Énergie spirituelle* (1919), may not actually have been read by Proust, who, as we have seen, had still not reached the point in 1910 of reading a work of Bergson's which had appeared in 1907.

[9] Green, p. 504.

[10] Ibid., p. 500.

[11] Poulet, pp. 396–397.

[12] John Martin Cocking, *Proust* (London: Bowes and Bowes, 1956), p. 24.

[13] Proust, *Correspondance générale de Marcel Proust*, II, 23.

Schopenhauer in the past. It seems quite possible that Proust, having fully assimilated the ideas of Schopenhauer, may well have been bored by hearing them again at second hand, without, for all that, renouncing their fecundating influence on his work. Mme de Noailles may have been annoyed by Proust's indifference, but indifference is the reaction one is likely to receive if one insists on preaching, if not to the converted, at least to those long since proselytized. Not only did Proust read at least some Schopenhauer in school, but he must have encountered, in many other authors, ideas which were either derived from or similar to those of Schopenhauer. As Patrick Gardiner points out, the French Symbolists borrowed heavily from Schopenhauer in constructing their aesthetic theories,[14] while many of Schopenhauer's basic preoccupations are also those of an entire family of philosophers, ranging from Herder to Bergson.[15] Proust's awareness of life as a dynamic process may be shown to derive from Schopenhauer just as plausibly as from Bergson;[16] again, Proust's concern with relation and relativity, which led some critics to compare him to Einstein, is also typical, as Hindus points out,[17] to a marked degree, of Schopenhauer. But, as Hindus also observes,[18] the most striking similarity between Proust and Schopenhauer lies in the nature of the contrast which both establish between life and art, with art figuring as a salvation and escape from life. Certainly, much of the Third Book of *The World as Will and Idea*, especially paragraphs 34, 36, and 38, could provide a striking theoretical basis for Proust's aesthetic claims. For Schopenhauer, the artist, by means of a detached, nonutilitarian contemplation, lifts the object contemplated out of flux, out of the categories of space and time, and makes of it, by incorporating it in an art work, something both universal and eternal. Art, he says, is everywhere at its goal: "For it plucks the object of its contemplation out of the stream of the world's course, and has it isolated before it. And this particular thing, which in that stream was a small perishing part, becomes to art the representative of the whole, an equivalent of the endless multitude in

---

[14] Patrick Gardiner, *Schopenhauer* (Harmondsworth: Penguin Books, 1963), p. 212.

[15] Ibid., p. 185.

[16] Arthur Schopenhauer, *The World as Will and Idea*, trans. R. B. Haldane and J. Kemp, 3 vols. (London: Routledge and Kegan Paul, 1883), I, 145–154, 208–215.

[17] Milton Hindus, *The Proustian Vision* (New York: Columbia University Press, 1954), p. 113; cf. Schopenhauer, I, 8–9.

[18] Hindus, p. 30.

space and time." [19] There is a definite similarity here between Schopenhauer's theory and Proust's account of his narrator's aesthetic experience. Gardiner sees a connection here too, especially in the stress which both Schopenhauer and Proust lay on the contrast between the selfish, utilitarian attitude of our everyday selves and the complete, selfless detachment required of the artist, who must lose all awareness of himself as an individual as he is swallowed up in the contemplation of the object he is to depict.[20] We have already noticed, in this connection, the importance which Proust attributes to contemplation as an aesthetic technique. Also, although I do not think that either Hindus or Gardiner points this out, the role of Proust's singularly featureless narrator is strongly reminiscent of Schopenhauer's description of the knowing subject:

That which knows all things and is known by none is the subject. Thus it is the supporter of the world, that condition of all phenomena, of all objects which is always presupposed throughout experience; for all that exists, exists only for the subject. Every one finds himself to be subject, yet only in so far as he knows, not in so far as he is an object of knowledge. But his body is object, and therefore from this point of view we call it idea. For the body is an object among objects, and is conditioned by the laws of objects, although it is an immediate object. Like all objects of perception, it lies within the universal forms of knowledge, time and space, which are the conditions of multiplicity. The subject, on the contrary, which is always the knower, never the known, does not come under these forms, but is presupposed by them; it has therefore neither multiplicity nor its opposite unity. We never know it, but it is always the knower wherever there is knowledge.

So then the world as idea, the only aspect in which we consider it at present, has two fundamental, necessary, and inseparable halves. The one half is the object, the forms of which are space and time, and through these multiplicity. The other half is the subject, which is not in space and time, for it is present, entire and undivided, in every percipient being. So that any one percipient being, with the object, constitutes the whole world as idea just as fully as the existing millions could do; but if this one were to disappear, then the whole world would cease to be.[21]

This fits in very well with the narrator's awareness of himself as essentially an unmodified spirit, at odds with matter (including his own corruptible body) and his superficial personality, and gifted with a vision of the world which must not be allowed to disappear when his body vanishes from that world, dragging his spirit with it.

Perhaps the most important feature of Schopenhauer's aesthetic

[19] Schopenhauer, I, 239.
[20] Gardiner, p. 202.
[21] Schopenhauer, I, 5–6.

is his belief that the artist of genius has some special access to the permanent forms which underly the constant apparent changes of the world:

That the Idea comes to us more easily from the work of art than directly from nature and the real world, arises from the fact that the artist, who knew only the Idea, no longer the actual, has reproduced in his work the pure Idea, has abstracted it from the actual, omitting all disturbing accidents. The artist lets us see the world through his eyes. That he has these eyes, that he knows the inner nature of things apart from all their relations, is the gift of genius, is inborn; but that he is able to lend us this gift, to let us see with his eyes, is acquired, and is the technical side of art.[22]

Proust says something very similar, in "Du Côté de chez Swann," about the music of Vinteuil:

Swann n'avait donc pas tort de croire que la phrase de la sonate existât réellement. Certes, humaine à ce point de vue, elle appartenait pourtant à un ordre de créatures surnaturelles et que nous n'avons jamais vues, mais que malgré cela nous reconnaissons avec ravissement quand quelque explorateur de l'invisible arrive à en capter une, a l'amener, du monde divin où il a accès, briller quelques instants au-dessus du nôtre. C'est ce que Vinteuil avait fait pour la petite phrase. Swann sentait que le compositeur s'était contenté, avec ses instruments de musique, de la dévoiler, de la rendre visible, d'en suivre et d'en respecter le dessin d'une main si tendre, si prudente, si délicate et si sûre que le son s'altérait à tout moment, s'estompant pour indiquer une ombre, revivifié quand il lui fallait suivre à la piste un plus hardi contour. Et une preuve que Swann ne se trompait pas quand il croyait à l'existence réelle de cette phrase, c'est que tout amateur un peu fin se fût tout de suite aperçu de l'imposture, si Vinteuil, ayant eu moins de puissance pour en voir et en rendre les formes, avait cherché à dissimuler, en ajoutant çà et là des traits de son cru, les lacunes de sa vision ou les défaillances de sa main [I, 350–351].

It sounds from this passage as if Proust, too, believed that the artist has access to some divine world of Forms and that he has only to copy them, without adding anything of his own, to produce a perfect work of art. But, in "Le Temps retrouvé," he corrects this suggestion by claiming that what the artist sees is the inner nature, not of some pseudo-Platonic Idea, but of his own emotional experience, and that everyone could perform the same feat as the artist, if he was only prepared to make the same effort of introspective analysis. At the same time, Proust differs from Schopenhauer in making no distinction between the artist's vision and "the technical side of art." For Proust, the artist's style is his vision, and it is impossible to

[22] Ibid., p. 252.

separate these two aspects of artistic creation. For him, they seem to be one and not two:

La vraie vie, la vie enfin découverte et éclaircie, la seule vie par conséquent réellement vécue, c'est la littérature; cette vie qui, en un sens, habite à chaque instant chez tous les hommes aussi bien que chez l'artiste. Mais ils ne la voient pas, parce qu'ils ne cherchent pas à l'éclaircir. Et ainsi leur passé est encombré d'innombrables clichés qui restent inutiles parce que l'intelligence ne les a pas "développés." Notre vie, et aussi la vie des autres; car le style pour l'écrivain, aussi bien que la couleur pour le peintre, est une question non de technique mais de vision. Il est la révélation, qui serait impossible par des moyens directs et conscients, de la différence qualitative qu'il y a dans la façon dont nous apparaît le monde, différence qui, s'il n'y avait pas l'art, resterait le secret éternel de chacun [III, 895].

It seems that neither Schopenhauer nor Bergson may be considered fully accountable for the ideas which Proust expresses in "Le Temps retrouvé." Cocking, for one, has expressed doubts as to whether Proust's aesthetic is philosophically tenable at all. In fact, he calls it "a kind of trick." [23] Poulet takes a much less severe view of Proust's aesthetic. He admires the way in which Proust's narrator has attained "cette structure totale de soi-même" [24] which had been lost in the history of European consciousness since the Middle Ages. Another critic, Hans Meyerhoff, also sees the problem with which Proust was confronted as an emotional, rather than an intellectual, one. In his *Time in Literature*,[25] Meyerhoff argues that modern science and philosophy (with the exception of Bergson's philosophy) have had a destructive effect on our awareness of experience. Time, matter, and perception have been divided, for the modern consciousness, into tiny, discontinuous units. In order to abolish the sensation that the personality, too, is crumbling away by a similar process, modern art and literature have had to reconstruct experience into continuous, whole units, and present them, as a life-weapon, to the threatened personality. An emotional need is being supplied by Proust's treatment of time. If this emotional need is at odds with our intellectual requirements, then this according to Meyerhoff, is not entirely Proust's fault, but rather the result of a modern dilemma in which Proust, too, found himself involved.

It would appear that Proust was primarily concerned, in "Le Temps retrouvé," with a religious problem — that of spiritual in-

[23] Cocking, p. 67.
[24] Poulet, p. 404.
[25] Hans Meyerhoff, *Time in Literature* (Berkeley and Los Angeles: University of California Press, 1955), *passim*.

tegration — although his approach to this religious problem was fully compatible with a philosophical attitude. He probably preferred Schopenhauer and Bergson to other philosophers because both are friendly to a certain type of mysticism. In fact, for Schopenhauer, the artist and the mystic meet on common ground, since both attain, through detachment, a vision of the Ideas.[26] But Proust's concern with spiritual matters probably antedated, as it accounted for, his interest in both these philosophers; it did not limit him to a slavish adherence to either of their philosophies. At the root of "Le Temps retrouvé" is an act of faith, faith in the belief that spirit must triumph over matter and lead to the integration of the personality, an integration which in turn leads to creative achievement. Artistic creation is the goal of this faith, not personal redemption, so it is fitting to call it a religion of art.

It has been suggested to me that it might be more appropriate to speak of a philosophy of art which eventually turned into a religion of art, as what was originally a philosophic concept acquired the ornament of a religious vocabulary. But I do not think that the philosophical impulse was ever entirely separate from the religious one in Proust's mind. In a very early text, "L'Irreligion d'état" (1892),[27] Proust declared simultaneously his belief in Christianity, his abhorrence of materialism, and his adherence to idealistic philosophy, in a way which suggests that these three things were, in the mind of the young Proust, very closely related. Later, his belief in the unconditional truth of Christianity faded, and it was on this condition that he was able to transfer religious values to art; but I think that the appeal which religion never lost for him continued throughout his life to be associated with a taste for the spiritual and the idealistic, whatever form they might take. His religion of art is a religion if one takes religion in the broadest possible sense of anything to which a person is closely bound, in a way completely involving his life and personality. But it also owes much to religion taken in a more traditional sense, partly because of Proust's use of religious vocabulary (although this is not to be taken literally), and partly because of his acute sense of being surrounded by spiritual mysteries.

It is to an analysis of this religion of art, with its struggle between spirit and matter, that this study is devoted. In the following chap-

[26] Schopenhauer, I, 239–240, 346, 405, 504–505.
[27] Proust, *Textes retrouvés*, recueillis et présentés par Philip Kolb et Larkin B. Price, avec une bibliographie des publications de Proust (1892–1967) (Urbana: University of Illinois Press, 1968), pp. 57–58.

ters we will consider, first, how Proust presents the struggle between spirit and matter, and then how he arrays his religion of art in the trappings of traditional Christianity, thereby giving it the prestige of an accepted religion. Finally, we will consider how Proust develops, in spite of his use of Christian language, an attitude which is more akin to oriental mysticism than to any other form of religious belief.

CHAPTER TWO

LITERATURE: REALITY
AND IMAGINATION

"Le Temps retrouvé" is both a beginning and an end. It is the end of *A la Recherche du temps perdu* but, since it establishes the vocation of the narrator as a novelist, it sends us back to the beginning of the work which springs from the realization of that vocation. Returning to the opening section of "Du Côté de chez Swann," we find the narrator, in a state between sleeping and waking, with his head so full of some book he has been reading that he can scarcely distinguish between his own consciousness and the book's contents: "Je voulais poser le volume que je croyais avoir encore dans les mains et souffler ma lumière; je n'avais pas cessé en dormant de faire des réflexions sur ce que je venais de lire, mais ces réflexions avaient pris un tour un peu particulier; il me semblait que j'étais moi-même ce dont parlait l'ouvrage: une église, un quatuor, la rivalité de Francois Ier et de Charles Quint" (I, 3). In this way, the importance for the narrator of reading is not only established from the beginning, but it is clearly connected with the important themes of various types of consciousness, illusion, and the creative imagination.

Books are the narrator's constant companions, being mixed in with his basic preoccupations and memories as well as affecting his dreams. His most easily recalled memories of Combray are full of literary associations and reminiscences. Books were frequently discussed in his home, and afforded at least some of his relatives with standards for judging life. So, for instance, in his opening pages, the narrator tells us how his grandmother used Mme de Sévigné as a standard for judging people's "distinction" — that is, their natural refinement. Having just met Jupien and his niece, she is delighted with them, and expresses this delight in literary terms:

Ma grand'mère avait trouvé ces gens parfaits, elle déclarait que la petite était une perle et que le giletier était l'homme le plus distingué, le mieux qu'elle eût jamais vu. Car pour elle, la distinction était quelque chose d'absolument indépendant du rang social. Elle s'extasiait sur une réponse que le giletier lui avait faite, disant à maman: "Sévigné n'aurait pas mieux dit!" et, en revanche, d'un neveu de Mme de Villeparisis qu'elle avait rencontré chez elle: "Ah ma fille, comme il est commun!" [I, 20].

The grandmother's remark is hardly unusual for a woman of culture; it is striking simply because it is one of the first things we hear about her, and because it turns out, as we get to know her character better, to be extremely typical.

The grandmother's sisters, Flora and Céline, judge life by aesthetic standards to an even more marked extent. For them, aesthetic and ethical values (which they appear to consider as more or less identical) are the only ones which count: "C'étaient des personnes d'aspirations élevées et qui à cause de cela même étaient incapables de s'intéresser à ce qu'on appelle un potin, eût-il même un intérêt historique, et d'une façon générale à tout ce qui ne se rattachait pas directement à un objet esthétique ou vertueux" (I, 21). Because of this attitude, they become deaf whenever the conversation touches on topics of purely personal or practical interest. This makes them seem absurd, even in the opening pages. Later they will reach even greater heights of absurdity by refusing to attend their sister's deathbed, on the grounds that they can express (or rather, egotistically experience) their affectionate sympathy much better by remaining in Combray and listening to chamber music. The narrator's grandfather treats them as if they were slightly mad.

The family is, in fact, divided into two camps, the aesthetic and the practical. Great-aunts Flora and Céline form the extremist element in the aesthetic camp, their extremism being what makes them ridiculous in the narrator's eyes, not the nature of their preferences. In the same way, the son of Christian parents can laugh affectionately at the excesses of an exaggeratedly devout aunt, without, for one moment, supposing that her eccentricity invalidates the truth of the religion in which they both believe. To the aesthetic camp also belong the narrator's mother and grandmother, the mother falling somewhat in the shadow of her own, more enthusiastic, more Romantic, less practical mother. But even the grandmother who, in many ways, represents the highest and best ideals that the narrator is ever to know, and who would not dream of substituting an aesthetic communion for a direct emotional contact, has a faintly ridiculous side. Very lovingly, very tenderly, and most acutely, Proust draws a line, in his delineation of the grandmother's character, between the admirable and the ridiculous. What is admirable about her cult of the beautiful is the disinterestedness which this cult both demonstrates and encourages. Of the ethical value of this disinterestedness (to which Schopenhauer would have given his blessing) she is herself aware, as we see in the following passage describing her choice of gifts for her friends:

En réalité, elle ne se résignait jamais à rien acheter dont on ne pût tirer un profit intellectuel, et surtout celui que nous procurent les belles choses en nous apprenant à chercher notre plaisir ailleurs que dans les satisfactions du bien-être et de la vanité. Même quand elle avait à faire à quelqu'un un cadeau dit utile, quand elle avait à donner un fauteuil, des couverts, une canne, elle les cherchait "anciens," comme si, leur longue désuétude ayant effacé leur caractère d'utilité, ils paraissaient plutôt disposés pour nous raconter la vie des hommes d'autrefois que pour servir aux besoins de la nôtre [I, 40].

Our admiration of the beautiful at the expense of the useful teaches us to look for satisfactions which do not derive from the pleasures of physical well-being and vanity, says Proust: that is, they diminish our egocentricity. Disinterestedness is, in many respects, a virtue. But, from the practical point of view, it becomes tainted with folly when it leads the grandmother to neglect entirely the usefulness of the objects she selects for the sake of their aesthetic or historical value. A chair is, after all, intended to be sat on, and, unless one wishes to present it to a museum, there is no purpose in buying a chair whose use is so far outweighed by its beauty that it collapses under anyone who attempts to sit on it:

On ne pouvait plus faire le compte à la maison, quand ma grand'tante avait à dresser un réquisitoire contre ma grand'mère, des fauteuils offerts par elle à de jeunes fiancés ou à de vieux époux qui, à la première tentative qu'on avait fait pour s'en servir, s'étaient immédiatement effondrés sous le poids d'un des destinataires. Mais ma grand'mère aurait cru mesquin de trop s'occuper de la solidité d'une boiserie où se distinguaient encore une fleurette, un sourire, quelquefois une belle imagination du passé [I, 41].

Disinterestedness, when carried to such an extreme, loses its positive moral value and becomes, so far as the business of living is concerned, a dubious, not to say destructive, quality. In this connection, it is difficult not to think of another admirer of Schopenhauer,

Thomas Mann, who, in his *Buddenbrooks*, shows with cruel clarity the way in which the purely practical virtues disintegrate as the spirit gains more and more control over a family.

It seems reasonable to suppose that Proust intends to prepare us, by such examples, for a much more clearly recognized conflict between life and art later in the book. But it is the narrator who will become aware of this conflict. A conscious awareness of it is lacking in the narrator's mother and, to a greater degree, in his grandmother, who actually goes so far as to choose, for her grandson's fête, books which, by her own conservative moral standards, are highly unsuitable for a child. The books in question are the poems of Musset, a volume of Rousseau (which volume is not stated), and *Indiana*. This choice is prompted by her conviction that any work of art and genius must have a good effect on any mind, no matter how immature and undeveloped the mind in question may be. Only the strenuous objections of the child's father, who insists that she must be mad, can induce her to exchange these works for something less stimulating. In the end, she selects the four pastoral novels of George Sand, saying to her daughter that she simply could not bring herself to give the child anything badly written. Obviously, she considers a clumsy style far more dangerous than a highly emotional approach and excessively "adult" subject matter.

The amusing thing about this selection on the part of the grandmother is that, if she were to meet someone whom she knew to be leading the life of George Sand, she would be unable, for moral reasons, to speak to her, or even of her. (It is fortunate for their friendship, for instance, that no one makes any revelations to her about the private life of Mme de Villeparisis.) She has taught her daughter to feel the same way. Neither of them could possibly meet or even, at one point, refer to Swann's wife, who is known to have led the life of a cocotte before her marriage. It takes all the kindness and ingenuity of the narrator's mother to make even an indirect allusion to this woman, when talking to Swann, in the opening pages of the book. She had been talking to him about his daughter, when their conversation was interrupted: "Ma mère fut obligée de s'interrompre, mais elle tira de cette contrainte même une pensée délicate de plus, comme les bons poètes que la tyrannie de la rime force à trouver leurs plus grandes beautés: 'Nous reparlerons d'elle quand nous serons tous les deux, dit-elle à mi-voix à Swann. Il n'y a qu'une maman qui soit digne de vous comprendre. Je suis sûre que la sienne serait de mon avis' " (I, 24). By this comparison to "les bons poètes,"

Proust appears to attribute an aesthetic, as well as an ethical, value to her remark. The simile is based on the fact that the narrator's mother is yielding to a purely arbitrary convention in appearance, in order to elude it, by a feat of disinterested intellectual ingenuity, in fact. Disinterestedness, as already observed, provides us with a meeting ground for the ethical and aesthetic. So, for the moment, simple human kindness and a poetic type of intelligence have triumphed over respectable middle-class standards. Life and art are, fleetingly, at one. But, on the whole, the narrator's mother and grandmother cope with this conflict and, more particularly, with the morally disturbing elements in their favorite authors by turning a blind eye to these disturbing factors and concentrating instead on those qualities of intelligence and kindness, in their reading, of which they can wholeheartedly approve. This becomes apparent from the way in which the narrator's mother reads *François le Champi* aloud to him. She expurgates the love passages extempore and takes care to express, by her intonation "cette bonté, cette distinction morale que maman avait appris de ma grand'mère à tenir supérieures à tout dans la vie, et que je ne devais lui apprendre que bien plus tard à ne pas tenir également pour supérieures à tout dans les livres . . ." (I, 42). We see from this passage that the narrator's mother has adopted her own mother's standards, but that, being more practical, she is inclined to stress the ethical elements in a book, at the expense of its aesthetic integrity, for the sake of the benefit which this will have on her son's character. But, as this passage also indicates, the narrator will in later life become conscious of the conflict between ethical and aesthetic considerations, and will persuade his mother to put a higher price on aesthetic values, at least in literature, if not in life.

Once art has truly been made into a supreme value, the life of the individual whose supreme value it has become is liable to suffer. He is likely to repeat, in more important instances, the mistake which the grandmother made in selecting chairs too beautiful to be used as such, with results both ridiculous and heartbreaking. Art may be used to judge life, but it cannot really be used to support it without certain compromises being made to the detriment of either aesthetic or ethical integrity — that is, if the ethical values of the narrator's mother and grandmother are taken as really supreme. It requires a certain willful blindness on the part of these ladies to ignore it. The narrator, who is both more sharp-sighted and less concerned with traditional moral values than they, will come to realize the existence of this conflict and to condone moral failings, however much suffering they may entail, if they lead to artistic profit. But this question will be discussed more fully in a later chapter.

Between the camps of the aesthetic and the practical stands (or rather lies!) Tante Léonie. Being completely self-obsessed, she can hardly be said to have any opinion whatever on matters literary and artistic, except insofar as she enjoys having her meals served to her on plates painted with scenes from the *Arabian Nights*. She might, however, be considered as a parodic version of the creative artist. Living chiefly to gaze from her window and comment on what she sees, her existence reminds one of the Lady of Shalott, that perfect symbol of the creative artist, able only to observe and reflect life, and doomed to disaster should the artist attempt to engage in it. Later, as the narrator nears middle life, he will comment on the extent to which he is becoming a reincarnation of his relatives in general, and of Tante Léonie in particular. It may well be that it is the Tante Léonie element in him which will eventually enable him to use his creative talent, in spite of the total lack of such talent, or appreciation for it, in Tante Léonie herself.

In the practical camp of the family we find the narrator's father, grandfather and great-aunt (Tante Léonie's mother). The narrator's father shows no particular interest in literature, apart from his censorship of the grandmother's choice of books for his child. We are given to understand that he is a powerful person, friendly with influential people. The youthful narrator presumes that the father's influence might reach so far as to endow him miraculously with the literary gifts for which he longs, although he is not altogether certain of this. The narrator's grandfather shows somewhat more interest in literature, although his interest is more of a biographical and historical nature. Thus, he thoroughly enjoys listening to anecdotes from Saint-Simon retailed to him by their visitor Swann, and murmurs a line of poetry, taught to him by his daughter, to cheer himself up when he becomes too annoyed with the other-worldliness of his sisters-in-law. Only the great-aunt on this side of the family is actively hostile to literature, regarding reading as a form of light entertainment, suitable only for Sundays. Reading on a weekday is, in her opinion, a childish waste of time. But her opinion is not to be taken seriously, since she is "la seule personne un peu vulgaire de notre famille" (I, 17). She feels an instinctive antagonism for the generous-hearted, idealistic grandmother, against whom she conducts a continual petty war.

Also influencing the child's attitude to literature are two friends of the family, Swann and Legrandin. Swann does not like to talk about art or literature in an enthusiastic manner. He prefers to adopt a tone of deliberate dryness, restricting himself to concrete, factual information on these topics. He has read the *Mémoires* of Saint-Simon often enough to be able to quote passages from memory, which certainly indicates a taste for literature. But when he expresses a preference for Pascal over the gossip columns and society news of the daily paper, he becomes suddenly embarrassed, as if he had allowed his feelings to carry him away into a social indiscretion. There has been some discussion of newspapers round the dinner table, in the course of which the narrator's great-aunts Flora and Céline have made an allusion, so subtle as to be incomprehensible to all but themselves, to the fact that Swann's collection of paintings has been mentioned in *Le Figaro*. Swann is more puzzled by the allusion than anyone, but continues his contribution to the conversation:

"Ce que je reproche aux journaux, c'est de nous faire faire attention tous les jours à des choses insignifiantes, tandis que nous lisons trois ou quatre fois dans notre vie les livres où il y a des choses essentielles. Du moment que nous déchirons fiévreusement chaque matin la bande du journal, alors on devrait changer les choses et mettre dans le journal, moi je ne sais pas, les . . . Pensées de Pascal! (il détacha ce mot d'un ton d'emphase ironique pour ne pas avoir l'air pédant). Et c'est dans le volume doré sur tranches que nous n'ouvrons qu'une fois tous les dix ans, ajouta-t-il en témoignant pour les choses mondaines ce dédain qu'affectent certains hommes du monde, que nous lirions que la reine de Grèce est allée à Cannes ou que la princesse de Léon a donné un bal costumé. Comme cela la juste proportion serait rétablie" Mais regrettant de s'être laissé aller à parler même légèrement de choses sérieuses: "Nous avons une bien belle conversation, dit-il ironiquement, je ne sais pas pourquoi nous abordons ces 'sommets' . . ." [I, 26].

Although Swann spends much of his time at social functions, he seems to feel that literature represents something more worthwhile. But here there seems to be a certain conflict. If literature represents something so worthwhile, why does Swann neglect it for activities of lesser importance? This contradiction will be analyzed at a later point in "Combray," when the narrator will also take occasion to point out the contradiction between Swann's horror of appearing enthusiastic about a work of art or literature, and the extreme importance which he attaches to the value of facts concerning that work.

Jusque-là cette horreur d'exprimer sérieusement son opinion m'avait paru
quelque chose qui devait être élégant et parisien et qui s'opposait au dog-
matisme provincial des soeurs de ma grand'mère; et je soupçonnais aussi
que c'était une des formes de l'esprit dans la coterie où vivait Swann et
où, par réaction sur le lyrisme des générations antérieures, on réhabilitait
à l'excès les petits faits précis, réputés vulgaires autrefois, et où on proscri-
vait les "phrases." Mais maintenant je trouvais quelque chose de choquant
dans cette attitude de Swann en face des choses. Il avait l'air de ne pas oser
avoir une opinion et de n'être tranquille que quand il pouvait donner
méticuleusement des renseignements précis. Mais il ne se rendait donc pas
compte que c'était professer l'opinion, postuler que l'exactitude de ces dé-
tails avait de l'importance. Je repensai alors à ce dîner où j'étais si triste
parce que maman ne devait pas monter dans ma chambre et où il avait
dit que les bals chez la princesse de Léon n'avait aucune importance. Mais
c'était pourtant à ce genre de plaisirs qu'il employait sa vie. Je trouvais
tout cela contradictoire. Pour quelle autre vie réservait-il de dire enfin
sérieusement ce qu'il pensait des choses, de formuler des jugements qu'il
pût ne pas mettre entre guillemets, et de ne plus se livrer avec une politesse pointilleuse à des occupations dont il professait en même temps
qu'elles sont ridicules? [I, 98].

The narrator's remarks have, at this point, a rather priggish ring.
This is almost the tone which an earnest young Christian might
adopt toward an uncle who had taken to worldly ways, while still
putting in an occasional and perfunctory attendance at church. The
youth's self-righteousness depends, in either case, upon the absence
of temptation. Before he enters the adult world, the narrator is con-
fident of his ability to withstand the lure of social life and devote
himself entirely to the cult of beauty. This is brought out, almost
too clearly, by the passage in which the narrator, as a child, bids
farewell to his beloved hawthorns: " 'O mes pauvres petites aubépines, disais-je en pleurant, ce n'est pas vous qui voudriez me faire du
chagrin, me forcer à partir. Vous, vous ne m'avez jamais fait de
peine! Aussi je vous aimerai toujours.' Et, essuyant mes larmes, je
leur promettais, quand je serais grand, de ne pas imiter la vie in-
sensée des autres hommes et, même à Paris, les jours du printemps,
au lieu d'aller faire des visites et écouter des niaiseries, de partir
dans la campagne voir les premières aubépines" (I, 145). This is one
of the few implausible passages in the novel. For once, Proust has
allowed his didactic urge to subordinate his gift for conveying an
impression or telling a story. This betrayal of his own narrative instinct shows the importance to him of the message which he is attempting to convey. However unlikely it may seem in the context
of a child's view of life, Proust feels it necessary to show the frivolities of social life as a real, and clearly recognized, threat to the love

of beauty. In fact, once the narrator enters adult life, he does succumb to these temptations. Literature, music, the visual arts, and the beauties of nature will still command his enthusiastic attention, but only at those moments when he is not engaged with trifles. His eventual realization of his vocation as a writer will take on the aspect of a reconversion, after years of straying from the true path.

But, for the moment, we are concerned, not with the narrator, but with what Proust presents as defective in Swann's attitude. Completely self-possessed in his dealings with the aristocracy, Swann shows, in his attitude to art, the awkwardness of a timid lover. The dryness of his tone and his insistence on the importance of facts, when discussing art works, betray, as the narrator seems half to realize, an intense emotional attachment to the works of art in question. Fear is what really hinders Swann, rather than frivolity. He separates art and life as much as do the narrator's great-aunts, but in order to set art to one side of life, behind an emotional barrier, rather than above it. The sincerity of his feeling for art appears in many of his remarks and actions, at moments when he does not feel himself to be observed. He is, for instance, a personal friend of Bergotte, and one of his earliest admirers. This shows unusual perspicacity since, as Proust observes, most people have great difficulty in appreciating the talent either of a close friend or of an author who has not yet won public recognition. Bergotte falls into both these categories, and yet Swann is able to admire him, although without realizing the full extent of his genius. Not only does Swann admire Bergotte, but he strives to awaken this admiration in others. He is not actually the first to recommend Bergotte to the narrator — the boy's school friend, Bloch, has already done this — but he encourages him in his liking for this author, and gives him information about Bergotte's other works and his personal tastes. Bergotte has written a monograph on Racine, Swann tells the narrator, and likes to visit old towns, cathedrals, and castles with Swann's daughter, Gilberte. So we see that, in spite of his false shame about his feeling for literature, Swann has a true feeling for and just appreciation of literature, and encourages such feelings in others.

Legrandin, another family friend who divides his time between Paris and Combray, is superficially similar to Swann in the division of his interests between literature and social climbing, but he is, in fact, Swann's direct antithesis. So far from being a successful worldling, he is a frustrated snob, striving to conceal his snobbery behind a mask of indifference. He claims to despise social life and live only for art and literature. He backs up these claims, partly by an ostentatiously artless style of dress, and partly by an elaborately flowery style of speech. Although an engineer by profession, he writes in his spare time, and his normal conversation is so "literary" as to astonish his acquaintance. His remarkable dinner invitation to the narrator may serve as an example of this:

"Venez tenir compagnie à votre vieil ami, m'avait-il dit. Comme le bouquet qu'un voyageur nous envoie d'un pays où nous ne retournerons plus, faites-moi respirer du lointain de votre adolescence ces fleurs des printemps que j'ai traversés moi aussi il y a bien des années. Venez avec la primevère, la barbe de chanoine, le bassin d'or, venez avec le sédum dont est fait le bouquet de dilection de la flore balzacienne, avec la fleur du jour de la Résurrection, la pâquerette et la boule de neige des jardins qui commence à embaumer dans les allées de votre grand'tante, quand ne sont pas encore fondues les dernières boules de neige des giboulées de Pâques. Venez avec la glorieuse vêture de soie du lis digne de Salomon, et l'émail polychrome des pensées, mais venez surtout avec la brise fraîche encore des dernières gelées et qui va entr'ouvrir, pour les deux papillons qui depuis ce matin attendent à la porte, la première rose de Jérusalem" [I, 126].

It is difficult to imagine anyone actually uttering these words without losing control of his syntax and his breath. Legrandin talks like a flamboyant writer. But his oratory is just as self-protective as Swann's dryness, and even further removed from a total devotion to art. It is a form of exhibitionism: Legrandin wants to put his own talent and sensitivity on display for his neighbors' admiration — a wish quite different from the disinterested creative urge of a literary genius. The basic difference between Swann and Legrandin is that, while the former masks his feelings out of a kind of nervous shrinking, being one of those who are ashamed of the Gospel of art and who will be rejected in consequence, the latter is a deliberate and conscious hypocrite. The narrator who, although he has not yet received the revelation of the Gospel of art in its fullness, is one of the elect, is able, in spite of his youth and inexperience, to perceive the flaws in both these attitudes. Legrandin's hypocrisy is evident, not only in his denial of snobbery in himself and condemnation of it in others, but also in his use of literature as an emotional smokescreen to conceal his real preoccupations. The "literature" which results is necessarily false, since, as Proust makes abundantly clear in "Le Temps retrouvé," literature of genuine worth can result only from a writer's determination to convey the truth of a real impression. What the impression is hardly matters, and the occasion of the impression matters even less. The obviously arbitrary nature of the examples of involuntary memory and spatial perspective given in "Le Temps retrouvé" may be taken as proof of this. What matters is the exactness with which an arbitrary impression is conveyed. But the idea of conveying his real impressions could never occur to Legrandin. Swann may be a timid lover of beauty who has espoused "real life" because he feels unable to approach the object of his desire; but Legrandin is a lover of society who pays court to beauty because he fears a rejection from his real love. Consequently, Legrandin's decorative conversation may be understood as a mere manipulation of language, not as a true expression of thought or feeling. In adopting this line of behavior, Legrandin is reacting, at a distance, to the attitudes of the society he longs to approach. As Gilles Deleuze points out,[1] society, in Proust's depiction of it, puts a fairly strong pressure upon its members to use language falsely. The latter, whether they are at the level of the Duchesse de Guermantes or at that of Mme Verdurin, use words in such a way that they become signs void of content. Society, Proust gives us to understand, is dangerous to a writer because it vitiates language, and does so systematically, in order to destroy any possibility of real communication. Legrandin is simply doing individually, in his own elaborate way, what society people do in general, by means of established formulas.

Perhaps the most flagrant example of Legrandin's use of imitation literature to conceal his genuine snobbery appears in a metaphysico-aesthetical discourse which he delivers to the narrator's father, at a moment's notice, to dissuade him from sending the boy to Balbec:

"Mais les choses elles-mêmes y semblent des personnes, des personnes rares, d'une essence délicate et que la vie aurait déçues. Parfois c'est un castel que vous rencontrez sur la falaise, au bord du chemin où il s'est arrêté pour confronter son chagrin au soir encore rose où monte la lune d'or et dont les barques qui rentrent en striant l'eau diaprée hissent à leurs mâts la flamme et portent les couleurs; parfois c'est une simple maison solitaire, plutôt laide, l'air timide mais romanesque, qui cache à tous les yeux quelque secret impérissable de bonheur et de désenchantement. Ce pays sans vérité, ajouta-t-il avec une délicatesse machiavélique, ce pays de pure fiction est d'une mauvaise lecture pour un enfant, et ce n'est certes pas lui que je choisirais et recomanderais pour mon petit ami déjà si enclin à la tristesse, pour son coeur prédisposé. Les climats de confidence amoureuse et de regret inutile peuvent convenir au vieux désabusé que je suis, ils sont toujours malsains pour un tempérament qui n'est pas formé" [I, 132].

[1] Gilles Deleuze, *Marcel Proust et les signes* (Paris: Presses Universitaires de France, 1964), p. 4.

However, his real reason for insisting on the harmful effect of such a place on the emotions of a growing boy is his wish to avoid giving the family an introduction to his sister, now a Marquise, who lives near Balbec. And the narrator's family is fully aware of this:

Comme cet escroc érudit qui employait à fabriquer de faux palimpsestes un labeur et une science dont la centième partie eût suffi à lui assurer une situation plus lucrative, mais honorable, M. Legrandin, si nous avions insisté encore, aurait fini par édifier toute une éthique de paysage et une géographie céleste de la basse Normandie, plutôt que de nous avouer qu'à deux kilomètres de Balbec habitait sa propre soeur, et d'être obligé à nous offrir une lettre d'introduction . . . [I, 132].

Altogether, Swann, Legrandin, the narrator's family and his teachters and friends constitute a cultural climate, providing the narrator with various influences, among which he makes a more or less conscious choice. He is most inclined, for the time being, to accept the values of his mother and grandmother, in preference to the rest, although later on, as we have seen, he will modify these views, and even cause his mother to modify hers. His acute, although not yet mature, critical ability makes him aware of certain inconsistencies in their attitude; but he is deeply impressed by their attempt to integrate the values of truth, beauty, and goodness with the realities of daily life, while finding constant inspiration for this endeavor in works of literature and objects of beauty. Furthermore, it is his mother and grandmother, between them, who first open to him the world of books, in which he hopes to find the key to unknown, but deeply alluring, mysteries.

His initiation to creative literature forms the culminating point of the *drame du coucher*, the episode of greatest emotional importance in his boyhood. Having obtained, by a desperate act of insubordination, the supreme favor of his mother's company throughout the night, he is in a state of nervous collapse. To soothe both him and herself, his mother reads aloud from *François le Champi*, one of the books selected for his fête by his grandmother. The child's first impression, on hearing the book read aloud, is one of mystery. This sense of mystery had already been present in his mind, owing to his ignorance of the nature of novels in general. It is now reinforced by his unfamiliarity with narrative techniques, and also by his mother's impromptu expurgation of the love passages. The book seems not only individual, but special, extraordinary, and unique:

Maman s'assit à côté de mon lit; elle avait pris *François le Champi* à qui sa couverture rougeâtre et son titre incompréhensible donnaient pour moi une personnalité distincte et un attrait mystérieux. Je n'avais jamais lu encore de vrais romans. J'avais entendu dire que George Sand était le type du romancier. Cela me disposait déjà à imaginer dans *François le Champi* quelque chose d'indéfinissable et de délicieux. Les procédés de narration destinés à exciter la curiosité ou l'attendrissement, certaines façons de dire qui éveillent l'inquiétude et la mélancolie, et qu'un lecteur un peu instruit reconnaît pour communs à beaucoup de romans, me paraissaient simplement — à moi qui considérais un livre nouveau non comme une chose ayant beaucoup de semblables, mais comme une personne unique, n'ayant de raison d'exister qu'en soi — une émanation troublante de l'essence particulière à *François le Champi* [I, 41].

The charm of the unknown and unfamiliar is actively at work in the receptive imagination and over-excited sensibility of the child, combined with the element of the familiar and reassuring provided by his mother's tones.

In this manner, literature has received the special sanction of the narrator's mother and grandmother, while the circumstances of his initiation have implanted in him the hope that books will provide access to some realm beyond the world of immediate reality. Truth and beauty are what he seeks from literature, but (insofar as the two are separable) more particularly truth. However these values are sought, throughout the greater part of his life, in a somewhat confused way. This confusion is particularly apparent in the narrator's account of what he sought and what he found in his reading as a child and as an adolescent. While guided by a certain instinctive awareness of the kind of spiritual nourishment which he really needs, his efforts to define the object of his search lead him continually into the twin errors of excessive materialism and excessive spirituality. Explaining his motives for reading, he says:

Dans l'espèce d'écran diapré d'états différents que, tandis que je lisais, déployait simultanément ma conscience, et qui allaient des aspirations les plus profondément cachées en moi-même jusqu'à la vision tout extérieure de l'horizon que j'avais, au bout du jardin, sous les yeux, ce qu'il y avait d'abord en moi de plus intime, la poignée sans cesse en mouvement qui gouvernait le reste, c'était ma croyance en la richesse philosophique, en la beauté du livre que je lisais, et mon désir de me les approprier, quel que fût ce livre. Car, même si je l'avais acheté à Combray, en l'apercevant devant l'épicerie Borange, trop distante de la maison pour que Françoise pût s'y fournir comme chez Camus, mais mieux achalandée comme papeterie et librairie, retenu par des ficelles dans la mosaïque des brochures et des livraisons qui revêtaient les deux vantaux de sa porte, plus mystérieuse, plus semée de pensées qu'une porte de cathédrale, c'est que je l'avais reconnu pour m'avoir été cité comme un ouvrage remarquable par le profes-

seur ou le camarade qui me paraissait à cette époque détenir le secret de
la vérité et de la beauté à demi pressenties, à demi incompréhensibles, dont
la connaissance était le but vague mais permanent de ma pensée [I, 84].

Together with a vague awareness of what he is actually looking for,
this passage displays two basic misconceptions on the part of the
narrator. On the one hand, he supposes that there are in existence
truths so elevated that he could never discover them for himself and,
on the other, that these truths have a kind of concrete quality which
allows them to be possessed by one individual and handed over to
another, specifically in the form of a book. In a sense, both these
ideas are true, and yet the way in which the narrator understands
them is fundamentally false. It is true that he might never entertain
certain ideas if it were not for his reading; but he is making the
basic mistake of failing to realize that he could never reach these
truths unless he was capable of re-creating them in his own mind,
even if the occasion of this re-creation was his contact with a book.
At the same time, he is making the even more serious mistake of supposing that the secret of truth and beauty, as absolute ideals rather
than as partial and incomplete approximations, can be possessed by
anyone, and handed over in consequence.

Convinced of the overwhelming superiority of his favorite authors, the narrator reads them in a spirit of submission and grati-
tude. From Bergotte he obtains an idea of the beauty of certain
natural objects and works of art in which he had previously been
unable to see beauty for himself. His expectation of finding truth
and beauty in a book is consequently gratified, in spite of the false
and exaggerated nature of that expectation:

Chaque fois qu'il parlait de quelque chose dont la beauté m'était restée
jusque-là cachée, des forêts de pins, de la grêle, de Notre-Dame de Paris,
d'*Athalie* ou de *Phèdre*, il faisait dans une image exploser cette beauté
jusqu'à moi [I, 95].

Because of this, the boy regards Bergotte as an oracle, whose opinion
on everything he would like to have:

Aussi sentant combien il y avait de parties de l'univers que ma perception
infirme ne distinguerait pas s'il ne les rapprochait de moi, j'aurais voulu
posséder une opinion de lui, une métaphore de lui, sur toutes choses, surtout sur celles que j'aurais l'occasion de voir moi-même, et entre celles-là,
particulièrement sur d'anciens monuments français et certains paysages
maritimes, parce que l'insistance avec laquelle il les citait dans ses livres
prouvait qu'il les tenait pour riches de signification et de beauté [I, 95].

The narrator feels that Bergotte is doing him a personal favor by
letting him know his opinions. He can only regret not having an

opinion by Bergotte on every conceivable subject, and when he discovers, in one of Bergotte's works, an idea which had already occurred to himself, he is as happy and grateful as if that author had
made a present of it:

Malheureusement sur presque toutes choses j'ignorais son opinion. Je ne
doutais pas qu'elle ne fût entièrement différente des miennes, puisqu'elle
descendait d'un monde inconnu vers lequel je cherchais à m'élever: per-
suadé que mes pensées eussent paru pure ineptie à cet esprit parfait,
j'avais tellement fait table rase de toutes, que quand par hasard il m'arriva
d'en rencontrer, dans tel de ses livres, une que j'avais déjà eue moi-même,
mon coeur se gonflait comme si un dieu dans sa bonté me l'avait rendue,
l'avait déclarée légitime et belle [I, 95–96].

That the narrator is potentially Bergotte's equal never occurs to him,
at this stage. Perhaps if this idea had occurred to him he might
never have become Bergotte's equal; this entire submission is part
of the learning process.

As we see in the passage quoted above, the narrator hardly thinks
of Bergotte as human at all. Regarding him as the physical equivalent of his style, the narrator visualizes Bergotte as an eternally
ancient, languorous, white-haired singer, living somewhere beyond
the actual world. His disillusionment, years later, on meeting Bergotte in the flesh, is described in terms which are intentionally
comic. The narrator is deeply disconcerted by seeing before him a
young man with a black goatee beard and a nose like a snail shell.
In his disappointment, he feels that he can no longer believe in the
beauty of Bergotte's work. It seems impossible to him that the mind
of the active, self-satisfied man he sees before him can ever have
been capable of the kind of intelligence which he had found in the
works of Bergotte. However, up to the time of this rude awakening,
the narrator has no difficulty in maintaining his faith in the transcendental nature of literary men.

The only incident which shakes his faith in literature (albeit momentarily) occurs when his friend, the gifted but nonsensical Bloch,
tells him that certain lines of poetry are beautiful precisely insofar
as they are devoid of meaning. The idea of a beauty from which not
only truth, but also meaning, is altogether absent worries the narrator so much that he becomes quite tired and ill. Such a beauty is to
him a contradiction in terms, since what he seeks in poetry is "rien
de moins que la révélation de la vérité" (I, 91). It is a godsend for
his peace of mind when his family, for reasons quite unconnected
with literature, forbids Bloch to enter the house again.

In his search for truth, the narrator, as we have already observed, finds both truth and error. Some of the truths which he actually finds he fails to recognize as such, and some of the truths which he thinks he finds are self-created errors — errors which will have serious consequences for years to come. So, to deal first with the unrecognized truths, he says that in his reading he was looking for truth first of all, and for excitement only second:

Après cette croyance centrale qui, pendant ma lecture, exécutait d'incessants mouvements du dedans au dehors, vers la découverte de la vérité, venaient les émotions que me donnaient l'action à laquelle je prenais part, car ces après-midi-là étaient plus remplis d'événements dramatiques que ne l'est souvent toute une vie [I, 84].

But this excitement is, in fact, connected with the discovery of a special kind of truth: the psychological truth conveyed by the behavior of the novelist's invented characters. The reader obtains from his novel-reading not merely information about these invented characters, but also, by a logical extension, information about human nature in general, and his own character in particular. Some of these insights might never have been gained by any other means, because we live at too slow a rate to get a complete picture of the development of our own emotions:

[Le romancier] déchaîne en nous pendant une heure tous les bonheurs et tous les malheurs possibles dont nous mettrions dans la vie des années à connaître quelques-uns, et dont les plus intenses ne nous seraient jamais révélés parce que la lenteur avec laquelle ils se produisent nous en ôte la perception . . . [I, 85].

But, at the time, the narrator fails to qualify these truths as Truth, because they are insufficiently transcendental.

Besides conveying psychological truths to the reader, a novel also provides access to the novelist's inner nature. It does so, not directly, but by the indirect means of displaying his reactions to certain landscapes, objects, and emotional events. The boy, however, compensating for the excessively spiritual nature of his expectations of transcendental truth, takes an excessively materialistic view of these descriptions. He wishes to visit the landscapes described in his favorite novels because he imagines that these landscapes have some intrinsic value which he can appropriate for himself, by seeing them in reality. He fails to realize that the truth which these descriptions actually convey is the truth of the novelist's state of mind, as mirrored in the landscape:

C'est ainsi que pendant deux étés, dans la chaleur du jardin de Combray, j'ai eu, à cause du livre que je lisais alors, la nostalgie d'un pays montueux et fluviatile, où je verrais beaucoup de scieries et où, au fond de l'eau claire, des morceaux de bois pourrissaient sous des touffes de cresson: non loin montaient le long des murs bas des grappes de fleurs violettes et rougeâtres. Et comme le rêve d'une femme qui m'aurait aimé était toujours présent à ma pensée, ces étés-là ce rêve fut imprégné de la fraîcheur des eaux courantes; et quelle que fût la femme que j'évoquais, des grappes de fleurs violettes et rougeâtres s'élevaient aussitôt de chaque côté d'elle comme des couleurs complémentaires.

Ce n'était pas seulement parce qu'une image dont nous rêvons reste toujours marquée, s'embellit et bénéficie du reflet des couleurs étrangères qui par hasard l'entourent dans notre rêverie; car ces paysages des livres que je lisais n'étaient pas pour moi que des paysages plus vivement représentés à mon imagination que ceux que Combray mettait sous mes yeux, mais qui eussent été analogues. Par le choix qu'en avait fait l'auteur, par la foi avec laquelle ma pensée allait au-devant de sa parole comme d'une révélation, ils me semblaient être — impression que ne me donnait guère le pays où je me trouvais, produit sans prestige de la correcte fantaisie du jardinier que méprisait ma grand'mère — une part véritable de la Nature elle-même, digne d'etre étudiée et approfondie.

Si mes parents m'avaient permis, quand je lisais un livre, d'aller visiter la région qu'il décrivait, j'aurais cru faire un pas inestimable dans la conquête de la vérité [I, 86].

This is a striking example of the way in which the narrator tends to combine the errors of excessive materialism and excessive spirituality in his search for truth. He places the longed-for truth on far too exalted a plane, and then is far too materialistic in his assumption that getting into physical contact with these landscapes will help him to obtain the truth in question.

The narrator's desire to see the landscapes of which he has read is common enough, but his association of the idea of travel with love is less usual. The explanation which he offers for this — that the idea of love was continually present at the back of his mind and tended to get mixed in with every other notion — is not really quite sufficient. A little further on, Proust indicates that the bond between love and travel is the hope they both inspire (deceptively, however) of escaping from the narrow bounds of the individual mind and personality:

Car si on a la sensation d'être toujours entouré de son âme, ce n'est pas comme d'une prison immobile; plutôt on est comme emporté avec elle dans un perpétuel élan pour la dépasser, pour atteindre à l'extérieur, avec une sorte de découragement, en entendant toujours autour de soi cette sonorité identique qui n'est pas écho du dehors, mais retentissement d'une vibration interne. On cherche à retrouver dans les choses, devenues par là précieuses, le reflet que notre âme a projeté sur elles; on est déçu en constatant qu'elles semblent dépourvues dans la nature du charme qu'elles devaient, dans notre pensée, au voisinage de certaines idées; parfois on convertit toutes les forces de cette âme en habileté, en splendeur pour agir sur des êtres dont nous sentons bien qu'ils sont situés en dehors de nous et que nous ne les atteindrons jamais. Aussi, si j'imaginais toujours autour de la femme que j'aimais les lieux que je désirais le plus alors, si j'eusse voulu que ce fût elle qui me les fît visiter, qui m'ouvrît l'accès d'un monde inconnu, ce n'était pas par le hasard d'une simple association de pensée: non, c'est que mes rêves de voyage et d'amour n'étaient que des moments — que je sépare artificiellement aujourd'hui comme si je pratiquais des sections à des hauteurs différentes d'un jet d'eau irisé et en apparence immobile — dans un même et infléchissable jaillissement de toutes les forces de ma vie [I, 86–87].

The hopelessness of the attempt to get outside oneself and penetrate some other entity, whether by love, or travel, or both combined, is made quite apparent in this passage; and yet the narrator will continue to make this attempt throughout the greater part of the novel. Eventually, in "Le Temps retrouvé," the narrator will realize that the art work offers the only possibility for the communion of minds. Before that time, however, he will make attempt after attempt to get into contact with the inner quality of a person or place by other, personal means, and especially by love and travel.[2] He will make this attempt all the more assiduously since love will often appear to him to offer the key to a particular place or milieu.

The simplest expression of this idea appears in his longing, when out on country walks, for a local girl to appear and spontaneously impart to him, through physical contact, the essence of the country-side.

J'avais le désir d'une paysanne de Méséglise ou de Roussainville, d'une pêcheuse de Balbec, comme j'avais le désir de Méséglise et de Balbec. Le plaisir qu'elles pouvaient me donner m'aurait paru moins vrai, je n'aurais plus cru en lui, si j'en avais modifié à ma guise les conditions. Connaître à Paris une pêcheuse de Balbec ou une paysanne de Méséglise, c'eût été recevoir des coquillages que je n'aurais pas vus sur la plage, une fougère que je n'aurais pas trouvée dans les bois, c'eût été retrancher au plaisir que la femme me donnerait tous ceux au milieu desquels l'avait enveloppée mon imagination. Mais errer ainsi dans les bois de Roussainville sans une paysanne à embrasser, c'était ne pas connaître de ces bois le trésor caché, la beauté profonde. Cette fille que je ne voyais que criblée de feuillages, elle était elle-même pour moi comme une plante locale d'une espèce plus élevée seulement que les autres et dont la structure permet d'approcher de plus près qu'en elles la saveur profonde du pays [I, 157].

The same desire is expressed, in a more spiritual way, when he explains that his special interest in Gilberte Swann dated from the day when he heard her father remark that she frequently went on excursions with Bergotte:

[2] Cf. Cocking, p. 57.

Le plus souvent maintenant quand je pensais à elle, je la voyais devant le porche d'une cathédrale, m'expliquant la signification des statues, et, avec un sourire qui disait du bien de moi, me présentant comme son ami, à Bergotte. Et toujours le charme de toutes les idées que faisaient naître en moi les cathédrales, le charme des coteaux de l'Ile-de-France et des plaines de la Normandie faisait refluer ses reflets sur l'image que je me formais de Mlle Swann: c'était être tout prêt à l'aimer. Que nous croyions qu'un être participe à une vie inconnue où son amour nous ferait pénétrer, c'est, de tout ce qu'exige l'amour pour naître, ce à quoi il tient le plus, et qui lui fait faire bon marché du reste [I, 100].

This shows a somewhat more complex association of ideas, since literature here subordinates both love and travel. Gilberte's journeys would be of no interest to the narrator if they were not undertaken in the company of Bergotte, whom he already reveres. Her association with Bergotte gives her a reflected prestige which fills the narrator with a sense of deep inadequacy: "Alors je sentis, en même temps que le prix d'un être comme Mlle Swann, combien je lui paraîtrais grossier et ignorant, et j'éprouvai si vivement la douceur et l'impossibilité qu'il y aurait pour moi à être son ami, que je fus rempli à la fois de désir et de désespoir" (I, 100). When he finally hears the name Gilberte applied to the strange little blond girl he sees in Swann's park, this is all that is needed to carry him to a paroxysm of frustrated desire. His love had been present, in precipitation, ever since he heard her name mentioned in connection with Bergotte; now his love has crystallized.

As we see from these examples, the narrator's interest in Gilberte was connected from the start with literary associations, fear of rejection in love, and a frustrated desire to travel. Oddly enough, the reawakening of his interest in Gilberte, some years later, will follow directly on a period in which he has indulged in a longing for travel, heightened by literature, to such an extent that he has made himself ill and has to be forbidden to travel.

His reborn love for Gilberte is described in the third part of "Du Côté de chez Swann," which bears the subtitle, "Noms de Pays: le nom." At the beginning of this section, the narrator indulges in longings for Balbec which are based partly on Legrandin's account, and partly on more factual (but equally misleading) information which he has received from Swann. What particularly draws him to Balbec is his expectation of finding there something somehow more real than himself: "Je n'étais curieux, je n'étais avide de connaître que ce que je croyais plus vrai que moi-même, ce qui avait pour moi le prix de me montrer un peu la pensée d'un grand génie, ou de la force ou de la grâce de la nature telle qu'elle se manifeste livrée à elle-même, sans l'intervention des hommes" (I, 384). Balbec is on a coast where storms frequently occur (and where Nature may therefore be seen in its strength) and, according to Swann, it has an almost Persian church. This makes a trip to Balbec particularly appealing to the narrator, since it offers him the special realities of Art and Nature combined. Then his dreams of Balbec fade, because his parents have promised him a trip to northern Italy. He conjures up visions of Italian towns based solely on a few facts, some literary associations, and the sound of their names, and then proceeds to take these visions for realities:

> Pendant ce mois — où je ressassai comme une mélodie, sans pouvoir m'en rassasier, ces images de Florence, de Venise et de Pise, desquelles le désir qu'elles excitaient en moi gardait quelque chose d'aussi profondément individuel que si ç'avait été un amour, un amour pour une personne — je ne cessai pas de croire qu'elles correspondaient à une réalité indépendante de moi, et elles me firent connaître une aussi belle espérance que pouvait en nourrir un chrétien des premiers âges à la veille d'entrer dans le paradis [I, 391].

Among the incantations which he uses to keep his excitement at fever pitch are phrases translated from Ruskin's *Modern Painters*.[3] These quotations are identified as quotations, in Proust's text, but without mention of their origin. Thus Venice is "l'école de Giorgione, la demeure du Titien, le plus complet musée de l'architecture domestique du moyen âge";[4] it is a city made of marble and gold, "rehaussée de jaspe et pavée d'émeraudes";[5] it is inhabited by men who are "majestueux et terribles comme la mer, portant leur armure aux reflets de bronze sous les plis de leur manteau sanglant."[6] The literary nature of his longing and the complete impossibility that Venice could come up to his expectations are only too obvious. His vision of Venice is all the more divorced from reality in that these descriptions of the city and its inhabitants are, for the most part, prose-poem renderings, not of any immediate actuality, but of paintings. As in the taste which the narrator's grandmother shows in selecting reproductions, "plusieurs épaisseurs d'art" (I, 40) are involved. Art and imagination combine to construct a hope so fla-

---

[3] John Ruskin, *Modern Painters*, 5 vols. (London: G. Allen, 1904). Cf. Jean Autret, *L'Influence de Ruskin sur la vie, les idées et l'œuvre de Marcel Proust* (Genève: Droz, 1955), pp. 110–111 and fn.

[4] I, 391; Ruskin, V, 316.

[5] I, 392; Ruskin, V, 315.

[6] I, 393; Ruskin, V, 315.

grantly impossible, since what has sprung from art can only lead back to art and not towards some material reality, as to cast serious doubts upon the "amour pour une personne," not to mention the Christian's hope of paradise (since the religion of art can brook no rival near the throne), which it is said to resemble. But this issue is not elaborated here. Proust simply goes on to write that, because of the fever which his longing for Italy has given him, the narrator is forced to stay at home in Paris and go for healthful walks in the Champs-Elysées. There he meets Gilberte once more, plays games with her, and falls in love with her for the second time.

If Gilberte may be considered his first love, because she was the first girl to focus his imagination and desire, then the Duchess de Guermantes must rank as his second. Again, the narrator's interest is aroused by hearing the lady talked of, before he has any opportunity or expectation of meeting her; again, his feeling for her is connected with travel in a landscape strongly tinged with literary associations; and again, he thinks of this love as initiating him into the secrets of the landscape of which she forms a part:

Puis il arriva que sur le côté de Guermantes je passai parfois devant de petits enclos humides où montaient des grappes de fleurs sombres. Je m'arrêtais, croyant acquérir une notion précieuse, car il me semblait avoir sous les yeux un fragment de cette région fluviatile que je désirais tant connaître depuis que je l'avais vue décrite par un des mes écrivains préférés. Et ce fut avec elle, avec son sol imaginaire traversé de cours d'eau bouillonnants, que Guermantes, changeant d'aspect dans ma pensée, s'identifia, quand j'eus entendu le docteur Percepied nous parler des fleurs et des belles eaux vives qu'il y avait dans le parc du château. Je rêvais que Mme de Guermantes m'y faisait venir, éprise pour moi d'un soudain caprice; tout le jour elle y pêchait la truite avec moi. Et le soir, me tenant par la main, en passant devant les petits jardins de ses vassaux, elle me montrait, le long des murs bas, les fleurs qui y appuient leurs quenouilles violettes et rouges et m'apprenait leurs noms [I, 172].

When he finally sees her, in church, at the wedding of Dr. Percepied's daughter, he will be staggered, in the same way as when he meets Bergotte, by the refractoriness of her material reality. It worries him to have to recognize that she is a real woman and not a character in a novel. However, after a short struggle, he will succeed in investing her appearance once more with all the charm of poetry and romance. He does this mainly by repeating a kind of private incantation to the glory of the Guermantes, who have so long appeared to him "enveloppés du mystère des temps mérovingiens et baignant, comme dans un coucher de soleil, dans la lumière orangée qui émane de cette syllable 'antes'" (I, 171). Self-hypnosis through art and imagination will form the basis for the narrator's unwelcome, unfulfilled, and somewhat ridiculous love for the duchess, years later, when they become neighbors in Paris.

Love and travel are even more closely connected in the case of the narrator's passion for Albertine, the great love of his life, since his first meeting with her takes place away from home, on his first trip to Balbec. He arrives at Balbec in a state of nervous excitement for which a certain kind of literature (that is, Legrandin's conversation) is partly responsible. Looking forward to the place of misty, melancholy, insidious Celtic charm for which Legrandin had prepared him, he is disappointed to find day after day of unbroken sunshine; but he does encounter the deceitful magic against which Legrandin had warned him, in the person of Albertine. Albertine will, in fact, become for the narrator, as Gilles Deleuze remarks,[7] an incarnation of the spirit of Balbec, the mystery of Albertine and the mystery of Balbec becoming inseparable in the narrator's mind.

Besides being associated for the narrator with a real place, arrived at by an actual journey, Albertine is also associated with an impossible voyage: that is, with a trip to Venice. It is not ill health which prevents the narrator from going to Venice, in this instance, but fear of the encounters which would be so easy for Albertine, and the winding waterways through which she could so easily disappear. There seems to be some necessary connection between the convolutions of Venice and the secretive nature, with its endless ramifications, of Albertine. In "La Prisonnière," he says that he feels unable to visit Venice so long as Albertine is with him, because it would test his jealousy too much: "C'était moi qui me désolais de penser que, s'il n'y avait pas eu Albertine (car avec elle j'eusse trop souffert de la jalousie dans un hôtel où elle eût toute la journée subi le contact de tant d'êtres), je pourrais en ce moment dîner à Venise dans une de ces petites salles à manger surbaissées comme une cale de navire et où on voit le Grand Canal par de petites fenêtres cintrées qu'entourent des moulures mauresques" (III, 176). One could well see a Baudelairian *correspondance* between Albertine and these cities by the sea. But, just as one feels that the lovers' journey, in *Le Voyage*, is too beautiful ever to take place, so the narrator and Albertine — so long as Albertine is alive and in possession of her elusive, fugitive will to escape the narrator's possessiveness — can never go to Venice.

[7] Deleuze, p. 5.

Conequently, the narrator does not visit Venice until some time after Albertine's death, when he does so in the company of his mother. There, the last vestige of his feeling for Albertine fades away. When he receives a telegram signed "Albertine," announcing that the sender is alive and wishes to discuss marriage with him, he reacts by realizing that his love is completely dead. His later discovery that the telegram was really from Gilberte (who affects a complicated, almost illegible signature), concerning her marriage to Robert de Saint-Loup, does not affect his attitude one way or the other. For him, Albertine is finally dead. Venice seems fated to witness the death of passion, and not only for the narrator, since it is there that we perceive M. de Norpois and Mme de Villeparisis, bound together by habit, like ghostly survivors of their former love. Conversely, it is in Venice that the love between the narrator and his mother is most openly displayed, since his mother no longer fears to spoil him by showing the full warmth of her affection. Her love is most apparent in the smile with which she greets him from her window: "Dès que de la gondole je l'appelais elle envoyait vers moi, du fond de son cœur, son amour qui ne s'arrêtait que là où il n'y avait plus de matière pour le soutenir à la surface de son regard passionné qu'elle faisait aussi proche de moi que possible, qu'elle cherchait à exhausser, à l'avancée de ses lèvres, en un sourire qui semblait m'embrasser, dans le cadre et sous le dais du sourire plus discret de l'ogive illuminée par le soleil de midi . . ." (III, 625). This love is so passionate, exclusive, and pure that the narrator's numerous, highly unromantic affairs with Venetian shopgirls cannot damage it.

It is a little difficult to think of an aesthetic reason for making Venice the place where romantic passion dies and maternal love triumphs. A biographical reason lies readily to hand, in the very happy trip which Proust took to Venice with his own mother.[8] One might, perhaps, argue that the narrator is shedding his illusions, one by one, in order to arrive at the state of detachment which is so essential to the creative artist. The illusion of romantic love disappears in Venice. Later, the illusion of travel will vanish, too. In the previous chapter, we have already discussed the narrator's disappointment, in "Le Temps retrouvé," on his return to Combray, his sense of futility on gazing from a train window (in contrast to the intense excitement which he felt on his first trip to Balbec), and his

<hr/>

[8] George Duncan Painter, *Marcel Proust: A Biography,* 2 vols. (London: Chatto and Windus, 1959–65), I, 268–269.

conviction that the Venice and Balbec resurrected by involuntary memory are superior to these places in reality. Love and travel are illusions; society is a snare; it remains for the narrator to devote himself to literature, since it was from literature that love, travel, and the aristocracy first derived their prestige. Neither love nor travel offers any hope of penetrating or possessing another entity; one possesses the essential nature of a person or object only in one's mind, and the only contact between minds is afforded by the work of art.

The full realization of his vocation dawns on the narrator fairly late in life; but, in a dim, instinctive way, he knew of his talent and sought to develop it from his earliest years. He was, for instance, always convinced that there was something special about his reaction to certain experiences. He felt, at the same time, the need to make his reactions clear to himself and convey them to others; but it was only by trial and error that he came to realize that the words which express one's meaning to oneself do not always convey it to others. To brandish one's umbrella and exclaim "Zut! zut!," he realizes, on a walk near Combray, may relieve one's own soul of a superabundance of delight, but conveys neither pleasure nor meaning to any other mind. We are expecting the impossible, Proust says, if we suppose that other people will be in the same mood as ourselves at the same moment, and ready to listen to an account of our state of mind, whether eloquently or awkwardly expressed.

A further drawback to a purely emotional, merely approximate expression of feeling is the ease with which it vanishes from one's mind. The only hope for the recovery of a feeling so incompletely defined lies in its semi-miraculous restoration by involuntary memory. The impressions which the narrator carries home from his walks around Combray are doomed to fade, because of his failure to preserve them in words:

Alors je ne m'occupais plus de cette chose inconnue qui s'enveloppait d'une forme ou d'un parfum, bien tranquille parce que je la ramenais à la maison, protégée par le revêtement d'images sous laquelle je la trouverais vivante, comme les poissons que, les jours où on m'avait laissé aller à la pêche, je rapportais dans mon panier, couverts par une couche d'herbe qui préservait leur fraîcheur. Une fois à la maison je songeais à autre chose et ainsi s'entassaient dans mon esprit (comme dans ma chambre les fleurs que j'avais cueillies dans mes promenades ou les objets qu'on m'avait donnés) une pierre où jouait un reflet, un toit, un son de cloche, une odeur de feuilles, bien des images différentes sous lesquelles il y a longtemps qu'est morte la réalité pressentie que je n'ai pas eu assez de volonté pour arriver à découvrir [I, 179].

There is just one exception to this failure on his part, and that is his written analysis of the impression made upon him by the spires of Martinville and Vieuxvicq. Once he has succeeded in writing down a description which conveys his impression, he is so full of joy in his obedience to his creative instinct that he begins to chant at the top of his voice, like (he says) a hen which has laid an egg!

The only other moments when he conveys his feelings adequately in writing happen when the idea of literary creation is furthest from his mind; that is, when he is wholly intent on making himself understood by his mother and grandmother, in the little notes he sends them. Oddly enough, it is in these messages that he strikes out phrases similar to the style of his admired Bergotte:

Il arrivait parfois qu'une page de lui disait les mêmes chose que j'écrivais souvent la nuit à ma grand'mère et à ma mère quand je ne pouvais pas dormir, si bien que cette page de Bergotte avait l'air d'un recueil d'épigraphes pour être placées en tête de mes lettres. Même plus tard, quand je commençai de composer un livre, certaines phrases, dont la qualité ne suffit pas pour me décider à le continuer, j'en retrouvai l'équivalent en Bergotte. Mais ce n'était qu'alors, quand je les lisais dans son œuvre, que je pouvais en jouir; quand c'était moi qui les composais, préoccupé qu'elles reflétassent exactement ce que j'apercevais dans ma pensée, craignant de ne pas "faire ressemblant," j'avais bien le temps de me demander si ce que j'écrivais était agréable! [I, 96].

All his feeling of frustration, when he despairs of realizing his ambition of becoming a writer, spring from the one basic mistake of assuming that the truth is to be found somewhere outside him, whether embodied in some person or object, or else existing on some transcendental plane. Thus, when he dreams of becoming a great writer in order to impress Mme de Guermantes, he adds, somewhat ruefully: "Et ces rêves m'avertissaient que, puisque je voulais un jour être un écrivain, il était temps de savoir ce que je comptais écrire. Mais dès que je me le demandais, tâchant de trouver un sujet où je pusse faire tenir une signification philosophique infinie, mon esprit s'arrêtait de fonctionner, je ne voyais plus que le vide en face de mon attention, je sentais que je n'avais pas de génie ou peut-être une maladie cérébrale l'empêchait de naître" (I, 172–173). The revelation of "Le Temps retrouvé" is basically the revelation that the truth, like the Kingdom of Heaven for the Christian, is within him. It remains only for him to bring that truth, the truth of his individual reactions to his personal experiences, out from within himself and incorporate it in a book.

CHAPTER THREE

VISION AND THE VISUAL ARTS

In the two preceding chapters, we observed a struggle, in the narrator's mind, between reality and imagination. In the first chapter we saw how the narrator, by deciding to quit the world in order to write a novel, chose imagination in preference to material reality. Henceforward, physical reality will be of importance to him only insofar as it may be used as material for works of the creative imagination. Imagination bestows upon material reality its only meaning and value; therefore, the narrator is justified in retreating from society (which he had been inclined, for a moment, to accept as the only true reality) in order to devote himself to creating works of imagination. These are, in turn, to bestow value, meaning, and a sense of enhanced reality upon the lives of others.

In the second chapter we saw how literature raised the question, in the narrator's mind, of the conflict between reality and imagination. As a child and adolescent, he looks for a guide to his adult existence and to the world of physical reality in works of literature (that is, of the creative imagination) and projects the figments of his own imagination onto the material world. Works of literature seem to him to represent something both more real and more valuable than his own existence and surroundings; yet he persists in searching for that superior reality in the (equally insignificant) existence of other human beings and the (by no means intrinsically superior) beauty of other landscapes. As we saw in the first chapter, persistence in this attitude leads inevitably to frustration, fatigue, and disillusionment, until imagination and reality are finally put into what Proust considers the proper relation. But whatever the importance of literature, it does not constitute the only means by which the value of physical reality is simultaneously enhanced and questioned. The visual arts have the same function, although exercised in a different way.

Things seen, whether real objects, works of art, visual memories, or visions in a dream, figure largely in the narrator's mind and form an important part of his adult preoccupations and childhood memories. If we look at the opening pages of *A la Recherche du temps perdu,* taking them as a preliminary statement of Proust's basic themes, it is quite difficult to determine whether literary associations or visual constructions are more important. The narrator's half-waking, half-dreaming thoughts on the first page of the novel are based on the volume which he thought he still had in his hands, which seems to put literature first. But he then opens his eyes upon his darkened, scarcely recognized room, "pour fixer le kaléidoscope de l'obscurité" (I, 4). The image of the kaleidoscope implies an unstable, constantly shifting pattern, composed of a limited number of fixed elements, multiplied by reflection and illumined by a single ray of light. The darkness becomes a kaleidoscope because of the fragmented efforts of the narrator to reconstruct the room in its hidden form. Guessed-at chairs, windows, and tables swim through his mind and vanish, as he attempts to fix his position in space before dropping off to sleep again. Visual memories, when he next awakens, help him to locate himself in time: "Je passais en une seconde par-dessus des siècles de civilisation, et l'image confusément entrevue de lampes à pétrole, puis de chemises à col rebattu, recomposaient peu à peu les traits originaux de mon moi" (I, 5–6). These memories are then compared to an early form of the cinema, the bioscope: "Ces évocations tournoyantes et confuses ne duraient jamais que quelques secondes; souvent ma brève incertitude du lieu où je me trouvais ne distinguait pas mieux les unes des autres les diverses suppositions dont elle était faite, que nous n'isolons, en voyant un cheval courir, les positions successives que nous montre le kinétoscope" (I, 7). Although the bioscope projects pictures in a way in which the kaleidoscope does not, there is a connection between the two images. In each case, it is a question of an optical toy which makes use of controlled changes in a visual pattern, over a period of time and with the help of directed lighting. The pattern, although constantly changing, is coherent. Moreover, the eye sees something which is really there, in appearance, although a trick is played upon the eye (with the willing cooperation of the imagination) to make it see more than is really there, in physical fact as opposed to appearance, or something different from what is really there. Both provide excellent metaphors for the visual imagination, since this starts with a physical reality and then proceeds to transform it.

Once he has established himself more or less correctly in his actual position in time and space, now quite awake, the narrator settles down to dwell on specific memories. The one which comes most readily to his mind is that of his bedroom in Combray, where, as a child, he used to watch the projections cast by his magic lantern as he waited to be called to dinner. This forms the introduction to the episode of the *drame du coucher*, which for so long constituted his primal memory of Combray, blotting out every other childhood association and memory. Having concluded his narration of this episode, he compares its destruction of his other memories to an effect of selected lighting:

C'est ainsi que, pendant longtemps, quand, réveillé la nuit, je me ressouvenais de Combray, je n'en revis jamais que cette sorte de pan lumineux, découpé au milieu d'indistinctes ténèbres, pareil à ceux que l'embrasement d'un feu de Bengale ou quelque projection électrique éclairent et sectionnent dans un édifice dont les autres parties restent plongées dans la nuit . . . [I, 43].

A second visual memory of Combray, infinitely richer and more varied, was vouchsafed to him, he remembers after this, by a non-visual stimulus (the consumption of *madeleine* crumbs soaked in tea). As he concludes the account of this second evocation of Combray, we find him still in his bed, confronting the ray of light which is to destroy the last remaining trace of illusion in his darkened room and in his sleep-clouded mind:

Mais à peine le jour — et non plus le reflet d'une dernière braise sur une tringle de cuivre que j'avais pris pour lui — traçait-il dans l'obscurité, et comme à la craie, sa première raie blanche et rectificative, que la fenêtre avec ses rideaux quittait le cadre de la porte où je l'avais située par erreur, tandis que, pour lui faire place, le bureau que ma mémoire avait maladroitement installé là se sauvait à toute vitesse, poussant devant lui la cheminée et écartant le mur mitoyen du couloir; une courette régnait à l'endroit où, il y a un instant encore, s'étendait le cabinet de toilette, et la demeure que j'avais rebâtie dans les ténèbres était allée rejoindre les demeures entrevues dans le tourbillon du réveil, mise en fuite par ce pâle signe qu'avait tracé au-dessus des rideaux le doigt levé du jour [I, 187].

By the way in which one illusion is succeeded by another, to culminate in illumination, "Combray" provides us with an extended metaphor for the narrator's spiritual progress throughout the entire novel, seen in terms of optics.

Optics is a key word in Roger Shattuck's *Proust's Binoculars,* which sets out to explain Proust's entire novel in terms of visual effects.[1] One feature of Proust's use of visual effects which interests Shattuck very much is their connection with time.[2] We have already noticed a similarity between the kaleidoscope and the bioscope, based on their mingling of the illusory and the real, and on their use of a visual pattern dependent on sequence in time. The magic lantern, which is associated with the narrator's childhood memories, belongs to the same group, in its projection of shifting images in a temporal sequence. It belongs more radically to the realm of the unreal, since the images it projects depict imagined events, painted directly onto the individual slides. The magic lantern slide is halfway between an optical toy and a picture, since each slide constitutes "une image": an individual, momentary view of a person or object, which may be seen in isolation. These pictures follow each other less rapidly, and are therefore more readily distinguished from one another, than are those of the bioscope. But a temporal sequence of views is involved in all three instruments.

As well as being connected with time, memory, illusion, and illumination, the projection of light is sometimes used by Proust as a metaphor for emotional bias. We have already noticed the way in which the narrator's primal memory of Combray was compared, in its selectivity, to an effect of controlled lighting. His intense attachment to this memory casts light upon it and shadow upon every surrounding circumstance, until an unexpected emotional jolt brings everything connected with Combray into a new perspective. An equally striking example of light being used in an emotional connection occurs in a passage describing the way in which the jealousy of Swann dies down when he is actually in the presence of Odette: "Alors à ces moments-là, pendant qu'elle leur faisait de l'orangeade, tout d'un coup, comme quand un réflecteur mal réglé d'abord promène autour d'un objet, sur la muraille, de grandes ombres fantastiques, qui viennent ensuite se replier et s'anéantir en lui, toutes les idées terribles et mouvantes qu'il se faisait d'Odette s'évanouissaient, rejoignaient le corps charmant que Swann avait

---

[1] Cf. Roger Shattuck, *Proust's Binoculars: a Study of Memory, Time and Recognition in "A la Recherche du temps perdu"* (New York: Random House, 1963), p. 6.
[2] Ibid., p. 23.

devant lui" (I, 298). This forms a variation on the search for truth, since one searches only for these truths which are of emotional importance to the seeker. The searchlight in Swann's mind is switched off when Odette is actually in front of him, for then he no longer needs to imagine what she is doing.

Coping with changes in people's physical appearance also involves the search for truth and leads, in consequence, to the use of optical imagery. Changes in people whom he knows well but who have grown older present the narrator with the problem of recognizing the substance which underlies the appearance. These changes are specifically compared to the operation of a magic lantern, a comparison which treats the underlying personal substance as the screen and the physical changes as the projection of the slides of the magic lantern. So the old people at the reception of the Princesse de Guermantes, in "Le Temps retrouvé," are compared to puppets upon whom Time has projected the slides of its magic lantern: "Des poupées baignant dans les couleurs immatérielles des années, des poupées extériorisant le Temps, le Temps qui d'habitude n'est pas visible, pour le devenir cherche des corps et, partout où il les rencontre, s'en empare pour montrer sur eux sa lanterne magique" (III 924).

Again, the changes which take place in one's impression of individual character take on a magic lantern aspect, although Proust does not actually use this image in this connection. Proust's acute interest in the interplay between truth and illusion, appearance and reality, is most strikingly exemplified by the narrator's unwearied inquiry into the tendencies, activities, and interests of his acquaintance. Time and again, one of the narrator's first impressions is canceled by information received at a later date, only to be reinstated, albeit in modified form, until the bewildered reader hardly knows what he is supposed to accept as truth and what as illusion. In the end (although Shattuck argues strongly for the superior validity of the "stereoscopic" view) the individual, fixed image may give a truer insight than the sequence of the images of the magic lantern. Perhaps the most outstanding example of this is provided by the narrator's tardy realization that his first impressions of Gilberte and Albertine were closer to the truth than any he had formed later on:

Et tout d'un coup, je me dis que la vraie Gilberte, la vraie Albertine, c'étaient peut-être celles qui s'étaient au premier instant livrées dans leur regard, l'une devant la haie d'épines roses, l'autre sur la plage. Et c'était moi qui, n'ayant pas su le comprendre, ne l'ayant repris que plus tard dans

ma mémoire, après un intervalle où par mes conversations tout un entre-
deux de sentiment leur avait fait craindre d'être aussi franches que dans la
première minute, avais tout gâté par ma maladresse. Je les avais "ratées"
plus complètement — bien qu'à vrai dire l'échec relatif avec elles fût moins
absurde — pour les mêmes raisons que Saint-Loup Rachel [III, 694].

The Proustian writer is both a painter and an oculist. He paints
pictures for us in words and provides us, at the same time, with spec-
tacles through which we may view both these pictures and the world
around us more clearly. The narrator will provide his readers, says
Proust, with a magnifying glass through which they may read in
themselves: "Car ils ne seraient pas, selon moi, mes lecteurs, mais
les propres lecteurs d'eux-mêmes, mon livre n'étant qu'une sorte
de ces verres grossissants comme ceux que tendait à un acheteur
l'opticien de Combray; mon livre, grâce auquel je leur fournirais le
moyen de lire en eux-mêmes" (III, 1033). By means of his style, the
writer, as does the artist by means of color, presents us with an insight into his particular vision of the universe:

Car le style pour l'écrivain, aussi bien que la couleur pour le peintre, est
une question non de technique mais de vision. Il est la révélation, qui
serait impossible par des moyens directs et conscients, de la différence
qualitative qu'il y a dans la façon dont nous apparaît le monde, différence
qui, s'il n'y avait pas l'art, resterait le secret éternel de chacun. Par l'art
seulement nous pouvons sortir de nous, savoir ce que voit un autre de cet
univers qui n'est pas le même que le nôtre, et dont les paysages nous seraient restés aussi inconnus que ceux qu'il peut y avoir dans la lune [III,
895].

In imparting his particular vision of the universe, Proust presents
us with two kinds of pictures: the moving and the static. The moving pictures we have already discussed. Typical of the static picture
is the window, whether the glass in it is transparent or stained.
Views through a window, which occur again and again in Proust's
work, have a great emotional importance, as Howard Moss has
pointed out.[3] But transparent window, magic lantern, and stained
glass window coalesce imaginatively.[4] The connection between these
varied elements is that of vision and light, which are inescapably
connected with imagination as illusion and emotional bias, on the
one hand, and with the creative imagination, especially as brought
into play by the visual arts, on the other. To sum up: in Proust's
narrative, visual effects have to do with the search for truth and the
encounter with illusion, these being further connected with emo-

[3] Howard Moss, The Magic Lantern of Marcel Proust (London: Faber and
Faber, 1963), chap. 3.
[4] Ibid.. p. 57.

tional bias and with the awareness of an unchanging substance underlying superficial change.

Light also has to do, throughout the novel, with the bestowal or removal of value. Sunlight, the prime giver of value, is of intense emotional importance to the narrator, being welcomed by him even before his eyes are open to see it:

Dès le matin, la tête encore tournée contre le mur et avant d'avoir vu, au-dessus des grands rideaux de la fenêtre, de quelle nuance était la raie du jour, je savais déjà le temps qu'il faisait. . . . Et peut-être ces bruits avaient-il été dévancés eux-mêmes par quelque émanation plus rapide et plus pénétrante qui, glissée au travers de mon sommeil, y répandait une tristesse annonciatrice de la neige ou faisait entonner à certain petit personnage intermittent de si nombreux cantiques à la gloire du soleil que ceux-ci finissaient par amener pour moi, qui encore endormi commençais à sourire et dont les paupières closes se préparaient à être éblouies, un étourdissant réveil en musique [III, 9].

He feels that on his deathbed the last part of his personality to die will be a certain little individual who rejoices instinctively in the sunlight. But this is not merely a personal, limited reaction on the part of the narrator. That sunlight is the greatest giver of value, the narrator's favorite paintings testify. The lesson taught by the Elstirs which he views at the Hôtel de Guermantes is that the most insignificant object appears charming if the light is shown to fall on it in a certain way:

Comme, dans un des tableaux que j'avais vus à Balbec, l'hôpital, aussi beau sous son ciel de lapis que la cathédrale elle-même, semblait, plus hardi qu'Elstir théoricien, qu'Elstir homme de goût et amoureux du moyen âge, chanter: "Il n'y a pas de gothique, il n'y a pas de chef-d'œuvre, l'hôpital sans style vaut le glorieux portail," de même j'entendais: "La dame un peu vulgaire qu'un dilettante en promenade éviterait de regarder, excepterait du tableau poétique que la nature compose devant lui, cette femme est belle aussi, sa robe reçoit la meme lumière que la voile du bateau, il n'y a pas de choses plus ou moins précieuses, la robe commune et la voile en elle-même jolie sont deux miroirs du même reflet. Tout le prix est dans les regards du peintre." Or celui-ci avait su immortellement arrêter le mouvement des heures à cet instant lumineux où la dame avait eu chaud et avait cessé de danser, où l'arbre était cerné d'un pourtour d'ombre, où les voiles semblaient glisser sur un vernis d'or [II, 421].

The all-importance of light is brought out even more strongly in a passage describing the trips which the narrator took to various Norman churches in the company of Albertine. The two of them survey the church of Marcouville l'Orgueilleuse with a certain ill will, having been informed by Elstir that it has been restored and thereby spoiled. But as the narrator watches its façade, swimming in sunlight, he feels that Elstir would have to be in contradiction with the principles of his own painting not to admire it at this moment:

Nous passions devant Marcouville l'Orgueilleuse. Sur son église, moitié neuve, moitié restaurée, le soleil déclinant étendait sa patine aussi belle que celle des siècles. A travers elle les grands bas-reliefs semblaient n'être vus que sous une couche fluide, moitié liquide, moitié lumineuse; la Sainte Vierge, sainte Élisabeth, saint Joachim, nageaient encore dans l'impalpable remous, presque à sec, à fleur d'eau ou à fleur de soleil. Surgissant dans une chaude poussière, les nombreuses statues modernes se dressaient sur des colonnes jusqu'à mi-hauteur des voiles dorés du couchant. . . . Pas plus qu'Elstir, je n'aimais cette église, c'est sans me faire plaisir que sa façade ensoleillée était venue se poser devant mes yeux, et je n'étais descendu la regarder que pour être agréable à Albertine. Et pourtant je trouvais que le grand impressionniste était en contradiction avec lui-même; pourquoi ce fétichisme attaché à la valeur architecturale objective, sans tenir compte de la transfiguration de l'église dans le couchant? [II, 1013–1014].

The value of sunlight is recognized by Elstir, as by the Impressionists whom he represents. Other painters give value to moonlight, lamplight, and firelight, as Proust acknowledges in descriptions of light effects which make use of pictorial comparisons for their full impact. Moonlight has a disintegrating dematerializing effect, as we see in an early description of Combray. The narrator and his family, returning at night from an unexpectedly lengthy walk, see before them an enchanted town, metamorphosed into a study of ruins by Hubert Robert:

Nous revenions par le boulevard de la gare, où étaient les plus agréables villas de la commune. Dans chaque jardin le clair de lune, comme Hubert Robert, semait ses degrés rompus de marbre blanc, ses jets d'eau, ses grilles entr'ouvertes. Sa lumière avait détruit le bureau du Télégraphe. Il n'en subsistait plus qu'une colonne à demi brisée, mais qui gardait la beauté d'une ruine immortelle [I, 114].

Lamplight, candlelight, and firelight give richness and warmth, with a certain fantastic quality, due to the erratic placing of shadow by the flickering light. This effect is conveyed very vividly in a passage describing the views which the narrator has through lighted windows as he walks through Doncières at night, on his way back to his hotel:

Ici le génie du feu me montrait en un tableau empourpré la taverne d'un marchand de marrons où deux sous-officiers, leurs ceinturons posés sur des chaises, jouaient aux cartes sans se douter qu'un magicien les faisait surgir de la nuit, comme dans une apparition de théâtre, et les évoquait tels qu'ils étaient effectivement à cette minute même, aux yeux d'un passant arrêté qu'ils ne pouvaient voir. Dans un petit magasin de bric-à-brac, une bougie à demi consumée, en projetant sa lueur rouge sur une gravure, la transformait en sanguine, pendant que, luttant contre l'ombre, la clarté de la grosse lampe basanait un morceau de cuir, niellait un poignard de paillettes étincelantes, sur des tableaux qui n'étaient que de mauvaises copies déposait une dorure précieuse comme la patine du passé ou le vernis d'un maître, et faisait enfin de ce taudis où il n'y avait que du toc et des croûtes, un inestimable Rembrandt [II, 96–97].

Sunlight, moonlight, lamplight, candlelight, and firelight are all the light effects of which the painter disposes, and Proust, in his turn, makes use of them all. But also found in nature, and exerting a particular fascination on Proust, are colored and broken light: the spectrum, the rainbow, the prism, and stained glass. The magic lantern, which provides the narrator with the first pictures to come within his ken, has a rainbow quality which makes it akin to stained glass: "A l'instar des premiers architectes et maîtres verriers de l'âge gothique, elle substituait à l'opacité des murs d'impalpables irisations, de surnaturelles apparitions multicolores, où des légendes étaient dépeintes comme dans un vitrail vacillant et momentané" (I, 9). It is this quality which fixes the attention of the narrator, as a child, almost more than the "literary" interest of the story which accompanies the slides. Not long after the description of the magic lantern in the child's bedroom, the stained glass windows in the church of Combray are celebrated in a passage which, among so many bravura descriptions, is perhaps the most remarkable of all. One particularly splendid window, mainly in blue, is described in terms of a fire, a peacock's tail, a flaming rain falling from the roof of a rainbow-hued grotto, a sapphire upon a breastplate, and forget-me-nots of glass. Proust can scarcely find words enough to convey the glory of its changing colors, with the glorious sun shining through. Yet even the most humble prism arouses the same enthusiasm in him. The cut glass knife-rests in a middle-class home, the narrator points out to Albertine, "projettent des feux multicolores et aussi beaux que les verrières de Chartres" (III, 168). Perhaps it would not be too fanciful to claim that the spectrum fascinates him as an example of the analysis of what is really complex and apparently simple, and also as an example of something which combines the real, the illusory, and the true. The divided light is as real as the single light; neither is more true than the other; which light one sees depends solely on the angle at which one sees it. At the same time, the colored light of the prism or of stained glass appears to have, for Proust, an emotional value which is greater than that of the white light of the moon or the sun; just as the narrator confesses to an infantile preference for cream cheese when stained pink over the same cheese left white and for the pink hawthorn over its white sister. But, whether the colored or the white light is brought into play, the effect of both is to detract from the obstinately material nature of reality, as things as solid as churches or bedroom walls dissolve in effects of light. What starts as the normal exercise of vision ends as the contemplation of a vision. As we shall see, it is the unreal and mystical quality of Elstir's painting, *Le Port de Carquethuit*, crowned as it is with a rainbow, which appeals especially strongly to the narrator. But many years are to elapse between the time when the narrator views his magic lantern slides and the stained glass windows of the parish church and the day on which he stands before his first Elstirs, at Balbec. For the moment, let us confine ourselves to the place of the visual arts in "Combray," in order to retrace from the beginning the narrator's progress toward a mature understanding of them.

It is, perhaps, typical of the austerity of his upbringing that the first real pictures of any artistic merit with which the narrator is presented should be black and white reproductions. These are obtained for the narrator by his grandmother, through Swann. They represent a typical attempt, on the part of the narrator's grandmother, to diminish the importance of the utilitarian element in a gift (the utility of these pictures being that of instruction), by a liberal admixture of aestheticism:

Elle eût aimé que j'eusse dans ma chambre des photographies des monuments ou des paysages les plus beaux. Mais au moment d'en faire l'emplette, et bien que la chose représentée eût une valeur esthétique, elle trouvait que la vulgarité, l'utilité reprenaient trop vite leur place dans le mode mécanique de la représentation, la photographie. Elle essayait de ruser et, sinon d'éliminer entièrement la banalité commerciale, du moins de la réduire, d'y substituer, pour la plus grande partie, de l'art encore, d'y introduire comme plusieurs "épaisseurs" d'art: au lieu de la Cathédrale de Chartres, des Grandes Eaux de Saint-Cloud, du Vésuve, elle se renseignait auprès de Swann si quelque grand peintre ne les avait pas représentés, et préférait me donner des photographies de la Cathédrale de Chartres par Corot, des Grandes Eaux de Saint-Cloud par Hubert Robert, du Vésuve par Turner, ce qui faisait un degré d'art de plus [I, 40].

The aesthetic wins heavily over the useful, in fact, since these pictures do not convey an exact impression of the scenes or monuments which they represent, and are consequently deficient as sources of information. As the narrator complains, photographs would have given him a better idea of what they actually looked like:

Il faut dire que les résultats de cette manière de comprendre l'art de faire un cadeau ne furent pas toujours très brillants. L'idée que je pris de Venise d'après un dessin du Titien qui est censé avoir pour fond la lagune, était certainement beaucoup moins exacte que celle que m'eussent donné de simples photographies [I, 40–41].

But, as he will learn, the object of art is to transform reality, not to provide factual information.

Other reproductions presented to the narrator by Swann (of his own free will, it seems, instead of at the grandmother's instigation) are an engraving, after Benozzo Gozzoli, of Abraham separating Sarah from Isaac, and certain of the *Vices* and *Virtues* of Padua, by Giotto. Photographs of Giotto's symbolic figures were pinned to the narrator's wall and formed the basis for a childish meditation on the similarities and differences between life and art. Giotto's *Charity* interests him most. To begin with, he is amused by the literal, somewhat clumsy way in which the allegory of Charity, trampling on riches and offering God her heart, is represented. She looks like a cook handing a corkscrew up from her basement, he says. He is also disappointed by the earthy, not to say vulgar, expression on her face; he thinks she ought to look more charitable. But later he will realize that this expectation is pure sentimentality on his part. When he compares this picture to the pregnant kitchen maid, he comes to realize that the painter has shown great psychological acumen in his representation of a fecund woman:

De même que l'image de cette fille était accrue par le symbole ajouté qu'elle portait devant son ventre, sans avoir l'air d'en comprendre le sens, sans que rien dans son visage en traduisît la beauté et l'esprit, comme un simple et pesant fardeau, de même c'est sans paraître s'en douter que la puissante ménagère qui est représentée à l'Arena au-dessous du nom "Caritas" et dont la reproduction était accrochée au mur de ma salle d'études, à Combray, incarne cette vertu, c'est sans qu'aucune pensée de charité semble avoir jamais pu être exprimée par son visage énergique et vulgaire [I, 81].

Later on, he will come to realize that the same acumen has been shown in Giotto's representation of a genuinely charitable person:

Et peut-être cette non-participation (du moins apparente) de l'âme d'un être à la vertu qui agit par lui, a aussi en dehors de sa valeur esthétique une réalité sinon psychologique, au moins, comme on dit, physiogno- monique. Quand, plus tard, j'ai eu l'occasion de rencontrer au cours de ma vie, dans des couvents par exemple, des incarnations vraiment saintes de la charité active, elles avaient généralement un air allègre, positif, indifférent et brusque de chirurgien pressé, ce visage où ne se lit aucune commisération, aucun attendrissement devant la souffrance humaine, aucune crainte de la heurter, et qui est le visage sans douceur, le visage antipathique et sublime de la vraie bonté [I, 82].

Thus it appears that a painting, although it may be deficient as a source of purely factual information, can give the same kind of psychological information, although in a different form, as a work of literature. It can be a source of truth (once the nature of that truth has been understood) in the same way as a novel.

A painting can also be a source of symbolic truth. As a child, the narrator, as we have noticed, is chiefly struck by the odd and almost comically literal way in which Giotto represents his symbols:

L'Envie, elle, aurait eu davantage une certaine expression d'envie. Mais dans cette fresque-là encore, le symbole tient tant de place et est représente comme si réel, le serpent qui siffle aux lèvres de l'Envie est si gros, il lui remplit si complètement sa bouche grande ouverte, que les muscles de sa figure sont distendus pour pouvoir le contenir, comme ceux d'un enfant qui gonfle un ballon avec son souffle, et que l'attention de l'Envie — et la nôtre du même coup — tout entière concentrée sur l'action de ses lèvres, n'a guère de temps à donner à d'envieuses pensées [I, 81].

But later, he will realize that the beauty of these symbols is dependent, to a large extent, on the literalness of their representation:

Mais plus tard j'ai compris que l'étrangeté saisissante, la beauté spéciale de ces fresques tenait à la grande place que le symbole y occupait, et que le fait qu'il fût représenté, non comme un symbole puisque la pensée symbolisée n'était pas exprimée, mais comme réel, comme effectivement subi ou matériellement manié, donnait à la signification de l'œuvre quelque chose de plus littéral et de plus précis, à son enseignement quelque chose de plus concret et de plus frappant [I, 82].

The changes in the narrator's attitude to painting are not unlike the changes in his attitude to literature. He looks at first for factual information and is disappointed or misled; later, he comes to realize the importance of the psychological truth conveyed by the work of literature or the painting; later again, he realizes the importance of the special atmosphere (whether conveyed by symbols or otherwise) of the work of literature or the painting. How much later he comes to recognize the importance of this last element in painting is not stated; but his awareness of the importance of literary symbols, and of a special atmosphere connected with the use of these symbols, is expressed by the narrator for the first time in his conversations with Albertine, in his Paris apartment. Perhaps his full awareness of the symbolic quality of certain paintings occurs at the same moment in his intellectual pilgrimage. At any rate, it is at this point in the narrative that he compares the recurrence of certain objects in Vermeer to the recurrence of certain situations in Dostoevsky:

Vous m'avez dit que vous aviez vu certains tableaux de Ver Meer, vous vous rendez compte que ce sont les fragments d'un même monde, que c'est toujours, quelque génie avec lequel elle soit recréée, la même table, le même tapis, la même femme, la même nouvelle et unique beauté, énigme à cette époque où rien ne lui ressemble ni ne l'explique, si on ne cherche pas à l'apparenter par les sujets, mais à dégager l'impression particulière que la couleur produit. Hé bien, cette beauté nouvelle, elle reste identique dans toutes les œuvres de Dostoïevsky . . . [III, 377].

The special atmosphere of Dostoevsky is created by the recurrence of particular themes; the special atmosphere of Vermeer is created by the recurrence of certain, not intrinsically significant, objects, bathed in a particular light. In fact, it is quite appropriate to speak of color in the picture and the novel alike: "Mais pour revenir à la beauté neuve que Dostoïevsky a apportée au monde, comme chez Ver Meer il y a création d'une certaine âme, d'une certaine couleur des étoffes et des lieux . . ." (III, 378).

It is, more than anything else, the coloring of Vermeer which impresses Bergotte. His last moments on earth are spent admiring the color of a wall in a Vermeer painting. This wall was praised in a newspaper article which Bergotte read before attending the exhibition in which the painting was displayed. The color of this wall, the article said, was put on so perfectly as to acquire an autonomous value: it is precious in itself.

Mais un critique ayant écrit que dans la *Vue de Delft* de Ver Meer prêté par le musée de la Haye pour une exposition hollandaise), tableau qu'il adorait et croyait connaître très bien, un petit pan de mur jaune (qu'il ne se rappelait pas) était si bien peint qu'il était, si on le regardait seul, comme une précieuse œuvre d'art chinoise, d'une beauté qui se suffirait à elle-même, Bergotte mangea quelques pommes de terre, sortit et entra à l'exposition [III, 186–187].

Looking at the picture, Bergotte entirely agrees with the author of the article, and feels that his own, most recent works suffer by comparison with Vermeer:

Enfin il fut devant le Ver Meer, qu'il se rappelait plus éclatant, plus différent de tout ce qu'il connaissait, mais où, grâce à l'article du critique, il remarqua pour la première fois des petits personnages en bleu, que le sable était rose, et enfin la précieuse matière du tout petit pan de mur jaune. Ses étourdissements augmentaient; il attachait son regard, comme un enfant à un papillon jaune qu'il veut saisir, au précieux petit pan de mur. "C'est ainsi que j'aurais dû écrire, disait-il. Mes derniers livres sont trop secs, il aurait fallu passer plusieurs couches de couleur, rendre ma phrase en elle-même précieuse, comme ce petit pan de mur jaune" [III, 187].

Although the symbolic paintings of Giotto are among the first real pictures which the narrator meets, he will come, in his maturity, to value pictures, like Bergotte, less for their subjects than for the light in which those subjects are displayed and the color which the artist has chosen for their portrayal. That is not to say that he is entirely indifferent to the choice of subject. He will even learn to appreciate the sights around him more because of their portrayal in pictures. And this is also true of his creator. Anyone who knows both Proust and Monet at all will realize the affinity between Proust's descriptions of water lilies on the Vivonne and Monet's series of *Nymphéas*. To select a less obvious example, there is, for me, a striking similarity between the sacrificial dawn which greets the narrator's eyes after he has decided that Albertine must be a Lesbian (II, 1128–1130), and Monet's famous *Impression: lever du soleil*. Chardin, like Elstir, teaches the narrator the beauties of the humble still life, while he learns to view Venice through the eyes of Veronese (III, 626). But, as we have already seen, it is the use of light and color which he most admires in such painters as Rembrandt and Vermeer. Most of all, he will see these qualities in Elstir, who represents both Turner and the Impressionists. Light is particularly important in this connection, for it was in the paintings of Turner and the Impressionists that light acquired so much importance as to destroy form, if not altogether, at least to a large extent.

My acquaintance with the works of these articles led me to believe that I might be able to say something new about Elstir's debt to them. But when I looked at Juliette Monnin-Hornung's study, *Proust et la peinture*, I found that in some cases she had been able to arrive at conclusions which had escaped me, while in other cases (although not all) I had merely repeated the conclusions which she had already reached. So I will, for the most part, refer to her conclusions, while adding a few suggestions of my own.

The first thing that is perceived upon entering Elstir's studio is a series of canvases, on one of which is seen "une vague de la mer écrasant avec colère sur le sable son écume lilas" and on another "un jeune homme en coutil blanc accoudé sur le pont d'un bateau" (I, 834). The description of the wave is so vague as to be applicable to any impressionist painting, but Monet and Renoir were particularly fond of shades of lilac in their shadows. The young man recalls, with some fairly basic changes, Manet's *Canotage à Argenteuil*.

Next, Proust invites us to inspect Elstir's *Port de Carquethuit*, a picture on which Monnin-Hornung can see the mark of several paintings by Turner, these being *Portsmouth seen from the Sea, Fishermen in the Wind, View of Plymouth with Mount Batten, The Castle and Regattas at East Cowes, Scarborough,* and *The Port of Dieppe.* Monnin-Hornung can also see in it the influence of two paintings by Manet, *Port-Goulphar* and *Port de Honfleur.*[5] When, later on, the narrator gives us other examples of Elstir's taste for painting the illusion which he can see rather than the reality which he knows to be there, Monnin-Hornung is able, in every instance, to point to a painting of Turner behind the painting of Elstir. A river which, because of a bend in its course, seems at one point to constitute a closed lake, recalls *The Mouth of the Avon* and *Yorkshire Coast near Whitby.*[6] In another picture, a section of the sea seems completely cut off from the main body of the sea, being enclosed by rocks. This makes Monnin-Hornung think of *Lulworth Cove.*[7] Formerly, the narrator says, Elstir had painted a castle the reflection of whose tower was so exactly mirrored in the water at its feet as to seem a continuation of the castle. Here Monnin-Hornung refers us to Turner's *Bernard Castle.*[8] Then Proust shows us a picture in which a river, passing through a town, appears completely dislocated, thereby recalling Turner's *The Crook of the Lune.*[9]

The portrait of *Miss Sacripant* which the narrator discovers as he rummages among Elstir's paintings makes Monnin-Hornung think simultaneously of Manet and of Whistler, partly because of the pose, partly because of the technique, and partly because of the subject matter.[10]

Elstir also paints still lifes, and the narrator is particularly impressed by an Elstir painting of the remains on a dinner table after the diners have left. It makes him see beauty in what had never before seemed to him to be a beautiful spectacle (I, 869). I do not know of any Impressionist painting which corresponds exactly to this, although there are two early Matisses which suggest it. One, *Table de dîner*, shows such a dinner table before the guests have arrived, while another, *Servante bretonne*, shows the remains of a

[5] Juliette Monnin-Hornung, *Proust et la peinture* (Genève: Droz, 1951), pp. 93–94.
[6] I, 838–839; cf. Monnin-Hornung, p. 92.
[7] I, 839; cf. Monnin-Hornung, p. 92.
[8] I, 839; cf. Monnin-Hornung, p. 91.
[9] Ibid.
[10] I, 848–849; cf. Monnin-Hornung, pp. 98–99.

very simple meal, without the bowls of fruit or the oysters which figure in the Elstir painting. Perhaps Proust was also thinking of Chardin, in such a way as to turn him into an Impressionist.

When Elstir shows the narrator and his girl friends sketches of "de jolies yachtswomen" (I, 897) or of a race track near Balbec, he makes us think of the paintings by Monet and Renoir entitled *La Grenouillère* or of *Voiture aux Courses* by Degas. This choice of subjects also makes Monnin-Hornung think of Helleu.[11] I myself am reminded of James Tissot who, while no more of an Impressionist than Helleu, had a taste for painting fashionable ladies on yachts. On the same visit, Elstir goes on to show the narrator a picture of rocks which appear to have been cut out into arches like those of a cathedral. Monnin-Hornung here sees an allusion to Monet's *Les Falaises d'Étretat*,[12] and it is true that there is a striking similarity between the rock formation described by Proust and that depicted on Monet's picture. However, the rocks are not pink in Monet's picture as they are in Proust's description (although they have some traces of russet), while below these rocks Monet has painted a violently stormy sea, beaten up to a yellowish-white froth with very few shadows, rather than the still, vaporous sea covered with shadows which Proust describes to us.

In "Le Côté de Guermantes," in a passage comparing Elstir to La Berma, Proust tells us that Elstir "avait trouvé le motif de deux tableaux qui se valent, dans un bâtiment scolaire sans caractère et dans une cathédrale qui est, par elle-même, un chef-d'oeuvre" (II, 51). Nobody's paintings of cathedrals can be more famous than the series which Monet painted, at different times of day, of Rouen Cathedral. I do not know of any painting by Monet of a school building, but he painted more than one successful picture of the *Gare Saint-Lazare*, which may be regarded as a fair equivalent, so far as the banality of the architecture is concerned, of a school building. In the same volume, Proust describes the narrator's wish to see more paintings by Elstir, a wish which had first been prompted by the narrator's interest in Elstir's choice of subjects and which is now based on a greater awareness of the value of his painting. Proust lists typical subjects of Elstir as being "un dégel véritable, une authentique place de province, de vivantes femmes sur la plage" (II, 125.) These are subjects which are found among the works of the Impressionists. Monet painted a *Dégel à Lavacourt*, Pissarro painted several

---

[11] Monnin-Hornung, pp. 99–100.
[12] I, 901; cf. Monnin-Hornung, p. 96.

views of provincial towns, and Monet, Manet, and Degas all painted
women at the seaside. On the same page, Proust informs us that Elstir had gone through a mythological phase and had also been influenced by Japanese art. The mythological paintings, which are
more fully described when the narrator sees the Elstir collection in
the Hôtel de Guermantes (II, 420), strike Monnin-Hornung as being
reminiscent both of Gustave Moreau and of Turner.[13] She says
nothing of Elstir's Japanese period, of which we have no descriptions, but it is not irrelevant to remark that Van Gogh went through
a Japanese stage, that Manet painted Zola in a room with Japanese
decorations, and that Mary Cassatt's lithographs and etchings are
typically Japanese in their treatment of line and mass.

When the narrator finally finds himself in front of the Elstir collection at the Hôtel de Guermantes, he is particularly taken by a
picture representing "une fête populaire au bord de l'eau" (II, 420).
This scene, which includes a gentleman in a frock coat and top hat
who is obviously the artist's friend or patron, is clearly based on
Renoir's *Le Déjeuner des canotiers*. I can only agree with Monnin-
Hornung when she says that the Elstir painting contains reminiscences of this picture, together with two other pictures by Renoir,
Le Moulin de la Galette (since a lady who has been dancing figures
in the Elstir picture) and *La Grenouillère* (since this gives an impression of boats and water which is entirely absent from *Le Déjeuner des canotiers*).[14] All three pictures convey that impression of the
capture of a fleeting moment which is so typical of the Elstir
painting.

In the course of the discussion of Elstir which subsequently takes
place around the Guermantes's dinner table, Mme de Guermantes
tells the narrator that Zola had written a study on Elstir. This, as
Monnin-Hornung informs us, equates him with Manet.[15] On the
same page, the narrator remarks that Elstir had been, at one time,
somewhat influenced by Manet. In his reply, the Duc de Guermantes
mentions that Swann had wanted them to buy a *Botte d'asperges*
by Elstir, but that they had thought it too expensive (II, 501). We
may connect this painting with the *Botte de radis* which the narrator considers Elstir's greatest painting (II, 223), and both of them
with a painting by Manet.[16]

[13] Monnin-Hornung, pp. 100–101.
[14] Ibid., pp. 96–97.
[15] II, 500; cf. Monnin-Hornung, p. 99.
[16] Monnin-Hornung, p. 99.

In "Sodome et Gomorrhe," the narrator and Albertine visit the church of Marcouville-l'Orgueilleuse, whose façade is so completely dissolved in light as to make it worthy of being painted by Elstir, in spite of the failure of the church to measure up to Elstir's standards in architecture (II, 1014). Here we may think of Monet's painting, *Cathédrale de Rouen: plein soleil*, in which the architectural details of the cathedral almost completely disappear, resolved as they are into a play of light and shadow, with light predominating. Finally, in "La Fugitive," we come back to Renoir, as a painting of Elstir's which makes the narrator think of Albertine is described in terms which immediately recall Renoir's *Baigneuses*.[17]

The narrator's education in the visual arts consists mainly of the changes in his attitude towards the paintings of Elstir. This artist is first encountered at Balbec, where he is valued primarily by the narrator as a means of getting closer to Albertine. However, from the moment when he enters Elstir's studio, the narrator does feel a special joy at the sight of the paintings with which he is surrounded. This joy depends very largely on the extent to which the subjects depicted by the painter are recognized as having been removed from the world of material reality, and placed in a world of purely aesthetic values. The narrator has come a long way from the time when he looked for confirmation of the reality of a painting in the reality of the world around him. Although, as we shall see, he is still capable of valuing a painting exclusively for its connection with material reality, he is now capable, at least at moments, of seeing that aesthetic reality is a thing apart:

Et l'atelier d'Elstir m'apparut comme le laboratoire d'une sorte de nouvelle création du monde, où, du chaos que sont toutes choses que nous voyons, il avait tiré, en les peignant sur divers rectangles de toile qui étaient posés dans tous les sens, ici une vague de la mer écrasant avec colère sur le sable son écume lilas, là un jeune homme en coutil blanc accoudé sur le pont d'un bateau. Le veston du jeune homme et la vague éclaboussante avaient pris une dignité nouvelle du fait qu'ils continuaient à être, encore que dépourvus de ce en quoi ils passaient pour consister, la vague ne pouvant plus mouiller, ni le veston habiller personne [I, 834].

However, this does not stop the narrator from bringing these dematerialized representations back into the world of material reality,

[17] III, 527; cf. Monnin-Hornung, p. 97. I should add, for the benefit of those readers who may be interested in comparing reproductions of these paintings with Proust's descriptions, that there are several reproductions, particularly of Turner, in Monnin-Hornung's study. Reproductions of most of the other paintings to which I have referred may be found in Phoebe Pool, *Impressionism* (London: Thames and Hudson, 1967).

and becoming eager to visit, in actual fact, the places which the
narrator has depicted, just as he had longed to visit the places
described in his favorite books. He is acutely disconcerted to discover that a particular spot which he wishes to visit, after having
seen Elstir's painting of it, is one which he has already seen many
times without feeling any particular enthusiasm. He is still not entirely free of the habit of supposing that the painting takes its value
from what it represents, instead of the other way around. He feels
pleased when he discovers a picture — the portrait of *Miss Sacripant* — which appears to justify this tendency:

Je me trouvai ainsi mettre au jour une aquarelle qui devait être d'un
temps bien plus ancien de la vie d'Elstir et me causa cette sorte particulière
d'enchantement que dispensent des œuvres, non seulement d'une exécution délicieuse, mais aussi d'un sujet si singulier et si séduisant que c'est
à lui que nous attribuons une partie de leur charme, comme si, ce charme,
le peintre n'avait eu qu'à le découvrir, qu'à l'observer, matériellement
réalisé déjà dans la nature et à le reproduire. Que de tels objets puissent
exister, beaux en dehors même de l'interprétation du peintre, cela contente
en nous un matérialisme inné, combattu par la raison, et sert de con-
trepoids aux abstractions de l'esthétique [I, 847–848].

Elstir himself is not entirely free from this idea. This appears in
the admiration which he feels for the appearance of his wife, who
represents the embodiment of his ideal. She is completely beautiful
in his eyes, but not, as yet, in those of the narrator. The narrator will
come to see her beauty later on, as a result of studying the representations of it in the art of Elstir:

Plus tard, quand je connus la peinture mythologique d'Elstir, Mme Elstir
prit pour moi aussi de la beauté. Je compris qu'à un certain type idéal
résumé en certaines lignes, en certaines arabesques qui se retrouvaient sans
cesse dans son œuvre, à un certain canon, il avait attribué en fait un
caractère presque divin, puisque tout son temps, tout l'effort de pensée
dont il était capable, en un mot toute sa vie, il l'avait consacrée à la
tâche de distinguer mieux ces lignes, de les reproduire plus exactement.
Ce qu'un tel idéal inspirait à Elstir, c'était vraiment un culte si grave, si
exigeant, qu'il ne lui permettait jamais d'être content; cet idéal, c'était la
partie la plus intime de lui-même: aussi n'avait-il pu le considérer avec
détachement, en tirer des émotions, jusqu'au jour où il le rencontra, réalisé
au dehors, dans le corps d'une femme, le corps de celle qui était par la
suite devenue madame Elstir et chez qui il avait pu — comme cela ne nous
est possible que pour ce qui n'est pas nous-mêmes — le trouver méritoire,
attendrissant, divin. Quel repos, d'ailleurs, de poser ses lèvres sur ce Beau
que jusqu'ici il fallait avec tant de peine extraire de soi, et qui maintenant,
mystérieusement incarné, s'offrait à lui pour une suite de communions
efficaces! [I, 850–851].

This materialism on Elstir's part is due to the fact that he is no longer young. Age is beginning to diminish his creative and imaginative faculties. Fatigue is what makes him see the beautiful incarnate in his wife — a fatigue which is not yet operative when he paints landscapes and still lifes, but which will one day come to affect every part of his work: "Et ainsi la beauté de la vie, mot en quelque sorte dépourvu de signification, stade situé en deçà de l'art et auquel j'avais vu s'arrêter Swann, était celui où, par ralentissement du génie créateur, idolatrie des formes qui l'avaient favorisé, désir du moindre effort, devait un jour rétrograder peu à peu un Elstir" (I, 852).

But even if this "idolatry" is wrong, there is a way of seeing material reality in terms of pictures which bestows an enhanced value on that reality, and which is the exact opposite of seeing a series of ready-made pictures in material reality. Just as Bergotte had made the beauty of things of which the narrator had never before been aware burst upon him by means of a metaphor, so shadows on the sea became valuable to the narrator because of the way in which Elstir has represented them. The sunlight on the sea, which is so still as to seem like a vapor, becomes beautiful in the narrator's eyes, by the same token, although only the stormy or misty sea had seemed beautiful to him before. Modern yachts, modern costumes, and horse races now also seem attractive to the narrator because their beauty has been shown to him by Elstir. Elstir's flower paintings constitute a revelation of the essential nature of the flowers such that the narrator would have liked to commission from him portraits of his favorite flowers: "C'était des fleurs, mais pas de celles dont j'eusse mieux aimer [sic] lui commander le portrait que celui d'une personne, afin d'apprendre par la révélation de son génie ce qui j'avais souvent cherché en vain devant elles — aubépines, épines roses, bluets, fleurs de pommiers" (I, 847). The narrator is, of course, on the wrong track here, for Elstir would reveal to him, not the inner meaning which the flowers intrinsically have (if such a thing exists), but the meaning which they have for him, Elstir. To obtain a portrait of the inner meaning which these flowers have for himself, the narrator would have to paint it himself. Finally, Elstir also reveals to him the beauty of the still life:

Depuis que j'en avais vu dans des aquarelles d'Elstir, je cherchais à retrouver dans la réalité, j'aimais comme quelque chose de poétique, le geste interrompu des couteaux encore de travers, la rondeur bombée d'une serviette défaite où le soleil intercale un morceau de velours jaune, le verre à demi vide qui montre mieux ainsi le noble évasement de ses formes et, au fond de son vitrage translucide et pareil à une condensation du jour, un reste de vin sombre mais scintillant de lumières, le déplacement des volumes, la transmutation des liquides par l'éclairage, l'altération des prunes qui passent du vert au bleu et du bleu à l'or dans le compotier déjà à demi dépouillé, la promenade des chaises vieillottes qui deux fois par jour viennent s'installer autour de la nappe, dressée sur la table ainsi que sur un autel où sont célébrées les fêtes de la gourmandise, et sur laquelle au fond des huîtres quelques gouttes d'eau lustrale restent comme dans de petits bénitiers de pierre; j'essayais de trouver la beauté là où je ne m'étais jamais figuré qu'elle fût, dans les choses les plus usuelles, dans la vie profonde des "natures mortes" [I, 869].

Elstir's paintings convey the inner truth of things (or at least the inner truth of what they mean for Elstir) and bestow enhanced value on the objects which they represent. But the impression which the narrator has on looking at his first Elstir paintings is also one of transformation and illusion. Both transformation and illusion consist of rendering objects in terms of one another — as the sea in terms of the land, and vice versa, in the *Port de Carquethuit*: "Naturellement, ce qu'il y avait dans son atelier, ce n'était guère que des marines prises ici, à Balbec. Mais j'y pouvais discerner que le charme de chacune consistait en une sorte de métamorphose des choses représentées, analogue à celle qu'en poésie on nomme métaphore, et que, si Dieu le Père avait créé les choses en les nommant, c'est en leur ôtant leur nom, ou en leur en donnant un autre, qu'Elstir les recréait" (I, 835). By his use of the word "metaphor" Proust establishes a parallel between literature and painting. But then he goes on to describe an effect which is usually only achieved by painting, although Proust can find examples of it in his favorite authors, such as Mme de Sévigné (I, 653). The actual impression made upon the eye by the scene, not the reconstruction of it by the intelligence, is what Elstir has represented, with an effect which appears unreal and mystical because of the way in which material reality has been melted down, in the crucible of the artist's mind, and given a new form which corresponds to the artist's vision:

C'est par exemple à une métaphore de ce genre — dans un tableau représentant le port de Carquethuit, tableau qu'il avait terminé depuis peu de jours et que je regardai longuement — qu'Elstir avait préparé l'esprit du spectateur en n'employant pour la petite ville que des termes marins et que des termes urbains pour la mer. Soit que les maisons cachassent une partie du port, un bassin de calfatage ou peut-être la mer même s'enfonçant en golfe dans les terres, ainsi que cela arrivait constamment dans ce pays de Balbec, de l'autre côté de la pointe avancée où était construite la ville, les toits étaient dépassés (comme ils l'eussent été par des cheminées

ou par des clochers) par des mâts, lesquels avaient l'air de faire des vais-
seaux auxquels ils appartenaient, quelque chose de citadin, de construit
sur terre, impression qu'augmentaient d'autres bateaux, demeurés le long
de la jetée, mais en rangs si pressés que les hommes y causaient d'un
bâtiment à l'autre sans qu'on pût distinguer leur séparation et l'interstice
de l'eau, et ainsi cette flottille de pêche avait moins l'air d'appartenir à
la mer que, par example, les églises de Criquebec qui, au loin, entourées
d'eau de tous côtés parce qu'on les voyait sans la ville, dans un poudroie-
ment de soleil et de vagues, semblaient sortir des eaux, soufflées en albâtre
ou en écume et, enfermées dans la ceinture d'un arc-en-ciel versicolore,
former un tableau irréel et mystique [I, 836].

Yet this picture which has so little correspondence with material
reality claims a value of superior reality.

Because of this value, it is in pictures, and especially in Elstir's
pictures, that the narrator will come to locate that transcendental
reality which he once sought in the works of Bergotte, and then, on
Bergotte's testimony, in the acting of La Berma, especially in
Phèdre:

A vrai dire je n'attachais aucun prix à cette possibilité d'entendre la
Berma qui, quelques années auparavant, m'avait causé tant d'agitation. Et
ce ne fut pas sans mélancolie que je constatai mon indifférence à ce que
jadis j'avais préféré à la santé, au repos. Ce n'est pas que fût moins passionné qu'alors mon désir de pouvoir contempler de près les parcelles précieuses de réalité qu'entrevoyait mon imagination. Mais celle-ci ne les
situait plus maintenant dans la diction d'une grande actrice; depuis mes
visites chez Elstir, c'est sur certaines tapisseries, sur certains tableaux modernes, que j'avais reporté la foi intérieure que j'avais eue jadis en ce jeu,
en cet art tragique de la Berma; ma foi, mon désir ne venant plus rendre
à la diction et aux attitudes de la Berma un culte incessant, le "double"
que je possédais d'eux, dans mon coeur, avait dépéri peu à peu comme
ces autres "doubles" des trépassés de l'ancienne Egypte qu'il fallait constamment nourrir pour entretenir leur vie [II, 36–37].

However, the memory of his past disenchantments causes the narrator to harbor a certain latent skepticism in the midst of this, his
latest enthusiasm:

Tel soir où, malade, je partais pour aller voir dans un château un tableau
d'Elstir, une tapisserie gothique, ressemblait tellement au jour où j'avais
dû partir pour Venise, à celui où j'étais allé entendre la Berma ou partir
pour Balbec, que d'avance je sentais que l'objet présent de mon sacrifice
me laisserait indifférent au bout de peu de temps, que je pourrais alors
passer très près de lui sans aller regarder ce tableau, ces tapisseries pour
lesquelles j'eusse en ce moment affronté tant de nuits sans sommeil, tant
de crises douloureuses [II, 45].

Later again, the narrator comes to value Elstir's pictures for their
own sake, not for what they represent or for any transcendental real-

ity into which they might initiate him. We see this as he hunts for a pretext which will allow him to ask Saint-Loup if he may visit his aunt, the Duchesse de Guermantes, who has a collection of Elstir paintings:

Or, ce prétexte me fut fourni par le désir que j'avais de revoir des tableaux d'Elstir, le grand peintre que Saint-Loup et moi nous avions connu à Balbec. Prétexte où il y avait, d'ailleurs, quelque vérité car si, dans mes visites à Elstir, j'avais demandé à sa peinture de me conduire à la compréhension et à l'amour de choses meilleures qu'elle-même, un dégel véritable, une authentique place de province, de vivantes femmes sur la plage (tout au plus lui eussé-je commandé le portrait des réalités que je n'avais pas su approfondir, comme un chemin d'aubépine, non pour qu'il me conservât leur beauté mais me la decouvrît), maintenant, au contraire, c'était l'originalité, la séduction de ces peintures qui excitaient mon désir, et ce que je voulais surtout voir, c'était d'autres tableaux d'Elstir [II, 125].

The narrator is beginning to see that what is special about Elstir's paintings is the insight which they afford into this particular artist's special vision of the world:

Il me semblait d'ailleurs que ses moindres tableaux, à lui, étaient quelque chose d'autre que les chefs-d'œuvre de peintres même plus grands. Son œuvre était comme un royaume clos, aux frontières infranchissables, à la matière sans seconde [II, 125].

The narrator's awareness of this special vision is reinforced when he finds himself in front of the Elstirs at the Hôtel de Guermantes:

De nouveau comme à Balbec j'avais devant moi les fragments de ce monde aux couleurs inconnues qui n'était que la projection de la manière de voir particulière à ce grand peintre et que ne traduisait nullement ses paroles. Les parties du mur couvertes de peintures de lui, toutes homogènes les unes aux autres, étaient comme les images lumineuses d'une lanterne magique laquelle eût été, dans le cas présent, la tête de l'artiste et dont on n'eût pu soupçonner l'étrangeté tant qu'on n'aurait fait que connaître l'homme, c'est-à-dire tant qu'on n'aurait fait que voir la lanterne coiffant la lampe, avant qu'aucun verre coloré eût encore été placé [II, 419].

The artist is himself a magic lantern, transfiguring and dematerializing the universe by the projection of colored light. Art is a matter, not of copying transcendental realities or objects beautiful in themselves, but of vision.

In Chapter One, we considered the question of Proust's debt to Schopenhauer. In this connection, we may raise this question again, since it is not beyond the bounds of possibility that Proust borrowed the image of the magic lantern from Schopenhauer. In view of the importance which Proust attributes to metaphor, this would be an important loan. Schopenhauer, too, has his magic lantern: "As the

magic lantern shows many different pictures, which are all made
visible by one and the same light, so in all the multifarious phenomena which fill the world together or throng after each other as
events, only *one will* manifests itself, of which everything is the visi-
bility, the objectivity, and which remains in the midst of this
change; it alone is thing-in-itself; all objects are manifestations, or,
to speak the language of Kant, phenomena." [18] As we can see from
this passage, Schopenhauer uses the image of the magic lantern to
suggest that the will, seen as the light behind the lantern, shines
through phenomena, which are like the slides. We have only to
adapt this metaphor a little, replacing the central importance of the
cosmic will by that of the artist's vision, to arrive at the Proustian
idea that the artist's mind both contains that single light which
illumines and projects phenomena and takes up and transforms
phenomena which, in their transformed state, still retain their function of magic lantern slides. This adaptation of Schopenhauer's
metaphor may be explained by the influence of another use of the
same metaphor, in Tolstoy's *War and Peace* (a novel which Proust
certainly knew well, since he refers to it in a conversation between
the narrator and Albertine) (III, 378). Tolstoy uses the metaphor of
the magic lantern to define the way in which emotion colors our
view of things. When Prince Andrei sees that his death is imminent,
the idea of death takes on, for him, the form of a cold, white light
without shadows, perspective, or outline, while everything which
had motivated him in his life appears like a series of magic lantern
pictures seen through artificial light.[19] The two uses of the same
basic metaphor may well have coalesced in Proust's memory and
imagination to result in his double use of the image of the magic
lantern to express both what Coleridge called Fancy, that is, the
delusive side of the imagination, as it leads the imaginative person
astray, and what Coleridge called Imagination, as it operates in the
mind of the creative artist.

  It is also possible that Proust, when he gave so much importance
to the prism, the spectrum, and the rainbow, was thinking of the
way in which Schopenhauer uses the metaphor of the rainbow.
Schopenhauer's use of this metaphor is very striking, in view of the
way in which it is connected with his doctrine of the ability of the

    [18] Schopenhauer, I, 199–200.
    [19] L. N. Tolstoy, *War and Peace*, trans. Rosemary Edmonds, 2 vols. (Harmonds-
worth: Penguin Books, 1968), II, 914.

contemplative mystic and the artistic genius to see through appearance to the reality beyond:

The method of viewing things which proceeds in accordance with the principle of sufficient reason is the rational method, and it alone is valid and of use in practical life and science. The method which looks away from the content of this principle is the method of genius, which is only valid and of use in art. The first is the method of Aristotle; the second is, on the whole, like that of Plato. The first is like the mighty storm, that rushes along without beginning and without aim, bending, agitating, and carrying away everything before it; the second is like the silent sunbeam that pierces through the storm quite unaffected by it. The first is like the innumerable showering drops of the waterfall, which, constantly changing, never rest for an instant; the second is like the rainbow, quietly resting on this raging torrent. Only through the pure contemplation described above, which rests entirely in the object, can Ideas be comprehended; and the nature of *genius* consists in pre-eminent capacity for such contemplation.[20]

In this connection, we may remember the rainbow which hung over the port in Elstir's painting, *Le Port de Carquethuit*, adding to its unreal and mystical appearance. The painter has bodied forth a representation of material reality, based on a type of contemplation which may be compared, in its serenity, to a rainbow, and, to give us what may be taken as visible evidence of this contemplation, he has attached a rainbow to his painting. Of course, what Elstir is seeing is not Schopenhauer's Ideas but his own idea; and yet Proust's use of the image of the rainbow recalls Schopenhauer's use of this image.

To return to the subject of the narrator's quest, we may say that, with the realization that art is a matter of vision, his pilgrimage, so far as the visual arts are concerned, is complete. But it is as possible to stray into false paths when traveling along the road of the visual arts as it is when traveling along that of literature. Once again, in his attitude to painting as in his attitude to literature, Charles Swann offers an instructive bad example. The temptation, in dealing with the visual arts, is, as we have seen, that of "idolatry" — the supposition that a picture derives its value from what it represents, instead of the other way around. Swann succumbs to this temptation in his dealings with Odette, whom he sees as a Botticelli painting. This would be permissible, in Proust's eyes, if his awareness of this resemblance were to lead Swann away from his infatuation with Odette toward a renewed cult for Botticelli, especially if this were to lead in turn toward some creative activity on his part. But, in actual fact, the reverse occurs.

[20] Schopenhauer, I, 239–240.

Swann has always had a taste for seeing his contemporaries as the modern equivalents of famous paintings. It was he, for instance, who pointed out to the narrator the resemblance between the pregnant kitchen maid and Giotto's *Charity*. Proust suggests various reasons for this tendency:

Peut-être, ayant toujours gardé un remords d'avoir borné sa vie aux relations mondaines, à la conversation, croyait-il trouver une sorte d'indulgent pardon à lui accordé par les grands artistes, dans ce fait qu'ils avaient eux aussi considéré avec plaisir, fait entrer dans leur œuvre, de tels visages qui donnent à celle-ci un singulier certificat de réalité et de vie, une saveur moderne; peut-être aussi s'était-il tellement laissé gagner par la frivolité des gens du monde qu'il éprouvait le besoin de trouver dans une œuvre ancienne ces allusions anticipées et rajeunissantes à des noms propres d'aujourd'hui. Peut-être, au contraire, avait-il gardé sufisamment une nature d'artiste pour que ces caractéristiques individuelles lui causassent du plaisir en prenant une signification plus générale, dès qu'il les apercevait, déracinées, délivrées, dans la ressemblance d'un portrait plus ancien avec un original qu'il ne représentait pas [I, 223].

The last-mentioned possibility suggests the hope that Swann will be able to extricate himself from the snare represented by Odette by turning her into an art work, and so elevating her from the sphere of the particular to that of the general. But, in fact, he comes to value Botticelli's painting as a portrait of Odette, and so brings Botticelli down from the sphere of the general to that of the particular. Having done this, if he then sees Odette as an art work, it is in such a particular, materialistic way that it does nothing to support his "nature d'artiste" but rather degrades it.

To begin with, Swann sees Odette as Botticelli's *Zipporah* in much the same spirit as that in which he sees his coachman as the portrait of a doge, or Dr. du Boulbon as a painting by Tintoretto. This spotting of similarities, whatever its motivation, is an intellectual game with him, and hardly anything else. But, in the case of Odette, her resemblance to a Botticelli painting becomes of great emotional importance:

Il n'estima plus le visage d'Odette selon la plus ou moins bonne qualité de ses joues et d'après la douceur purement carnée qu'il supposait devoir leur trouver avec ses lèvres si jamais il osait l'embrasser, mais comme un écheveau de lignes subtiles et belles que ses regards dévidèrent, poursuivant la courbe de leur enroulement, rejoignant la cadence de la nuque à l'effusion des cheveux et à la flexion des paupières, comme en un portrait d'elle en lequel son type devenait intelligible et clair.

Il la regardait; un fragment de la fresque apparaissait dans son visage et dans son corps, que dès lors il chercha toujours à y retrouver, soit qu'il fût auprès d'Odette, soit qu'il pensât seulement à elle; et bien qu'il ne tînt sans doute au chef-d'œuvre florentin que parce qu'il retrouvait en elle, pourtant cette ressemblance lui conférait à elle aussi une beauté, la rendait plus précieuse. Swann se reprocha d'avoir méconnu le prix d'un être qui eût paru adorable au grand Sandre, et il se félicita que le plaisir qu'il avait à voir Odette trouvât une justification dans sa propre culture esthétique. Il se dit qu'en associant la pensée d'Odette à ses rêves de bonheur, il ne s'était pas résigné à un pis aller aussi imparfait qu'il l'avait cru jusqu'ici, puisqu'elle contentait en lui ses goûts d'art les plus raffinés [I, 223–224].

Odette, who had seemed rather uninteresting to Swann to begin with, increases in value by this comparison, as does his love for her, in consequence:

Le mot d'"œuvre florentine" rendit un grand service à Swann. Il lui permit, comme un titre, de faire pénétrer l'image d'Odette dans un monde de rêves où elle n'avait pas eu accès jusqu'ici et où elle s'imprégna de noblesse. Et, tandis que la vue purement charnelle qu'il avait eue de cette femme, en renouvelant perpétuellement ses doutes sur la qualité de son visage, de son corps, de toute sa beauté, affaiblissait son amour, ces doutes furent détruits, cet amour assuré quand il eut à la place pour base les données d'une esthétique certaine; sans compter que le baiser et la possession qui semblaient naturels et médiocres s'ils lui étaient accordés par une chair abimée, venant couronner l'adoration d'une pièce de musée, lui parurent devoir être surnaturels et délicieux [I, 224].

In embracing her, he has the impression that he is possessing a work of art. But this is a way in which no work of art could, or should, be possessed. In his attitude to Odette, Swann is guilty of idolatry of the most extreme sort, as Monnin-Hornung points out.[21]

Apart from his taste for seeing people in terms of pictures, with the bad results we have observed, Swann treats works of art as objects of scholarship or of sensuous enjoyment, never of fervent admiration. In this, he is quite different from the true devotee of the religion of art who, as Proust observed in his preface to the *Bible d'Amiens* and in his article "En mémoire des églises assassinées," is as far as possible from being a dilettante who spends his time in the voluptuous contemplation of works of art. The true worshiper of art has to love beauty for itself, as something real existing beyond himself and infinitely more important than the joy it gives him.[22] Swann is very far from having such an enthusiastic, altruistic attitude. His attitude to art veers from the sensuous to the cold. He once started a study of Vermeer, which he uses, before falling in love

[21] Monnin-Hornung, pp. 42–43.
[22] Proust, *Pastiches et mélanges* (Paris: N.R.F., 1958), p. 154; Ruskin, *La Bible d'Amiens*, traduction, notes et préface par Marcel Proust (Paris: Mercure de France, 1926), p. 54.

with Odette, as a pretext to see her less often than he might; but at that moment he had not worked on it for some time. He does take it up again, but we understand that it is never completed. He has a collection of paintings, but makes only the driest comments on pictures, preferring to restrict himself to purely factual information. He uses his quite real knowledge of and taste for painting in order to advise society ladies in their selection of pictures. Altogether, his attitude toward the visual arts is the reverse of edifying, being (in Proust's opinion) typical of his general habit of setting life above art and subordinating his intellectual enthusiasms to mediocre ends. And yet, as we noticed in the previous chapter, Swann would have been capable of cultivating a genuine passion for art, if fear, specifically the fear of making himself ridiculous, had not held him back. There does come a moment, at the beginning of the *soirée* of Mme de Saint-Euverte, when Swann, owing to his state of detachment from everything which is not Odette, sees the people around him in terms of pictures with a detail, intensity and continuity which makes his view of them seem more like that of an artist than a dilettante. But when his suffering overcomes him once more, as the "petite phrase" of Vinteuil's sonata brings back memories of the time when Odette loved him, he becomes incapable of entertaining any aesthetic impressions other than those which the sonata is bringing to him, and, as his life continues, the memories both of his response to the music and of his moment of detached, creative vision fade away, never to be recalled.

The narrator shows some slight tendency to fall into the same error as Swann, but he does this to a much lesser extent, and chiefly when he is very young. His admiration for the Duchesse de Guermantes, for instance, is based not only on the works of literature with which his fancy has associated her; she also acquires a borrowed glory from the stained glass windows in the parish church of Combray and from the magic lantern slides.[23] But this borrowed glory which is the work of Fancy, will fade away, to a large extent, as time goes on. If Gilberte, by the same token, attracts the boy's attention, it is not only because of the prestige she has derived from her association with Bergotte. It is also because the narrator sees her for the first time immediately after his aesthetic perceptions and infantile greed have been roused, together, to the highest pitch, by the sight of the pink hawthorn which she, in a way, resembles. Al-

[23] Cf. Moss, p. 57.

bertine, too, acquires some borrowed prestige from the fact that it was Elstir who introduced the narrator to her. But the narrator never acquires the fixed habit of thinking of any of his loves as an art work. Although he does think of Albertine as an art work at moments, these moments never last long, and the moments when he thinks of her in this way are the ones when she seems least desirable to him as a woman; he is hardly ever able to think of her as a woman and as an art work at the same time:

Tout ce coin de la chambre semblait réduit à n'être plus que le sanctuaire éclairé, la crèche de cet ange musicien, œuvre d'art qui, tout à l'heure, par une douce magie, allait se détacher de sa niche et offrir à mes baisers sa substance précieuse et rose. Mais non; Albertine n'était nullement pour moi une œuvre d'art. Je savais ce que c'etait qu'admirer une femme d'une façon artistique, j'avais connu Swann. . . . Même, pour dire vrai, quand je commençais à regarder Albertine comme un ange musicien merveilleusement patiné et que je me félicitais de posséder, elle ne tardait pas à me devenir indifférente; je m'ennuyais bientôt auprès d'elle, mais ces instants-là duraient peu: on n'aime que ce en quoi on poursuit quelque chose d'inaccessible, on n'aime que ce qu'on ne possède pas, et bien vite je me remettais à me rendre compte que je ne possédais pas Albertine [III, 383–384].

There are moments when Albertine acquires an enhanced value from her association, in the narrator's mind, with works of art. But, on a closer inspection, it appears that this enhancement of her value takes place in her absence and is due, in part, to the resurrection of ideas connected with the narrator's first enthusiasm for her:

Les jours où je ne descendais pas chez Mme de Guermantes, pour que le temps me semblât moins long durant cette heure qui précédait le retour de mon amie, je feuilletais un album d'Elstir, un livre de Bergotte, la sonate de Vinteuil. Alors — comme les œuvres mêmes qui semblant s'addresser seulement à la vue et à l'ouïe exigent que pour les goûter notre intelligence éveillée collabore étroitement avec ces deux sens — je faisais sans m'en douter sortir de moi les rêves qu'Albertine y avait jadis suscités quand je ne la connaissais pas encore, et qu'avait éteints la vie quotidienne. Je les jetais dans la phrase du musicien ou l'image du peintre comme dans un creuset, j'en nourrissais l'œuvre que je lisais. Et sans doute celle-ci m'en paraissait plus vivante. Mais Albertine ne gagnait pas moins à être ainsi transportée de l'un dans l'autre des deux mondes où nous avons accès et où nous pouvons situer tour à tour un même objet, à echapper ainsi à l'écrasante pression de la matière pour se jouer dans les fluides espaces de la pensée. Je me trouvais tout d'un coup et pour un instant, pouvoir éprouver pour la fastidieuse jeune fille des sentiments ardents. Elle avait à ce moment-là l'apparence d'une œuvre d'Elstir ou de Bergotte, j'éprouvais une exaltation momentanée pour elle, la voyant dans le recul de l'imagination et de l'art [III, 56].

This state of excitement is only momentary; it does not survive Albertine's return. This may be at least partly due to the fact that the narrator, as he says himself, can only associate her with art by turning her into something immaterial; her physical presence brings him back once more to the fact that she is a living woman. He would have to have Swann's disastrously sensual attitude to art to be able to combine the two ideas of an art work and a creature of flesh and blood.

Finally, after her death, Albertine becomes associated, in the narrator's mind, with works of art. Having heard from Aimé that she used to play Lesbian games with young washerwomen on the banks of the Loire, the narrator visualizes the scene in terms of two paintings:

J'avais justement vu deux peintures d'Elstir où dans un paysage touffu il y a des femmes nues. Dans l'une, l'une des jeunes filles lève le pied comme Albertine devait faire quand elle l'offrait à la blanchisseuse. De l'autre elle pousse à l'eau l'autre jeune fille qui gaîment résiste, la cuisse levée, son pied trempant à peine dans l'eau bleue. Je me rappelais maintenant que la levée de la cuisse y faisait le même méandre de cou de cygne avec l'angle du genou, que faisait la chute de la cuisse d'Albertine quand elle était à côté de moi sur le lit, et j'avais voulu souvent lui dire qu'elle me rappelait ces peintures [III, 527].

Since Albertine no longer has any existence save in his mind, it is, at last, permissible to treat her as a work of the creative imagination. Even so, this incarnation of Albertine as an Elstir painting does not last long. And there is no evidence that the narrator ever dwelled on the resemblance between Albertine and this picture in order to heighten his enjoyment in making love to her — quite the reverse is true, in fact, since the picture has always been associated in his mind with his dread of Albertine's Lesbian tendencies. At any rate, the narrator is, in his years of maturity, entirely free from the temptation to idolatry which had led Swann away from the true aesthetic path.

As Proust continues his narrative, paintings seem to be mentioned progressively less. This is due partly to the increasing importance of music and partly to the increasingly abstract turn of the narrator's thoughts. There is little discussion of pictures in "Le Temps retrouvé," but this section does contain a discussion of word-painting, phrased in terms which suggest a certain rivalry between the novelist and the painter:

Le littérateur envie le peintre, il aimerait prendre des croquis, des notes, il est perdu s'il le fait. Mais quand il écrit, il n'est pas un geste de ses personnages, un tic, un accent, qui n'ait été apporté à son inspiration par sa mémoire; il n'est pas un nom de personnage inventé sous lequel il ne puisse mettre soixante noms de personnages vus, dont l'un a posé pour la grimace, l'autre pour le monocle, tel pour la colère, tel pour le mouvement avantageux du bras, etc. Et alors l'écrivain se rend compte que si son rêve d'être un peintre n'était pas réalisable d'une manière consciente et volontaire, il se trouve pourtant avoir été réalisé et que l'écrivain, lui aussi, a fait son carnet de croquis sans le savoir [III, 899–900].

The novelist would like to be a painter himself, and is actually tempted to keep a "sketch book" (in the style of the Goncourts, whose writing has such a depressing effect on the narrator). He can succeed in becoming a word-painter, in fact, but only by giving a truthful account of the impression which certain sights, tones, and gestures have made on him, not by keeping a notebook. By remaining true to this principle he becomes not only a painter but an Impressionist painter, like Elstir. He intends to represent sensations and characters according to Impressionist principles, the narrator says. This will help to insure the truth of his work: "Seule l'impression, si chétive qu'en semble la matière, si insaisissable la trace, est un critérium de vérité, et à cause de cela mérite seule d'être appréhendée par l'esprit, car elle est seule capable, s'il sait en dégager cette vérité, de l'amener à une plus grande perfection et de lui donner une pure joie" (III, 880). In his fidelity to the impression, the narrator will truly resemble Elstir, who represents the world in terms of transfiguration and illusion, because of his fidelity to the truth of the impression. This aspect of Elstir's work is pointed out by Proust in his description of the Elstir paintings in the Hôtel de Guermantes:

Parmi ces tableaux, quelques-uns de ceux qui semblaient le plus ridicules aux gens du monde m'intéressaient plus que les autres en ce qu'ils recréaient ces illusions d'optique qui nous prouvent que nous n'identiferions pas les objets si nous ne faisions pas intervenir le raisonnement. Que de fois en voiture ne découvrons-nous pas une longue rue claire qui commence à quelques mètres de nous, alors que nous n'avons devant nous qu'un pan de mur violemment éclairé qui nous a donné le mirage de la profondeur. Dès lors, n'est-il pas logique, non par artifice de symbolisme mais par retour sincère à la racine même de l'impression, de représenter une chose par cette autre que dans l'éclair d'une illusion première nous avons prise pour elle? Les surfaces et les volumes sont en réalité indépendants des noms d'objets que notre mémoire leur impose quand nous les avons reconnus. Elstir tâchait d'arracher à ce qu'il venait de sentir ce qu'il savait; son effort avait souvent été de dissoudre cet aggrégat de raisonnements que nous appelons vision [II, 419].

In his use of light effects, especially those light effects which give a transfigured or dematerialized appearance to the objects he depicts, and in his joyful indifference to the conventional value of the subjects he selects, Proust also resembles Elstir. He becomes a second Elstir.[24] The artist whom he himself has created is his rival, but a rival whom he transcends and who justifies him.

Proust welcomed a type of painting in which light triumphed over form. If light may be taken as the equivalent of spirit and form that of matter, this suggests that he also came to welcome a triumph of spirit over matter, thereby going beyond his earlier statement, in "En Mémoire des églises assassinées," that "La matière est réelle parce qu'elle est une expression de l'esprit." [25] If we view Impressionist painting in this perspective, it seems natural to move from it to the still more spiritual world of music.

[24] Cf. Monnin-Hornung, pp. 80–81.
[25] Proust, *Pastiches et mélanges*, p. 156.

CHAPTER FOUR

MUSIC: FROM THE MATERIAL
TO THE SPIRITUAL

Works of music are conspicuously absent from the narrator's child-hood. This is, at first sight, surprising, since Vinteuil, the great com-poser, lives at Combray and is known to the narrator's family. He is, in fact, the music teacher of the narrator's great-aunts. But he is much too shy to offer to play his works. He makes tentative gestures in that direction, placing his music on the piano before visitors ar-rive, but when his visitors are actually in the room, he claims that he does not know who put the music there, and hastens to hide it again. The narrator's mother presses him, in vain, to play, but she does this only out of politeness. For the people of Combray, Vinteuil is simply an obscure music teacher who is remarkable for nothing but the questionable relationship of his daughter with another woman. So music, the most spiritual of the arts, fails to form a part of the narrator's early education.

This comes as all the more of a surprise when one considers the importance of the village church in "Combray." One would expect a passage on organ playing, at some point in the description of the church. At the wedding of Dr. Percepied's daughter, for instance, some music would be a natural accompaniment. But if there is any music at the ceremony, we do not hear about it, for the narrator's attention is totally absorbed by studying the appearance of the Duchesse de Guermantes. When she advances, smiling, from the church, at the end of the ceremony, it is to the strains of a purely metaphorical music, provided by the sunlight:

Le soileil, menacé par un nuage mais dardant encore de toute sa force sur la place et dans la sacristie, donnait une carnation de géranium aux tapis rouges qu'on y avait étendus par terre pour la solennité et sur lesquels s'avançait en souriant Mme de Guermantes, et ajoutait à leur lainage un velouté rose, un épiderme de lumière, cette sorte de tendresse, de sérieuse douceur dans la pompe et dans la joie qui caractérisent certaines pages de *Lohengrin*, certaines peintures de Carpaccio, et qui font comprendre que Baudelaire ait pu appliquer au son de la trompette l'épithète de délicieux [I, 178].

Some other musical metaphors may be found in "Combray." The most striking are those based on spatial relationships. In these cases, music is thought of as something very abstract, in that the geometrical relationship between the various parts is considered as the essential factor, and yet quite concrete, in that this geometry is, after all, spatial. Thus, the hawthorns in Swann's park fascinate the narrator by what he thinks of as musical intervals between the flowers:

Mais j'avais beau rester devant les aubépines à respirer, à porter devant ma pensée qui ne savait ce qu'elle devait en faire, à perdre, à retrouver leur invisible et fixe odeur, à m'unir au rythme qui jetait leurs fleurs, ici et là, avec une allégresse juvénile et à des intervalles inattendus comme certains intervalles musicaux, elles m'offraient indéfiniment le même charme avec une profusion inépuisable, mais sans me laisser approfondir davantage, comme ces mélodies qu'on rejoue cent fois de suite sans descendre plus avant dans leur secret [I, 138].

The steeple of the parish church is also "musical" in its proportions — a musicality which is observed, without being analyzed, by the narrator's grandmother:

Ignorante en architecture, elle disait: "Mes enfants, moquez-vous de moi si vous voulez, il n'est peut-être pas beau dans les règles, mais sa vieille figure bizarre me plaît. Je suis sûre que s'il jouait du piano, il ne jouerait pas *sec*." Et en le regardant, en suivant des yeux la douce tension, l'inclinaison fervente de ses pentes de pierre qui se rapprochaient en s'élevant comme des mains jointes qui prient, elle s'unissait si bien à l'effusion de la flèche, que son regard semblait s'élancer avec elle; et en même temps elle souriait amicalement aux vieux pierres usées dont le couchant n'éclairait plus que le faîte et qui, à partir du moment où elles entraient dans cette zone ensoleillée, adoucies par la lumière, paraissaient tout d'un coup montées bien plus haut, lointaines, comme un chant repris "en voix de tête" une octave au-dessus [I, 64].

But, in spite of the music lessons received by the narrator's great-aunts, the only music which he actually hears during his childhood is "la musique de chambre de l'été" (I, 83) executed by the flies in his bedroom. We can only suppose that this omission is deliberate. Proust presumably wishes to show his narrator at grips with works of visual art, which display the beautiful in its most material form, and with works of literature, which must, by necessity, use "real" situations and a vocabulary created by the needs of daily life to convey even the most exalted notions of spiritual beauty, before confronting him with the more unequivocally spiritual power of music.

Music does not actually make its appearance in the narrative until "Un Amour de Swann." As Swann has been used as an instructive bad example in the other arts, so he is used to show how the narrator might have failed to be fully and creatively inspired by music. But, interestingly enough, Swann comes closer to a genuine aesthetic response to music than to the other arts. This suggests the surpassing power of music. His potentially fruitful encounter with music begins, in the company of Odette, in the home of the Verdurins, who patronize all the most modern manifestations of the arts and constantly regale their guests with Wagner. Here Swann hears, for the second time, a piece of music which he had heard the previous year and which had made a great impression on him:

L'année précédente, dans une soirée, il avait entendu une œuvre musicale exécutée au piano et au violon. D'abord, il n'avait goûté que la qualité matérielle des sons sécrétés par les instruments. Et ç'avait déjà été un grand plaisir quand, au-dessous de la petite ligne du violon, mince, résistante, dense et directrice, il avait vu tout d'un coup chercher à s'élever en un clapotement liquide, la masse de la partie du piano, multiforme, indivise, plane et entrechoquée comme la mauve agitation des flots que charme et bémolise le clair de lune. Mais à un moment donné, sans pouvoir nettement distinguer un contour, donner un nom à ce qui lui plaisait, charmé tout d'un coup, il avait cherché à recueillir la phrase ou l'harmonie — il ne savait lui-même — qui passait et qui lui avait ouvert plus largement l'âme, comme certaines odeurs de roses circulant dans l'air humide du soir ont la propriété de dilater nos narines [I, 208–209].

It is not surprising to find Swann taking a sensuous pleasure in a work of art. But it is something new, in our experience of him, to find him feeling that this work of art has expanded his soul. It is the first indication we have had that Swann actually has a soul.

A particular phrase in the piece of music had held a special charm for him. As he listened to the music, this phrase recurred, more easily distinguishable as Swann became more aware of the construction of the work as a whole, "cette chose qui n'est plus de la musique pure, qui est du dessin, de l'architecture, de la pensée, et qui permet de se rappeler la musique" (I, 209). He experienced a kind of love for the phrase in question: "Cette fois il avait distingué

nettement une phrase s'élevant pendant quelques instants au-dessus
des ondes sonores. Elle lui avait proposé aussitôt des voluptés particulières, dont il n'avait jamais eu l'idée avant de l'entendre, dont il
sentait que rien d'autre qu'elle ne pourrait les lui faire connaître,
et il avait éprouvé pour elle comme un amour inconnu" (I, 209–
210). He passionately longed for the phrase, which appeared to offer
"un bonheur noble, inintelligible et précis" (I, 210), to appear for
the third time. It did so, but without increasing his pleasure. In fact,
he felt "une volupté moins profonde" (I, 210). But the need for this
piece of music remained with him: "Mais, rentré chez lui, il eut
besoin d'elle: il était comme un homme dans la vie de qui une pas-
sante qu'il a aperçue un moment vient de faire entrer l'image d'une
beauté nouvelle qui donne à sa propre sensibilité une valeur plus
grande, sans qu'il sache seulement s'il pourra revoir jamais celle qu'il
aime déjà et dont il ignore jusqu'au nom" (I, 210). Proust obviously
wishes to suggest that Swann has been offered the chance of falling
in love with the "petite phrase" instead of with Odette. He is confronted, although he fails to realize it, with the choice between an
agonizing and degrading obsession and a happiness which is both
noble and clearly defined in a way in which no happiness afforded
by love (in Proust's opinion) can be. Swann has not yet met Odette
when he hears the phrase for the first time, so there is no external
obstacle to the love he might feel for it. But, just as in the parable
of the Sower and the Seed, the seed of a true aesthetic joy which has
been sown in Swann's mind finds a shallow soil and springs up
briefly, only to wither again.

   Swann's love for the phrase gave him, for a while, a renewed
spiritual life, in the midst of the deliberate aridity of his existence:
"Swann trouvait en lui, dans le souvenir de la phrase qu'il avait en-
tendue, dans certaines sonates qu'il s'était fait jouer, pour voir s'il
ne l'y découvrirait pas, la présence d'une de ces réalités invisibles
auxquelles il avait cessé de croire et auxquelles, comme si la musique avait eu sur la sécheresse morale dont il souffrait une sorte
d'influence élective, il sentait de nouveau le désir et presque la force
de consacrer sa vie" (I, 211). There is in this passage a faint, but
identifiable, religious allusion. "Dryness" is a state of which the
mystics frequently complain. It is the state of soul in which one no
longer responds to spiritual things. For the mystic, it is a relatively
rare and consequently painful state. But for one who is not a mystic,
it may be the usual state in which he passes his life, of which he is
consequently unaware, and from which nothing may come to rescue

him. Swann is luckier than most, in that the little phrase has come
to rescue him from his dryness. But, since he was unable to find out
what work it was he had heard, or even who had composed it, he
failed to hear it a second time, and had even stopped thinking about
it, until the moment when he heard it again, by chance or fate, at
the Verdurins'. By a special dispensation of artistic Providence, the
seed has been sown a second time. Once more, it is the one phrase
which catches his attention: "Et elle était si particulière, elle avait
un charme si individuel et qu'aucun autre n'aurait pu remplacer,
que ce fut pour Swann comme s'il eût recontré dans un salon ami
une personne qu'il avait admirée dans la rue et désespérait de jamais
retrouver" (I, 211–212). At last he can discover the identity of the
phrase: it is the andante of Vinteuil's *Sonata for piano and violin*,
although played, for the Verdurins, on the piano alone.

Swann expresses his admiration of the little phrase so fervently
that it is played for him every time he joins Odette at the Verdurins'.
It has become "l'air national de leur amour" (I, 218). In spite of its
beauty and charm, he no longer values it for itself but for its association with Odette. Just as he subordinates the Botticelli painting to
his love for Odette, so he subordinates the little phrase, turning
what might have been a source of spiritual enlightenment into a
source of sensual satisfaction. It is at once a souvenir of his love and
an assurance of the continuity of that love, because everyone in the
Verdurin circle who hears it thinks of Swann and Odette. So, even
when the two of them are not physically united, they are, by the
intermediary of Vinteuil's music, united in the minds of others.

This one phrase has become so important to Swann that, at Odette's request, he has given up his intention of hearing the entire
sonata played, and restricts himself to hearing the little phrase. If
Odette were not so stupid, one might almost suppose that she recognizes that the sonata is her rival, and insists on this rival's being
relegated to a second place. Every time he goes to see Odette, he
asks her to play the little phrase, although she plays extremely
badly. He does this, partly because the phrase continues to be, for
him, the "national anthem" of their love, but also because it foments
the love which he feels for Odette. He feels that, without this stimulus, his love might disappear, since, at this stage in their relationship, he is aware that Odette is not, by any objective standards,
worthy of his time and attention:

Il sentait bien que cet amour, c'était quelque chose qui ne correspondait
à rien d'extérieur, de constatable par d'autres que lui; il se rendait compte

que les qualités d'Odette ne justifiaient pas qu'il attachât tant de prix aux moments passés auprès d'elle. Et souvent, quand c'était l'intelligence positive qui régnait seul en Swann, il voulait cesser de sacrifier tant d'intérêts intellectuels et sociaux à ce plaisir imaginaire. Mais la petite phrase, dès qu'il l'entendait, savait rendre libre en lui l'espace qui pour elle était nécessaire, les proportions de l'âme de Swann s'en trouvaient changées; une marge y était réservée à une jouissance qui elle non plus ne correspondait à aucun objet extérieur et qui, pourtant, au lieu d'être purement individuelle comme celle de l'amour, s'imposait à Swann comme une réalité supérieure aux choses concrètes. Cette soif d'un charme inconnu, la petite phrase l'éveillait en lui, mais ne lui apportait rien de précis pour l'assouvir. De sorte que ces parties de l'âme de Swann où la petite phrase avait effacé le souci des intérêts matériels, les considérations humaines et valables pour tous, elle les avait laissées vacantes et en blanc, et il était libre d'y inscrire le nom d'Odette [I, 236–237].

Vinteuil's sonata is being forced to bestow a borrowed value on Odette, to its own detriment, and in spite of the message which it bears of detachment from love. Swann even insists that Odette should play it and kiss him at the same time, so that its value should be more effectually bestowed on her:

Il commençait à se rendre compte de tout ce qu'il y avait de douloureux, peut-être même de secrètement inapaisé au fond de la douceur de cette phrase, mais il ne pouvait en souffrir. Qu'importait qu'elle lui dît que l'amour est fragile, le sien était si fort! Il jouait avec la tristesse qu'elle répandait, il la sentait passer sur lui, mais comme une caresse qui rendait plus profond et plus doux le sentiment qu'il avait de son bonheur. Il la faisait rejouer dix fois, vingt fois à Odette, exigeant qu'en même temps elle ne cessât pas de l'embrasser [I, 237–238].

This constant playing of the little phrase makes it completely subservient to his feeling for Odette. As his feeling for Odette grows, he becomes less and less discriminating in his attitude toward music, and toward the arts in general. He even cultivates tastes which he really knows to be bad — although he tries to persuade himself that there are no objective standards in taste and that it is all a matter of fashion — simply because he knows them to be hers.

At this point in the narrative, the peace of Swann's love for Odette is destroyed by his jealousy of her new admirer, Forcheville, who is received by the Verdurins and encouraged by them to see Odette in their company. In his attack of jealousy, Swann launches a passionate tirade against Forcheville, the Verdurins, and everything which might conspire to bring Odette and Forcheville together. He gives the epithet of "entremetteuse" to Mme Verdurin first and to music second: " 'Entremetteuse', c'était le nom qu'il donnait aussi à la musique qui les convierait à se taire, à rêver ensemble, à se regarder, à se prendre la main" (I, 287). But if music is an "entremetteuse," it was Swann who made it into one, by treating it as the accompaniment of his love and refusing to value it for its own sake.

Odette continues to see Swann, with an air of indifference which distresses him, but which he does his best to ignore. He does everything he can to avoid all reminders of the happy time when she was more in love with him than he was with her. Consequently, he avoids listening to the Vinteuil sonata, in whole or in part, although his constant suffering gives him a constant need to find comfort in music, until one evening when he goes to a charity concert at the Marquise de Saint-Euverte's. Without being aware of the fact, he arrives at the concert in a frame of mind which is particularly conducive to aesthetic receptivity. Love and suffering have detached him, for the time being, from the idolatry of snobbery which had done so much to dry up his early enthusiasm for art, and he takes in the impressions he receives from the reception in a state of emotional detachment which is highly favorable to the appreciation of art. Love and snobbery are both enemies of art, but love first detaches the lover from snobbery and then leads him, through suffering, to a state of detachment in which he becomes open to art. So, if love does not reclaim the lover for its own, it may lead him back to art, after having led him away from it. Swann's state of aesthetic receptivity becomes apparent from the moment he enters the house. As we saw in the previous chapter, he has always been inclined to see his contemporaries in the guise of famous paintings, but the servants and guests at Mme de Saint-Euverte's now form, in his eyes, a series of grandiose or grotesque tableaux, hardly appearing as living people at all: "La disposition particulière qu'il avait toujours eue à chercher des analogies entre les êtres vivants et les portraits des musées, s'exerçait encore mais d'une façon plus constante et plus génerale; c'est la vie mondaine tout entière, maintenant qu'il en était détaché, qui se présentait à lui comme une suite de tableaux" (I, 323). Love has detached him from the idolatry of snobbery; this could be the moment when music might detach him from the idolatry of love and lead him into a state of creative spiritual awareness.

As the concert begins, however, there seems little sign of this. Swann listens to various pieces — a melody on the flute, a piano piece by Liszt and another by Chopin — without feeling any particular enlightenment or emotion. He does, however, observe his neighbors with a curiosity which betokens a certain detachment from practical or mundane considerations. At the same time, he suffers from the feeling that he is among people who would have no comprehension of his love, and no interest in it. He longs to return to Odette, but suddenly he feels as if she had come in. Before Swann has time to realize what it is that is reminding him of Odette, all his memories of the time when she was in love with him have returned, cruelly contrasting his former happiness with his present misfortune. What has reminded him of that period in his life is the little phrase of the Vinteuil sonata, to which he has responded emotionally before being consciously aware that it is being played. Because the phrase was so closely connected with his love for Odette, it is impossible for him to hear it without being reminded of that love. Not only does the little phrase remind him of his moments of happiness, but it seems like "une déesse protectrice et confidente de son amour" (I, 348). Swann feels a rush of affection in response to the sympathy which he feels the phrase is bestowing upon him. He even makes a movement with his lips as if to kiss the music as it passes by. No longer does he feel lonely and in exile, because he has the little phrase for company.

At the same time as the phrase brings him a message of sympathy for his sufferings, it also brings him one of detachment from them. It was this detachment, exercised toward joy and suffering alike, which Swann had noticed when he heard it at the Verdurins'. This is the impression which it had then made upon him:

Elle passait à plis simples et immortels, distribuant ça et là les dons de sa grâce, avec le même ineffable sourire; mais Swann y croyait distinguer maintenant du désenchantement. Elle semblait connaître la vanité de ce bonheur dont elle montrait la voie. Dans sa grâce légère, elle avait quelque chose d'accompli, comme le détachement qui succède au regret [I, 218].

The mixture of sympathy and detachment which Swann finds in the little phrase is deeply welcome to him. He had been unable to bear the indifference of the people around him, for whom his love was simply "une divagation sans importance" (I, 348). But the detachment of the little phrase is one which comes from recognizing the importance of these states of mind, expressing them at the same time as it rises above them:

C'est que la petite phrase, au contraire, quelque opinion qu'elle pût avoir sur la brève durée de ces états d'âme, y voyait quelque chose, non pas comme faisaient tous ces gens, de moins sérieux que la vie positive, mais au contraire de si supérieur à elle que seul il valait la peine d'être exprimé. Ces charmes d'une tristesse intime, cétait eux qu'elle essayait d'imiter, de recréer, et jusqu'à leur essence qui est pourtant d'être incommunicables et de sembler frivoles à tout autre qu'à celui qui les éprouve, la petite phrase l'avait captée, rendue visible [I, 348–349].

It is not only sympathy which Swann finds in the Vinteuil sonata, but a reality of another kind from that of ordinary human life, quite different but at least equally valid. He had come to believe in this different, and perhaps superior, reality when he first heard the Vinteuil sonata, even though he had neglected this belief in the interval. Music, he recognizes, contains ideas, none the less real for being expressed in nonconceptual terms:

Sans doute la forme sous laquelle elle les avait codifiés ne pouvait se résoudre en raisonnements. Mais depuis plus d'une année que, lui révélant à lui-même bien des richesses de son âme, l'amour de la musique était, pour quelque temps au moins, né en lui, Swann tenait les motifs musicaux pour de véritables idées, d'un autre monde, d'un autre ordre, idées voilées de ténèbres, inconnues, impénétrables à l'intelligence, mais qui n'en sont pas moins parfaitement distinctes les unes des autres, inégales entre elles de valeur et de signification [I, 349].

The special ideas conveyed by music are encouraging and comforting for us, since they show us "quelle richesse, quelle variété, cache à notre insu cette grande nuit impénétrée et décourageante de notre âme que nous prenons pour du vide et du néant" (I, 350). With the idea of renewed spiritual life which we derive from music, our present life seems more real, and its extinction even seems less likely: "Nous périrons, mais nous avons pour otages ces captives divines qui suivront notre chance. Et la mort avec elles a quelque chose de moins amer, de moins inglorieux, peut-être de moins probable" (I, 350). As Deleuze observes, the little phrase belongs to a world of superior, because immaterial, reality.[1] It is its spirituality which makes art superior to life.[2] Because the world in which we live and the world to which the spiritual, immaterial forms of art belong are capable of overlapping (for otherwise we could not respond to art), this means that, in a sense, we belong to that spiritual world ourselves, and therefore have some slight hope of not disappearing in our entirety when our bodies disappear. In the religion of art, the hope of immortality which traditional religions offer as a gift of God is held out by the art work itself, even if Proust cannot bring himself to express this hope in very positive terms.

That there is something religious about the little phrase is suggested by the allusions to the supernatural which come into Swann's mind as he listens to it. An intriguing feature of these allusions is

[1] Deleuze, p. 34.
[2] Ibid., p. 36.

the variety of types of the supernatural which they represent. The little phrase has been brought from a divine world; it is like a goddess, a fairy, or else like the spirit possessing a medium; the stand on which it is being played, thereby evoking the spirit of Vinteuil, is "un des plus nobles autels où pût s'accomplir une cérémonie surnaturelle" (I, 352–353). Proust begins with types of the supernatural in which no modern men believe, to approach gradually, through the intermediate stage of spiritualism, the idea of the Christian altar, which represents a serious belief for at least some moderns. One has the impression that he does not want to shock his readers by making claims for the religion of art too suddenly and obtrusively. Rather, he wishes to insinuate the notion that there is something supernatural, and in fact quite seriously religious, about Vinteuil's music into the reader's minds, before the readers are fully aware of what is going on. In a later chapter, we shall see that this is typical of the way in which Proust propagates his religion of art in general.

But, however deeply Swann may have been moved for the moment, the memory of his quasi-religious reaction to the Vinteuil sonata fades away as he falls once more into the grip of his obsession with Odette. Love, having brought him to the threshold of aesthetic illumination, has reclaimed him. He continues to suffer for Odette until his passion dies, having run its course, and he sinks back into the uninspired life he led before it began. As the husband of Odette, listening to her play the Vinteuil sonata years later, Swann will have nothing to say about supernatural visitations in the form of music. Instead, what he has to say about the music, although appreciative, is fairly banal. To the narrator, who is visiting them, Swann remarks that the Vinteuil sonata evokes a still, moonlit night in the Bois de Boulogne. One can almost hear someone saying that it is light enough to read the newspaper, Swann remarks. As the narrator realizes, what Swann is expressing is not an aesthetic impression, but simply an association of ideas: "Je compris par d'autres propos de lui que ces feuillages nocturnes étaient tout simplement ceux sous l'épaisseur desquels, dans maint restaurant des environs de Paris, il avait entendu, bien des soirs, la petite phrase" (I, 553). The phrase now conveys hardly anything to Swann beyond the physical circumstances of one of the occasions on which it was played.

But even though the Vinteuil sonata now conveys little to Swann, it makes some impression on the narrator. When he is grown up and living in his Paris apartment, he acquires a pianola, rolls of music, and the scores of various pieces of music, including the Vinteuil sonata. When Albertine is out at the Trocadéro, he plays it for himself. The sonata, cutting through his preoccupation with the absent Albertine's behavior, carries him back to the time when he had thought of becoming an artist, and raises, by the same token, the question of the reality of art: "En abandonnant, en fait, cette ambition, avais-je renoncé à quelque chose de réel? La vie pouvait-elle me consoler de l'art? Y avait-il dans l'art une réalité plus profonde où notre personnalité véritable trouve une expression que ne lui donnent pas les actions de la vie?" (III, 158). Certainly, music helps the narrator to enter into the truth of his own inner nature as nothing else can. And what he finds within himself, by this means, has a particular value for him: "La musique, bien différente en cela de la société d'Albertine, m'aidait à descendre en moi-même, à y trouver du nouveau: la variété que j'avais en vain cherchée dans la vie, dans le voyage, dont pourtant la nostalgie m'était donnée par ce flot sonore qui faisait mourir à côté de moi ses vagues ensoleillées" (III, 159). Wagner, of whom Vinteuil reminds him so strongly that he sets the score of *Tristan* beside the score of the Vinteuil sonata in order to compare them, also appears to him to offer access to this superior reality. In Wagner's case, the impression of superior reality is connected with his use of recurrent themes: "Je me rendais compte de tout ce qu'a de réel l'oeuvre de Wagner, en revoyant ces thèmes insistants et fugaces qui visitent un acte, ne s'éloignent que pour revenir, et parfois lointains, assoupis, presque détachés, sont, à d'autres moments, tout en restant vagues, si pressants et si proches, si internes, si organiques, si viscéraux qu'on dirait la reprise moins d'un motif que d'une névralgie" (III, 159).

The word "reality" as applied to art seems to bear a rather complex meaning for Proust. When he speaks of the "réalité supérieure aux choses concrètes" (I, 237) which Swann finds in the Vinteuil sonata, one has the impression that what Swann thinks he has found is a purely transcendental reality. Here, in discussing Wagner, Proust finds evidence of a special reality in a quality which appears to be more closely allied to physical sensations than to anything transcendental. The reality which he finds in art is, at the same time, immaterial, superior to the material, and more immediate, because experienced internally, than the material. As we shall see in the next chapter, Proust finds what one might speak of as a "food value" in art. Art is like food because it is nourishing for the spirit, by which it can be absorbed as can nothing else. In the field of human relationships, there is always a barrier between mind and mind.

Neither love nor friendship can break down this barrier, still less casual social contacts, which are based solely on self-interest and the wish for diversion. But the art work can be taken up into the spirit because of the immateriality and immediacy of its form, against which such barriers are powerless. Here we find the final proof that the narrator was wrong in searching for a reality which would be at once intensely material and unequivocally transcendental. The art work is not both transcendental and material; it is both spiritual and sensuous. Of course, it would be foolish to deny that whatever is brought to us by our senses is material in origin. The sensuousness of the art work is a very particular type of sensuousness, in that it is a kind of halfway house between material reality and the spirit. As the narrator says of those impressions on which he intended to base his own novel: "Car les vérités que l'intelligence saisit directement à claire-voie dans le monde de la pleine lumière ont quelque chose de moins profond, de moins nécessaire que celles que la vie nous a malgré nous communiquées sur une impression, matérielle parce qu'elle est entrée par nos sens, mais dont nous pouvons dégager l'esprit" (III, 878). The art work appeals to our senses, but in such a way that we are led away from the material reality which it represents and toward the spirit. It is in failing to realize this that Swann went wrong. Proust condemns Swann's sensuousness, not because the art work appealed to his senses, but because it did not appeal to them sufficiently strongly for him to find a total satisfaction in the art work alone; he had to turn to a material object, that is to say Odette, to obtain the satisfaction which the art work made him crave and which his sensuousness was not sufficiently spiritual to allow him to find in the art work itself. It is clear that the sensuous element in the art work is justified and redeemed by its spiritual goal. And sometimes, as we shall see at the end of this chapter, Proustian aesthetic sensuousness — even the highly spiritualized sensuousness of music — ends by being devoured by the spirit.

To return to the question of the reality of art, it appears that the impression of reality which Wagner's music affords is accompanied by a feeling of joy — a joy which, in Wagner's case, was really felt by the composer: "Chez lui, quelle que soit la tristesse du poète, elle est consolée, surpassée — c'est-à-dire malheureusement un peu détruite — par l'allégresse du fabricateur" (III, 161). And yet this very quality leads the narrator to doubt the existence of the superior reality to which both Wagner and Vinteuil appear to offer access.

Is it, perhaps, nothing but an illusion? "Mais alors, autant que par l'identité que j'avais remarquée tout à l'heure entre la phrase de Vinteuil et celle de Wagner, j'étais troublé par cette habileté vulcanienne. Serait-ce elle qui donnerait chez les grands artistes l'illusion d'une originalité foncière, irréductible, en apparence d'une réalité plus qu'humaine, en fait produit d'un labeur industrieux? Si l'art n'est que cela, il n'est pas plus réel que la vie, et je n'avais pas tant de regrets à avoir" (III, 161–162). Proust has allowed us to perceive the special nature of the reality offered by the work of art, but his narrator is still groping, it appears, among his old illusions, in spite of the light which has just dawned. In fact, he is now entertaining a totally new heresy: the idea that what the work of art presents is not the vision of its creator, but a mere simulacrum created by technical skills and which could be imitated by any industrious person having the skills in question. The angel which the narrator has glimpsed (so to speak) is, perhaps, far from being a real angel, not even a handsome mortal or even a mirage; it may be only the projection of a film, created by clever montage.

On Albertine's return from the Trocadéro, the narrator forgets music for the time being as his jealous obsession with her secret activities revives. He has decided to go the Verdurins' concert, although he had originally thrown their invitation into the wastebasket, simply because he wants to find out whom Albertine had intended to meet there. She had wanted to go there, some time previously, and had changed her mind when he had said that he would go too. Obviously, there was someone whom she wanted to meet at the Verdurins' and whom he could prevent her from meeting by accompanying her or going in her place. On his arrival at the Verdurins', a remark made by the Baron de Charlus gives him reason to suspect that the "someone" in question was Mlle Vinteuil and her friend, who were expected to come but who fail to arrive. The narrator's distress at the news is so great that even the Baron de Charlus notices it and is concerned for his health. Consequently, like Swann brooding over Odette at Mme de Saint-Euverte's, it is with gloomy thoughts of Albertine's Lesbian tendencies that the narrator settles down to listen to the concert, given by the Verdurins and the Baron de Charlus together in order to "star" Morel.

The narrator knows that a work by Vinteuil will be played, but he is surprised when he sees other musicians on the stand besides Morel, since he had imagined that Vinteuil's only known work was his *Sonata for piano and violin*. He supposes that some other music will be played, and listens without any idea of what he is hearing until he suddenly recognizes a passage from the Vinteuil sonata:

Tout d'un coup, je me reconnus, au milieu de cette musique nouvelle pour moi, en pleine sonate de Vinteuil; et, plus merveilleuse qu'une adolescente, la petite phrase, enveloppée, harnachée d'argent, toute ruisselante de sonorités brillantes, légères et douces comme des écharpes, vint à moi, reconnaissable sous ces parures nouvelles [III, 249].

This passage is simply a passing allusion to the sonata, but it leaves the narrator knowing that he is listening to a work by Vinteuil. The basic structure is one of seven notes, instead of five as in the sonata, and the entire atmosphere is somehow more violent, tense, electric:

Tandis que la Sonate s'ouvrait sur une aube liliale et champêtre, divisant sa candeur légère mais pour se suspendre à l'emmêlement léger et pourtant consistant d'un berceau rustique de chèvrefeuilles sur des géraniums blancs, c'était sur des surfaces unies et planes comme celles de la mer que, par un matin d'orage, commençait, au milieu d'un aigre silence, dans un vide infini, l'œuvre nouvelle, et c'est dans un rose d'aurore que, pour se construire progressivement devant moi, cet univers inconnu était tiré du silence et de la nuit. Ce rouge si nouveau, si absent de la tendre, champêtre et candide Sonate, teignait tout le ciel, comme l'aurore, d'un espoir mystérieux. Et un chant perçait déjà l'air, différent de tout ce que j'eusse jamais imaginé, à la fois ineffable et criard, non plus roucoulement de colombe comme dans la Sonate, mais déchirant l'air, aussi vif que la nuance écarlate dans laquelle le début était noyé, quelque chose comme un mystique chant de coq, un appel, ineffable mais suraigu, de l'éternel matin. [III, 250].

This opening is followed by a passage in which a theme of joy is expressed in an almost awkwardly noisy way:

À midi pourtant, dans un ensoleillement brûlant et passager, elle semblait s'accomplir en un bonheur lourd, villageois et presque rustique, où la titubation des cloches retentissantes et déchaînées (pareilles à celles qui incendiaient de chaleur la place de l'église à Combray, et que Vinteuil, qui avait dû souvent les entendre, avait peut-être trouvées à ce moment-là dans sa mémoire comme une couleur qu'on a à portée de sa main sur une palette) semblait matérialiser la plus épaisse joie. A vrai dire, esthétiquement ce motif de joie ne me plaisait pas; je le trouvais presque laid, le rythme s'en traînait si péniblement à terre qu'en aurait pu en imiter presque tout l'essentiel, rien qu'avec des bruits, en frappant d'une certaine manière des baguettes sur une table [III, 250–251].

Offended by what he considers the awkwardness of this theme, the narrator allows his attention to wander. He watches the audience, then the musicians, among whom are a cellist and a harpist. But then he returns to the music once more. This septet seems to him infinitely above the sonata, which was simply a first attempt to reach the same heights, just as his own early loves were preliminary sketches of the love he feels for Albertine. The thought of Albertine distracts him from the music for a while. Then his thoughts coincide once more with the music, as he hears a tender phrase which makes him think of the sleeping Albertine. But the music seems to offer more than reminiscences of his beloved: "Et pourtant, me dis-je, quelque chose de plus mystérieux que l'amour d'Albertine semblait promis au début de cette œuvre, dans ces premiers cris d'aurore. J'essayai de chasser la pensée de mon amie pour ne plus songer qu'au musicien" (III, 253). The narrator succeeds in plunging himself into the music so completely that, at a pause, when the other members of the audience feel compelled to exchange their impressions, the contrast between the superior reality which he has been enjoying and the mediocre reality to which he has returned makes him feel like an angel fallen from paradise: "Mais qu'étaient leurs paroles, qui, comme toute parole humaine extérieure, me laissaient si indifférent, à côté de la céleste phrase musicale avec laquelle je venais de m'entretenir? J'étais vraiment comme un ange qui, déchu des ivresses du Paradis, tombe dans la plus insignifiante réalité" (III, 258). Even if we had no other indication of Proust's contempt for material reality when compared with the superior reality of art, this passage would be sufficient to convince us of it.

The music starts up again, mingling several phrases, one of which affects the narrator much as he supposes the little phrase of the sonata must have affected Swann. This phrase is so feminine, so caressing, and yet so different from women in that the happiness it promises is really worth obtaining, that, the narrator says, it is "la seule Inconnue qu'il m'ait jamais été donné de rencontrer" (III, 260).

Two main themes are struggling together. One is the joyful theme of the beginning, while the other is a painful theme. Finally, the joyful theme emerges triumphant: "Enfin le motif joyeux resta triomphant; ce n'était plus un appel presque inquiet lancé derrière un ciel vide, c'était une joie ineffable qui semblait venir du paradis, une joie aussi différente de celle de la Sonate que, d'un ange doux et grave de Bellini, jouant du théorbe, pourrait être, vêtu d'une robe d'écarlate, quelque archange de Mantegna sonnant dans un buccin" (III, 260). This joy seems to offer a special challenge to the narrator, for it reminds him of the sensation he had already experienced before the spires of Martinville and before a row of trees near Balbec. Can he, the narrator seems to ask, attain an expression, in words, of joy in these experiences which would be equivalent to the joy which Vinteuil has expressed in music?

Je savais que cette nuance nouvelle de la joie, cet appel vers une joie supra-terrestre, je ne l'oublierais jamais. Mais serait-elle jamais réalisable pour moi? Cette question me paraissait d'autant plus importante que cette phrase était ce qui aurait pu le mieux caractériser — comme tranchant avec tout le reste de ma vie, avec le monde visible — ces impressions qu'à des intervalles éloignés je trouvais dans ma vie comme les points de repère, les amorces pour la construction d'une vie véritable: l'impression éprouvée devant les clochers de Martinville, devant une rangée d'arbres près de Balbec [III, 261].

What the narrator has received from Vinteuil's septet is a message of encouragement and inspiration, since it offers him "la promesse qu'il existait autre chose, réalisable par l'art sans doute, que le néant que j'avais trouvé dans tous les plaisirs et dans l'amour même, et que si ma vie me semblait si vaine, du moins n'avait-elle pas tout accompli" (III, 263).

The narrator, listening to the septet under conditions similar to those of Swann listening to the sonata, has arrived at that state of creative spiritual awareness which Swann failed to reach. He achieves this, not by superior virtue or greater knowledge of the arts, but by greater faith in art and by superior powers of concentration. He has the ability and will to pursue any idea, no matter how difficult or painful, to its ultimate conclusion, whereas Swann easily loses the thread of any idea which disturbs him, just as his father did. It is probably his inability to think things through which leads Swann into his sin of idolatry, for if he were to consider the matter fully, he would realize the intrinsic difference between a work of art and Odette, and so avoid confusing them.

Later, Albertine will play works by Vinteuil for the narrator upon the pianola. These occasions will serve to confirm and strengthen his belief in the reality of art and his conviction that those moments in his life which have given him a special joy have an importance which is artistic in nature:

Mais il n'est pas possible qu'une sculpture, une musique qui donne une émotion qu'on sent plus élevée, plus pure, plus vraie, ne corresponde à une certaine réalité spirituelle, ou la vie n'aurait aucun sens. Ainsi rien ne ressemblait plus qu'une belle phrase de Vinteuil à ce plaisir particulier que j'avais quelquefois éprouvé dans ma vie, par exemple devant les clochers de Martinville, certains arbres d'une route de Balbec ou plus simplement, au début de cet ouvrage, en buvant une certaine tasse de thé [III, 374].

Even though the narrator will lose hope and waste time before the final revelation of "Le Temps retrouvé," Vinteuil has shown him, by his example, the supreme importance of art, as well as the value which the narrator's own special experiences might have if incorporated in a work of art.

Vinteuil's music is not only a source of inspiration for the narrator; it has a very special flavor of its own. This is due partly to the way in which Proust convinces us of its quintessential quality, by such devices as his repetition of the word "ineffable" and his allusions to angels, partly to the very complex word-paintings which show its effect on the narrator, and partly to the variety of composers whom Proust has pillaged in order to build up the figure of Vinteuil. We have evidence of the fact that Vinteuil, like Elstir and Bergotte, is a composite figure, in a dedication which Proust wrote for Jacques de Lacretelle:

Dans la faible mesure où la réalité m'a servi, même très faible à vrai dire, la "petite phrase" de cette sonate, et je ne l'ai jamais dit à personne, est (pour commencer par la fin) dans la soirée de Saint-Euverte, la phrase charmante mais enfin médiocre d'une sonate pour piano et violon de Saint-Saëns, musicien que je n'aime pas. (Je vous indiquerai exactement le passage qui revient plusieurs fois et qui était le triomphe de Jacques Thibaud). Dans la même soirée, un peu plus loin, je ne serais pas surpris qu'en parlant de la même phrase j'eusse pensé à *l'Enchantement du vendredi saint*. Dans cette même soirée encore, quand le piano et le violon gémissent comme deux oiseaux qui se répondent, j'ai pensé à la *Sonate* de Franck (surtout jouée par Enesco) dont le quatuor apparaît dans les volumes suivants. Les trémolos qui couvrent la "petite phrase" chez les Verdurin m'ont été suggérés par un prélude de *Lohengrin*, mais elle-même à ce moment-là par une chose de Schubert. Elle est dans la même soirée Verdurin un ravissant morceau de piano de Fauré.[3]

But the similarity between the construction of Vinteuil's music and the construction of Proust's narrative makes of this music Proust's invention, not simply a reminiscence of several composers. In this connection, Germaine Brée points out that Vinteuil's music follows the same pattern as the narrative. She first establishes a parallel between the increasing density of themes in the septet and the increasing density of themes in the narrative, starting with the few simple notes of "Combray," and then goes on to see a parallel between the triumph of the joyful motif over the painful one in the

[3] *Hommage à Marcel Proust*, Les Cahiers Marcel Proust, I (Paris: Gallimard, 1927), 190.

septet and the expression of joy, triumphing over suffering, in "Le Temps retrouvé."[4]

Vinteuil's music both follows the pattern of the narrative and provides one of the moments of illumination which will inspire the narrator to literary composition. Thus, Vinteuil's music is doubly linked to the narrative. In addition, this music is described in terms which echo basic themes of the novel. We have just seen how Brée observes that the joyful theme of the septet is like the joyful mood which triumphs in "Le Temps retrouvé." There are other comparisons which could be made. When the sonata, for instance, is compared in its rustic simplicity to "l'emmêlement léger et pourtant consistant d'un berceau rustique de chèvrefeuilles sur des géraniums blancs," whilse the septet makes the narrator think of "des surfaces unies et planes comme celles de la mer" (III, 250), we have a contrast which is reminiscent of that of Combray and Balbec. The femininity of the phrase which is "plus merveilleuse qu'une adolescente" (III, 249) is like that of Albertine and her friends, and, as we have seen Proust observe, the progress of Vinteuil's music is like the sequence of the narrator's various loves.

Proust's description of both the sonata and the septet in terms of light also fits in with the importance of light effects in *A la Recherche du temps perdu*. There may, for instance, be a connection between the promise of the dawn in the septet and that early morning sky which so delights the narrator when he sees it from his railway carriage approaching Balbec. Again, the use of images derived from painting to bring out the special quality of Vinteuil's music is typical of the way in which such images are used throughout the novel. We find an example of this when Swann is listening to the sonata at Mme Verdurin's. The pianist, in the following passage, is playing the little phrase for Odette and Swann:

Il commençait par la tenue des trémolos de violon que pendant quelques mesures on entend seuls, occupant tout le premier plan, puis tout d'un coup ils semblaient s'écarter et, comme dans ces tableaux de Pieter de Hooch qu'approfondit le cadre étroit d'une porte entr'ouverte, tout au loin, d'une couleur autre, dans le velouté d'une lumière interposée, la petite phrase apparaissait, dansante, pastorale, intercalée, épisodique, appartenant à un autre monde [I, 218].

An even more striking example comes in the already quoted passage where the sonata is compared to a Bellini angel playing on the

---

[4] Germaine Brée, *Du Temps perdu au temps retrouvé: introduction à l'œuvre de Marcel Proust* (Paris: Les Belles Lettres, 1950), p. 224.

theorbo, while the septet is like a Mantegna archangel sounding a trumpet. The interaction of music and painting here becomes quite complex, as a piece of music is compared to a picture of an angel playing a piece of music. In such passages, Proust attains to a perfect Baudelairean *correspondance* of the visual and the auditory. Finally, Vinteuil is compared, in his creative joy, to Michelangelo:

La joie que lui avaient causée telles sonorités, les forces accrues qu'elle lui avait données pour en découvrir d'autres, menaient encore l'auditeur de trouvaille en trouvaille, ou plutôt c'était le créateur qui le conduisait lui-même, puisant dans les couleurs qu'il venait de trouver une joie éperdue qui lui donnait la puissance de découvrir, de se jeter sur celles qu'elles semblaient appeler, ravi, tressaillant comme au choc d'une étincelle quand le sublime naissait de lui-même des cuivres, haletant, grisé, affolé, vertigineux, tandis qu'il peignait sa grande fresque musicale, comme Michel-Ange, attaché à son echelle et lançant, la tête en bas, de tumultueux coups de brosse au plafond de la chapelle Sixtine [III, 254].

Michel Butor maintains that there is a deliberate linking of music, painting and literature in the sequence in which these themes are presented. Vinteuil's sonata is mentioned before the work of Elstir, which appears as a kind of intermediate stage between music and words; then Vinteuil's septet appears, indicating a more complex awareness of the connection between music, painting, and words; and finally the narrator is inspired to create his literary masterpiece.[5] Butor then goes on to say that he sees the changes in coloring between the sonata and the septet as equivalent to the breaking of the white light of the sonata into the prismatic colors of the septet, with the intercalation of Elstir as the prism which breaks the light.[6] It is an interesting idea. Certainly, the description of Vinteuil's music in visual terms, especially in terms appropriate to painting, does effect a bond between the visual and the auditory arts. The result is a Wagnerian "total spectacle" uniting all the arts, such as Georges Piroué claims that Proust must have wished to create.[7]

As Proust has told us, there is something Wagnerian about Vinteuil and, at the same time, there is a close connection between Vinteuil's manner of composition and the structure of *A la Recherche du temps perdu*. Many critics have seen a connection between Proust's use of recurrent themes and the Wagnerian leitmotiv. But Wagner and the imaginery Vinteuil are not the only musicians

[5] Michel Butor, *Essais sur les modernes* (Paris: Gallimard, 1964), p. 143.
[6] Ibid., pp. 179–180.
[7] Georges Piroué, *La Musique dans la vie, l'œuvre et l'esthétique de Proust* (Paris: Éditions Denoël, 1960), p. 115.

who have had an effect on Proust's style. Long ago, E. R. Curtius saw a marked similarity between Proust's description of a Chopin phrase and the construction of Proust's own sentences.[8] There are other explanations of Proust's sentence structure (all of which may be equally correct), but the resemblance between the structure of a phrase of Chopin and the language in which Proust describes it is certainly striking:

[Mme de Cambremer] avait appris dans sa jeunesse à caresser les phrases, au long col sinueux et démesuré, de Chopin, si libres, si flexibles, si tactiles, qui commencent par chercher et essayer leur place en dehors et bien loin de la direction de leur départ, bien loin du point où on avait pu espérer qu'atteindrait leur attouchement, et qui ne se jouent dans cet écart de fantaisie que pour revenir plus délibérément — d'un retour plus prémédité, avec plus de précision, comme sur un cristal qui résonnerait jusqu'à faire crier — vous frapper au coeur [I, 331].

This makes Proust's composition trebly musical, since not only the narrative and use of recurrent themes but also the sentence structure find their equivalent and their justification in music.

For Piroué, the moments of involuntary memory are musical, in that they balance the present, the past, and the future, bringing the past into the present and, by so doing, promising some future joy or recognition. He sees this as similar to the way in which musical themes, balancing one another, preparing and recalling one another, create their own form and their own self-justification.[9] Piroué maintains that what Proust finds in music is not only a number of stylistic procedures, but an example to be followed in its totality. Music is a closed system, inventing its own laws and creating a system of relationship which are self-sufficient. It is this self-sufficiency which Proust is imitating.[10] The use of metaphor to bring together the various parts of the work joins with the moments of involuntary memory to create an autonomous tension. It is this which makes the novel into something which produces and at the same time justifies itself.[11]

Piroué also finds in music the meeting place, in Proust's world, of the spiritual and the material, the abstract and the concrete.[12] I would prefer to speak of the union of the spiritual and the sensuous.

---

[8] Ernst Robert Curtius, *Marcel Proust*, traduit de l'allemand par Armand Pierhal (Paris: La Revue Nouvelle, 1928), p. 71.

[9] Piroué, p. 165.

[10] Ibid., pp. 162–163.

[11] Ibid., p. 267.

[12] Ibid., p. 10.

However, even this union is destroyed at moments by the intellect of the narrator. As he listens to a piece of music played again and again by Albertine, he transforms it into its spiritual equivalent to such an extent that he can no longer hear it as music:

De même que le volume de cet Ange musicien était constitué par les trajets multiples entre les différents points du passé que son souvenir occupait en moi et les différents signes, depuis la vue jusqu'aux sensations les plus intérieures de mon être, qui m'aidaient à descendre jusque dans l'intimité du sien, la musique qu'elle jouait avait aussi un volume, produit par la visibilité inégale des différentes phrases, selon que j'avais plus ou moins réussi à y mettre de la lumière et à rejoindre les unes aux autres les lignes d'une construction qui m'avait d'abord paru presque entière noyée dans le brouillard. Albertine savait qu'elle me faisait plaisir en ne proposant à ma pensée que des choses encore obscures et le modelage de ces nébuleuses. Elle devinait qu'à la troisième ou quatrième exécution, mon intelligence, en ayant atteint, par consequent mis à la même distance, toutes les parties, et n'ayant plus d'activité à déployer à leur égard, les avait réciproquement étendues et immobilisées sur un plan uniforme. Elle ne passait pas cependant encore à un nouveau morceau, car, sans peut-être bien se rendre compte du travail qui se faisait en moi, elle savait qu'au moment où le travail de mon intelligence était arrivé à dissiper le mystère d'une œuvre, il était bien rare qu'elle n'eût pas, au cours de sa tâche néfaste, attrapé par compensation telle ou telle réflexion profitable. Et le jour où Albertine disait: "Voila un rouleau que nous allons donner à Françoise pour qu'elle nous le fasse changer contre un autre", souvent il y avait pour moi sans doute un morceau de musique de moins dans le monde, mais une vérité de plus [III, 372].

In its double-natured reality, it is the "angelic" side of music which triumphs, even to the detriment of its own continued existence, just as, in spite of the sensuous origin of the moments of involuntary memory, it is the spiritual side of the narrator which triumphs in "Le Temps retrouvé"; and it is to this spiritual side that he gladly devotes what remains to him of physical existence.

At this point, it might be as well to pause and question the implicit assumption on which we have been proceeding that what is spiritual must also necessarily be religious. It is an assumption which is easily made (and which I think Proust expects us to make), for we are accustomed, because of the teachings of the New Testament, to associate the two ideas. What we tend to overlook is that the word "spirit" is used by us in a variety of senses, which range from that of the Holy Spirit as the third Person of the Trinity to the idea of that part of the human personality which responds to God, and from there, through the idea of spirit as a force operating in men's minds, and possibly outside them, but distinct from God

(Schopenhauer seems to use the word in this sense), to the simplest and most common idea of spirit as the opposite of matter. At the same time "esprit" is often translated simply as "mind." The trouble is that these several senses, because the word used is the same, tend to overlap. Consequently, when we use the word "spiritual" simply as the opposite of "material," we are inclined to suppose that what is spiritual is also virtuous. To take an example which fits in with what we have been discussing so far, we are material-minded if we regard a bunch of grapes, for instance, merely as something good to eat. If we pause to appreciate the color and shape of the grapes before eating them, we are infusing an element of the spiritual into the material. If, instead of eating grapes, we prefer to read a description or look at a picture of them, we are more spiritual, and if we listen to a piece of music from which we receive impressions of sweetness, shape, and color without a specific idea of "grapes" being evoked, we are more spiritual still. And if we suppose that this use of our faculties has brought us nearer to spirit-as-a-force, we are more spiritual yet. In fact, this further step may well be necessary in order to prevent us from infusing the spiritual with the material once more and so lapsing into that voluptuous contemplation of works of art which Proust said was insufficient for the practice of the religion of art.[13] But the question is, are we then being spiritual in the sense in which St. Paul, for example, used the word? Proust was too intelligent to entertain this idea, and we shall see in the next chapter that he was quite willing to admit that people could be spiritual in the aesthetic sense without performing actions which correspond to the values of the New Testament (although he did try to have it both ways by also suggesting that there is a parallel between the artist's act of creation and an act of loving-kindness). But, at the same time, he was ready to accept the prestige which the word "spiritual" has derived from the New Testament in order to enhance the aesthetic type of spirituality. We shall see other examples of this type of procedure on Proust's part in Chapter Seven.

[13] Proust, *Pastiches et mélanges*, p. 154; Ruskin, *La Bible d'Amiens*, p. 54.

CHAPTER FIVE

ETHICS AND ART

Combray is the place from which the narrator first derives his system of values. It constitutes a world of its own — as does each of the other places which are emotionally important to him. But Combray is particularly important because it is the primal world on the basis of which the later ones are first anticipated and then judged.[1] As a child in Combray, the narraor feels safe, warm, and contented, except at those dreadful moments when he has to climb up the stairs to his bedroom and entomb himself in his bed, far from his mother. Things follow an unquestioned and abiding pattern. The family goes to church and gives gifts and medical help to the servants who, in turn, are completely devoted to their masters. So, when Tante Léonie is enduring her last sickness, Françoise never leaves her for a moment, staying by her side until Tante Léonie is actually in her coffin. The narrator's mother differs from other charitable ladies in that she refuses to take part in philanthropic endeavors of an organized sort, but she is unstinting in her kindness to those who are close to her and to the poor and unfortunate whom she encounters on a personal basis. The grandmother, also, is completely devoted to those she loves, and gives of herself without reserve when they are ill or unhappy. So, when the narrator is feeling completely miserable in the unaccustomed surroundings of his hotel room at Balbec, his grandmother comes to him like a kind of ministering angel:

Elle portait une robe de chambre de percale qu'elle revêtait à la maison chaque fois que l'un de nous était malade (parce qu'elle s'y sentait plus à l'aise, disait-elle, attribuant toujours à ce qu'elle faisait des mobiles égo-

[1] Cf. Cocking, p. 39.

ïstes), et qui était pour nous soigner, pour nous veiller, sa blouse de servante et de garde, son habit de religieuse. Mais tandis que les soins de
celles-là, la bonté qu'elles ont, le mérite qu'on leur trouve et la reconnaissance qu'on leur doit, augmentent encore l'impression qu'on a d'être, pour
elles, un autre, de se sentir seul, gardant pour soi la charge de ses pensées,
de son propre désir de vivre, je savais, quand j'étais avec ma grand'mère,
si grand chagrin qu'il y eût en moi, qu'il serait reçu dans une pitié plus
vaste encore; que tout ce qui était mien, mes soucis, mon vouloir, serait,
en ma grand'mère, étayé sur un désir de conservation et d'accroissement
de ma propre vie autrement fort que celui que j'avais moi-même; et mes
pensées se prolongeaient en elle sans subir de déviation parce qu'elles passaient de mon esprit dans le sien sans changer de milieu, de personne [I,
667–668].

There are two ways in which one can interpret this passage, in view
of the fact that the narrator is making it clear that for him a charity
prompted only by Christian motives is not sufficient. Either one can
say that the narrator's grandmother is a true Christian who differs
from other saintly Christians only in the warmth of her personal
feeling for the narrator, a warmth for which the narrator, with his
customary egoism, chiefly values her, or else one can say that the
self-abnegation of the grandmother differs from Christian altruism,
since it exceeds the self-forgetfulness of even saintly souls. Which
interpretation we prefer must depend on whether we assume that
the scale of values at the back of Proust's mind is really Christian
or not. This is a question which we will have to consider more fully
later in this study. To return to the narrator's grandmother, she is
so incapable of self-assertion that she seems unable to express her
point of view with any force. When the narrator's great-aunt teases
her by offering brandy to the grandfather, whose health does not
permit him to drink, the grandmother, seeing her protests of no
avail, can only suffer in silence, with a smile which expresses at once
her feeling of irony toward herself and her passionate attachment
to those who are dear to her. For her own sufferings she is without
pity, thinking only of sparing others distress. So, when she has an
attack in the public convenience of the Champs-Elysées, her first
thought on emerging is to quote Mme de Sévigné to her grandson,
so as to appear as normal as possible and spare him alarm. She is
ready to participate completely in any suffering he may feel, but she
is unwilling to allow him the smallest anxiety on her own account.

As Cocking remarks,[2] the narrator's mother and grandmother represent a standard of kindness and self-abnegation which is far above

[2] Ibid., p. 41.

that of the other members of the family but by which the other members are judged. Françoise, in particular, falls short of these standards. She is something of a special case in the antiquity and, often, the ferocity of the standards she maintains: "Elle possédait à l'égard des choses qui peuvent ou ne peuvent pas se faire un code impérieux, abondant, subtil et intransigeant sur des distinctions insaisissables ou oiseuses (ce qui lui donnait l'apparence de ces lois antiques qui, à côté de prescriptions féroces comme de massacrer les enfants à la mamelle, défendent avec une délicatesse exagérée de faire bouillir le chevreau dans le lait de sa mère, ou de manger dans un animal le nerf de la cuisse)" (I, 28–29). This comparison of the attitude of Françoise to that of the Mosaic Code casts an interesting light upon her. One might suppose that she stands, in relation to the narrator's mother and grandmother, as the synagogue stands to the Christian church — that is, as an exemplar of idealistic tendencies to be more fully developed and freed of their taint of barbarism in a later age. (Whatever Proust's sympathy with the Judaism of his own mother and her family, he must have been aware of this idea, if only from the symbolism of medieval church architecture; at Balbec, as Elstir tells the narrator, one can see a statue of the Synagogue, whose reign is over, holding a broken scepter and dropping her crown and the Tables of the Law) (I, 841). Françoise has an idea of mourning which is so traditional that the narrator compares it to that of the *Chanson de Roland,* and she weeps over the suffering of others when she reads about it in the newspaper; but she has not the slightest sympathy for the agonies of the kitchen maid, to whom she gives asparagus to prepare simply because she knows that the smell of asparagus gives the girl attacks of asthma. In his unawareness of this side of her character, the narrator thinks of her for some time as a good and kindly person, compact of gentleness, compunction, and virtue. We see this in a passage where he describes her cooking: "Et cependant, Françoise tournait à la broche un de ces poulets, comme elle seule savait en rôtir, qui avaient porté loin dans Combray l'odeur de ses mérites, et qui, pendant qu'elle nous les servait à table, faisaient prédominer la douceur dans ma conception spéciale de son caractère, l'arome de cette chair qu'elle savait rendre si onctueuse et si tendre n'étant pour moi que le propre parfum d'une de ses vertus" (I, 121). But this very chicken whose taste and smell, when cooked, celebrate her virtues, surrounding them with what one might call the odor of sanctity, has been furiously slaughtered by Françoise beforehand, to cries of "Sale bête!" "Quand

je fus en bas, elle était en train, dans l'arrière-cuisine qui donnait
sur la basse-cour, de tuer un poulet qui, par sa résistance désespérée
et bien naturelle, mais accompagnée par Françoise hors d'elle, tandis
qu'elle cherchait à lui fendre le cou sous l'oreille, des cris de 'sale
bête! sale bête!', mettait la sainte douceur de notre servante un peu
moins en lumière qu'il n'eût fait, au dîner du lendemain, par sa
peau brodée d'or comme une chasuble et son jus précieux égoutté
d'un ciboire" (I, 121–122). To his dismay, the narrator realizes that
his impression of Françoise's goodness had been based, not on real
virtues, but on the excellence of her cooking.

If not all the members of the household share the virtues of the
mother and grandmother, they all uphold the standards of bourgeois
respectability and respect for class divisions. As we noticed in Chapter Two, it is all the narrator's mother can do to mention Mme
Swann, even when prompted by the wish to be kind, because
Mme Swann is a loose woman and Swann has disgraced himself by
marrying her. Later on, when the adolescent narrator is visiting Gilberte Swann regularly, he abandons the idea of inviting Gilberte to
his own home, because his mother refuses to promise that she will
ask Gilberte how her mother is. She does not know Mme Swann,
she says, and therefore she cannot ask after her health. The standards of Combray admit of no acquiescence in lax morality.

If Odette meets with the hostility of Combray, all the more so
does Mlle Vinteuil, whose father suffers agonies from his daughter's
Lesbian love affair, at the same time as he allows it to continue. He
is well known for his adherence to conventional morality and, in
fact, stopped coming to the narrator's house for fear of meeting
Swann, of whose marriage he disapproves. Consequently, his acceptance of his daughter's friendship with a notorious Lesbian causes
much comment in Combray. Dr. Percepied makes the curé laugh
until he cries with his sly comments on the amount of "music"
which is going on in the Vinteuil home (a reaction, by the
way, which reflects little credit on the way in which the curé acquits
himself of his duties as spiritual leader of his flock). The doctor's
cruelty is implicitly castigated by the narrator, who observes that
Vinteuil has every reason to think of his daughter's friend as a fine
person, precisely because their relationship brings out the best in
her: "L'amour physique, si injustement décrié, force tellement tout
être à manifester jusqu'aux moindres parcelles qu'il possède de
bonté, d'abandon de soi, qu'elles resplendissent jusqu'aux yeux de

l'entourage immédiat" (I, 147). Judged by the grandmother's standards of altruism and kindness, this infraction of the conventional
moral standards (which the grandmother also supports) becomes
positively beneficial. Even if the narrator derives his values from the
standards of Combray, he picks and chooses among these standards
and even allows himself to pass judgment on some of them. But Vinteuil, who does not share the narrator's emancipated attitude, weak-
ens visibly under the pressure which public opinion and his own
adherence to conventional standards bring to bear on him. He
avoids the people he knows, grows visibly older, and becomes incapable of any effort which does not have his daughter's happiness
as its goal. His manners become excessively humble, as he sees his
daughter and himself sunk to the lowest depths of degradation. In
his conviction of his own ignominy, Vinteuil is now delighted that
Swann should speak kindly to him and even invite his daughter to
Tansonville. He is so deeply moved by the honor of this invitation,
in fact, that he feels unable to accept it.

If illicit sexuality runs counter to the code of Combray, so does
any attempt to move out of the class into which one was born.
Swann is very secretive with the narrator's family about his mem-
bership in the Jockey Club and his friendship with the Comte de
Paris and the Prince of Wales. His reserve on this subject is due not
only to his wish to abstain from boasting but also to his awareness
that his brilliant social connections would not make the narrator's
family think more highly of him. When the family discovers,
through a newspaper article, that Swann is an intimate of the Duc
de X——, this pleases the narrator's grandfather, who is interested
in the information Swann will be able to give him, but it lowers
Swann in the opinion of the narrator's great-aunt:

Ma grand'tante au contraire interpréta cette nouvelle dans un sens dé-
favorable à Swann: quelqu'un qui choisissait ses fréquentations en dehors
de la classe où il était né, en dehors de sa "classe" sociale, subissait à ses
yeux un fâcheux déclassement. Il lui semblait qu'on renonçât tout d'un
coup au fruit de toutes les belles relations avec des gens bien posés, qu'a-
vaient honorablement entretenues et engrangées pour leurs enfants les
familles prévoyantes (ma grand'tante avait même cessé de voir le fils d'un
notaire de nos amis parce qu'il avait épousé une altesse et était par là
descendu pour elle du rang respecté de fils de notaire à celui d'un de ces
aventuriers, anciens valets de chambre ou garçons d'écurie, pour qui on
raconte que les reines eurent parfois des bontés) [I, 21].

This time, there is no suggestion that the great-aunt's opinion ought
to be discounted on account of her vulgarity. On the contrary, her

opinion on this subject is presented as having weight in the family council.

In a similar way, Legrandin sinks in the family's opinion when it learns of his snobbery. To begin with, he is, in its eyes, "le type de l'homme d'élite, prenant la vie de la façon la plus noble et la plus délicate" (I, 67). The narrator's grandmother, however, with her acute instinct for people's real worth, is offended by the lack of simplicity in his speech and puzzled by his tirades against snobbery, a failing which tempts her so little that she cannot imagine why anyone should waste his time inveighing against it. Legrandin's snobbery is finally exposed by his eagerness in paying court to members of the local gentry, before whom he does not wish to acknowledge the narrator's family. Once Legrandin has been found out, the family sees him much less frequently, while the narrator's mother treats his further manifestations of snobbery as a great joke. The narrator himself will not always abide by this point of view, since he, too, will fall under the spell of the aristocracy. But, in the end, he will be disenchanted and so return to the standards of Combray, although not for the reasons of his great-aunt.

Sex and snobbery may be outlawed by Combray but, as we have seen, there is a fair amount of hard-heartedness and actual cruelty in the town, to offset the selflessness of the narrator's mother and grandmother. When the narrator says of Giotto's *Justice* that this figure's features were precisely those of "certaines jolies bourgeoises pieuses et sèches . . . dont plusieurs étaient enrôlées d'avance dans les milices de réserve de l'Injustice" (I, 82), he needs to say no more to make us aware of the presence in Combray of a number of most uncharitable persons. Tante Léonie, again, tortures Françoise, just as Françoise tortures the kitchen maid, but not even for the understandable (although unadmirable) reason which prompts Françoise — the wish to get rid of a potential rival. She trumps up charges of stealing against Françoise simply for the sake of amusement. Sometimes she imagines scenes betwen herself and Françoise with herself as the triumphant judge and Françoise as the detected offender; at other times, she stages these scenes in reality. Tante Léonis treats Françoise so cruelly that the narrator's mother is afraid that Françoise will come to hate her, but the surprising thing is that Françoise, with all her fear of Tante Léonie, is passionately devoted to her. It is difficult to characterize their relationship as anything but sado-masochistic.

And yet the predominant impression which we have of Combray is one of righteousness and goodness. Is this only because of the presence of the narrator's mother and grandmother? They are equally present, later on, in Balbec and Paris, without bestowing any such certificate of good behavior on the towns in question. Is it because the narrator, as a child, accepts the goodness of those around him as a matter of course, even when their actions contradict his opinion of them? This appears to be the case, to quite a large extent. However, in spite of all the flaws which one can find in Combray, it does have certain authentic virtues which Paris and Balbec do not have. It is respectable, stable, caught up in a centuries-old tradition of ritual which is represented and guaranteed by the church.[3] It is with the church, seen as the focal point of the town, that the second evocation of Combray begins:

Combray, de loin, à dix lieues à la ronde, vu du chemin de fer quand nous y arrivions la dernière semaine avant Pâques, ce n'était qu'une église résumant la ville, la représentant, parlant d'elle et pour elle aux lointains, et, quand on approchait, tenant serrés autour de sa haute mante sombre, en plein champ, contre le vent, comme une pastoure ses brébis, les dos laineux et gris des maisons rassemblées qu'un reste de remparts du moyen âge cernait çà et là d'un trait aussi parfaitement circulaire qu'une petite ville dans un tableau de primitif [I, 48].

Although the narrator has nothing to say about the order of the mass, he attributes a great importance to the actual church building, which provides the town with a center of tradition and stability and even, in the proportions of its steeple, with that "distinction" which is a touchstone both of the aesthetic and the moral virtues (I, 64).

The town of Combray is also a repository of the domestic virtues. These are "represented" by the smells in Tante Léonie's rooms, the description of which follows immediately on that of the church and the town:

C'étaient de ces chambres de province qui — de même qu'en certains pays des parties entières de l'air ou de la mer sont illuminées ou parfumées par des myriades de protozoaires que nous ne voyons pas — nous enchantent de mille odeurs qu'y dégagent les vertus, la sagesse, les habitudes, toute une vie secrète, invisible, surabondante et morale que l'atmosphère y tient en suspens: odeurs naturelles encore, certes, et couleur du temps comme celles de la campagne voisine, mais déjà casanières, humaines et renfermées, gelée exquise, industrieuse et limpide de tous les fruits de l'année qui ont quitté le verger pour l'armoire; saisonnières, mais mobilières et domestiques, corrigeant le piquant de la gelée blanche par la douceur du pain chaud, oisives et ponctuelles comme une horloge de village, flâ-

---

[3] Cf. ibid., pp. 43–44.

neuses et rangées, insoucieuses et prévoyantes, lingères, matinales, dévotes, heureuses d'une paix qui n'apporte qu'un surcroît d'anxiété et d'un pro-saïsme qui sert de grand réservoir de poésie à celui qui les traverse sans y avoir vécu [I, 49].

Even if Tante Léonie spends her time lying in bed, the anthropo-morphized smells in her rooms take on the form of busy, active, routine-minded, devout housewives, who guarantee the virtues of tradition, stability, and hard work. Trusting to the instinctive re-action of our senses more than to any demonstration or argument, Proust provides the chief evidence of the goodness of Combray in the fact that it looks, tastes, and smells good.

None of the other milieux the narrator is to investigate will bear the same stamp of righteousness. Judged from the viewpoint of Combray, the Verdurin group first and then the Guermantes group will reveal a basic rottenness. On our first acquaintance with them, the Verdurins are presented as distinctly ridiculous. Their inverted snobbery (the result, at this point, of their despair of being received by the aristocracy) and their anxious desire to assert their own im-portance are apparent in the very first lines which introduce them to us. In their anxiety to keep around them only these persons who will believe in their value, and especially in their superiority to the aristocracy, the Verdurins neglect the bourgeois standards of caste and sexual respectability by encouraging the attendance of Odette, who is a demimondaine, and the pianist's aunt, who was once a con-cierge. The moral is obvious: outside the walls of Combray, sexual and caste standards go by the board. The only thing that counts any more is the assertion of the self and the persuasion of others to as-sent to this self-assertion. Mme Verdurin goes so far as to try to pre-vent Dr. Cottard from seeing his patients, if this should mean that he would miss one of her dinners, in whole or in part. Neither should any family or religious duties stand in the way of this at-tendance. The only thing in life which counts for her is that the "faithful" should come to her dinners and declare them preferable to every other activity, duty, or interest.

No friendship or love must stand in the way of absolute fidelity to the "clan." Any friend or lover of one of the "faithful" has to become one of the "faithful" too, or be banished. We see an ex-ample of this in the behavior of the Verdurins toward Swann. To begin with, when Swann acts like one of the "faithful," his relation-ship with Odette is encouraged and furthered by the Verdurins. Then, when Forcheville appears more amenable to the "clan" spirit,

Swann is no longer invited, and Odette is encouraged to deceive him with Forcheville. Later on, the Baron de Charlus and Morel are treated in a similar way. Morel comes to La Raspelière, the country house rented by the Verdurins, for regular violin recitals, and when he meets the Baron de Charlus he brings him along too. The Baron de Charlus arouses Mme Verdurin's resentment by talking of his pedigree, just as Swann had annoyed her by refusing to agree that the Duc and Duchesse de la Trémoïlle were ignorant and ill-behaved. She attempts to insult the Baron de Charlus at their first meeting, but her anxiety to keep him, for the sake of Morel and of the society ladies he might bring to the house, prevails for some time over her wish to be offensive. Little by little, because of his association with Morel, the Baron de Charlus becomes an habitué of the Verdurins, who give him every encouragement and, with complete disregard of traditional moral standards, do everything to facilitate his relationship with Morel. But, at the occasion of the Vinteuil concert, Mme Verdurin becomes furious with the Baron de Charlus because he has invited his friends of the Faubourg Saint-Germain in such a way that it appears as if he were giving the entertainment himself. The concert will consequently be of no use to her in the social climbing to which her inverted snobbery is giving way. What is even worse, he announces that Morel will give concerts for Mme de Duras. The Baron de Charlus fails to understand that Mme Verdurin is so passionately attached to the "faithful" that she cannot bear the idea of Morel's leaving her for anyone else, even to give just one concert. She has also long been jealous of the way in which the Baron de Charlus has been absorbing Morel's attention (III, 278). For these various reasons, she is determined to break up the relationship by telling Morel lies about the Baron de Charlus. She succeeds in this only too well, convincing Morel that the Baron de Charlus is a handicap to his career and has made him the laughing stock of the Conservatoire.

When the Verdurins do not have the excitement of breaking up a couple (whether normal or not) they entertain themselves by tormenting Saniette, whose gentleness and inability to defend himself make him the perfect butt. According to a passage added to the text in a footnote (III, 266), the Verdurins push matters to the point where M. Verdurin orders Saniette out of the house for a harmless remark. Saniette is so deeply affected that he has an attack in the courtyard and dies not long afterward. But according to another version, placed in the text some sixty pages further on, the Verdurins come to Saniette's aid when he loses a large amount of money on the Stock Exchange, and even have the delicacy to conceal the fact that the money comes from them. So even the Verdurins can be unexpectedly kind, confirming Proust's contention that "ce n'est pas le bon sens qui est 'la chose du monde la plus répandue', c'est la bonté" (although he goes on to add, "Mais la variété des défauts n'est pas moins admirable que la similitude des vertus.") (I, 741).

The Verdurins were never very highly thought of by the narrator's family. The narrator's grandfather thinks of M. Verdurin as "tombé — tout en gardant de nombreux millions — dans la bohème et la racaille" (I, 199), and disapproves strongly of Swann for associating with him. But the grandmother thinks highly of Mme de Villeparisis, with whom she went to school, and consequently of the Guermantes in general. The grandmother is very pleased when circumstances throw the narrator and herself together with Mme de Villeparisis at Balbec, although her first impulse had been to avoid the company of a lady whose station in life was so far above her own, because she thinks that the company of Mme de Villeparisis and her relatives will have a good effect on the nervous adolescent:

Comme on dit que c'est l'intérêt de l'espèce qui guide en amour les préférences de chacun et, pour que l'enfant soit constitué de la façon la plus normale, fait rechercher les femmes maigres aux hommes gras et les grasses aux maigres, de même c'était obscurément les exigences de mon bonheur menacé par le nervosisme, par mon penchant maladif à la tristesse, à l'isolement, qui lui faisaient donner le premier rang aux qualités de pondération et de jugement, particulières non seulement à Mme de Villeparisis, mais à une société où je pourrais trouver une distraction, un apaisement — une société pareille à celle où l'on vit fleurir l'esprit d'un Doudan, d'un M. de Rémusat, pour ne pas dire d'une Beausergent, d'un Joubert, d'une Sévigné, esprit qui met plus de bonheur, plus de dignité dans la vie que les raffinements opposés, lesquels ont conduit un Baudelaire, un Poe, un Verlaine, un Rimbaud, à des souffrances, à une déconsideration dont ma grand'mere ne voulait pas pour son petit-fils [I, 727].

It is with the grandmother's blessing, in consequence, that the narrator is introduced to Robert de Saint-Loup and the Baron de Charlus. She is particularly taken with the Baron de Charlus because of his feeling for Mme de Sévigné although, as the narrator is to discover later on, the Baron's taste for Mme de Sévigné has done nothing to introduce sobriety, order, or even normality into his life.

Caste standards are maintained in part, by the Guermantes, who are more noble than the House of France, "plus précieux et plus rares" (II, 438) than the rest of the aristocracy, and fully aware of their position in society. The Duc de Guermantes, for instance, is so deeply persuaded of his own importance that when he pays a visit to the narrator's family as the grandmother lies dying, he can think of nothing but the honor he is paying the family, and fails entirely to enter into their grief. His brother, the Baron de Charlus, is so preoccupied with his nobility that he is little short of a megalomaniac, while their cousin, the Prince de Guermantes, is so concerned with questions of rank and precedence that he is something of a family joke. But this does not prevent the Baron de Charlus and the Prince de Guermantes from pursuing handsome young men from the working class or the Prince de Guermantes from marrying Mme Verdurin, eventually, because he needs her money. Robert de Saint-Loup incurs the wrath of his family by his love for the actress Rachel and, even more, by his adoption of her attitudes and ideas. But he is simply more open and consistent than the other members of his family, who all lower caste barriers at times when their affections, passions, interest, or curiosity dictate it. The Duchesse de Guermantes, for instance, is doubly inconsistent in her attitudes. As a young woman, she delights in maintaining that she does not believe in titles and that she values only intelligence. But in spite of this she goes on to marry a very rich duke and to maintain the titles which are her due. At the end of her career, she will come to spend her time in the company of actresses, having begun to believe what she has so long maintained. As Brée points out, the aristocracy's attitude of defense against the encroachments of the lower orders is weakened by certain psychological tendencies: curiosity, fear of boredom, and the need for diversion.[4]

The Guermantes all talk about morality, but this does not necessarily affect their conduct:

Certes il y avait des Guermantes plus particulièrement intelligents, des Guermantes plus particulièrement moraux, et ce n'étaient pas d'habitude les mêmes. Mais les premiers — même un Guermantes qui avait fait des faux et trichait au jeu et était le plus délicieux de tous, ouvert à toutes les idées neuves et justes — traitaient encore mieux de la morale que les seconds, et de la même façon que Mme de Villeparisis, dans les moments où le Génie de la famille s'exprimait par la bouche de la vieille dame [II, 440–441].

Mme de Villeparisis, who regards Rachel as such a bad influence on her nephew, Robert de Saint-Loup, was once a wanton young

4 Brée, p. 101.

woman who ruined a number of men. This does not stop her from talking about modesty and kindness in a very intelligent way. Proust explains this, not by hypocrisy, but by the contention that one has to be at a certain distance from certain qualities to express them adequately: "Ceux qui non seulement parlent bien de certaines vertus, mais même en ressentent le charme et les comprennent à merveille (qui sauront en peindre dans leurs Mémoires une digne image), sont souvent issus, mais ne font pas eux-mêmes partie, de la génération muette, fruste et sans art, qui les pratiqua" (II, 184–185). The gap between life and art, which we noticed in Chapter Two, is coming to the fore once more, shedding an ironic light on the grandmother's hope that the narrator will benefit from contact with a classical type of literature and the society which fosters it. But even those Guermantes who are devoid of the intellectual and artistic pretensions of Mme de Villeparisis show the same discrepancy between their lip-service to morality and their actual conduct. Social punctilio, Proust observes, is more important to the Guermantes than any ethical considerations: "Le duc et la duchesse de Guermantes considéraient comme un devoir plus essentiel que ceux, assez souvent négligés, au moins par l'un d'eux, de la charité, de la chasteté, de la pitié et de la justice, celui, plus inflexible, de ne guère parler à la princesse de Parme qu'à la troisième personne" (II, 426). The Duc de Guermantes deceives his wife constantly and cruelly, forcing her to receive his ex-mistresses, while the reputation of the Duchesse for chastity may be "faite en réalité d'un nombre incalculable d'aventures habilement dissimulées" (III, 1023). (However, it is the Baron de Charlus, who is no authority on the subject, who puts this idea into the narrator's head.)

The Baron de Charlus, the Prince de Guermantes, and Robert de Saint-Loup all are or become homosexual. Whether we are to take this as a condemnation of them or not is not quite clear. We are given to understand, at several points in the novel, that this type of sexual behavior, while it may be more grotesque, more comic, and more pathetic in its manifestations than normal sexuality, is not intrinsically more disreputable. Thus, the narrator observes the encounter between the Baron de Charlus and Jupien in the courtyard of the Hôtel de Guermantes with an interest which appears strongly tinged with sympathy. In the description of this encounter, which is presented in terms of a rare insect bringing pollen to a flower which would otherwise remain unfertilized, Proust does everything, as Curtius points out,[5] to make the mutual attraction of the two homosexuals appear completely amoral. In fact, the choice of this comparison makes it appear natural, inevitable, and even desirable. Proust has much to say about the hypocrisy, gossip, deceitfulness, and generally pathetic and ludicrous behavior in which the Baron de Charlus's subservience to his ruling passion involves him. He also talks about his "déchéance morale" and his "vice" (e.g. III, 207). But when the narrator condemns the Baron de Charlus most strongly, for having himself tied to a bed in Jupien's brothel and whipped, an action which the narrator can only explain by the progress of a mental illness which has reached complete dementia, the narrator concludes, somewhat oddly, by condemning the Baron de Charlus for having allowed himself to be nailed by Force to the "rocher de la pure Matière" (III, 838). It sounds from this as if the extreme materialism of the nature of the Baron's satisfaction was what the narrator really had to reproach him with (a reproach which we have seen implicitly leveled against Swann for his dealings with Odette), and this impression is reinforced by the narrator's pious hope, expressed immediately after this condemnation, that some element of the spiritual still remained in the midst of this extreme materialism. We have already noticed the narrator's expression of sympathy with physical love, even in its least orthodox aspects, in his comments on Mlle Vinteuil. Yet there seems to be a certain ambivalence in the narrator's attitude. He is amused and interested by the behavior of Mlle Vinteuil and her friend, as he is by that of the Baron de Charlus and Jupien; yet the realization that Albertine may be a Lesbian comes upon him as a horrible shock, and his discovery that Robert de Saint-Loup is homosexual brings him close to shedding tears of distress and makes him regard the whole basis of their friendship as suspect. Then, when the narrator has become used to the idea of Saint-Loup's being homosexual, he comes to blame him, not for his attachment to Morel, but for the cruelty in which this involves him toward his wife, Gilberte. In order to conceal his real interests, Saint-Loup tortures her with lies, hysterical scenes, and pretended relationships with other women. Rather disingenuously, Proust gets out of the moral difficulty into which he has got his narrator by having him avow, whether naïvely or ironically is not quite clear, that he has no sense of morality (III,

291). The occasion for this avowal is the narrator's distress on see-ing the Baron de Charlus discomfited by Mme Verdurin.

But this very example makes it seem apparent that, in the eyes of Proust and his narrator, cruelty and indifference to the sufferings of others are much more grave offenses than sexual irregularities. The Guermantes are nearly all guilty of this cruelty, in spite of the charming attentions of which they are also capable. The most strik-ing examples of this are the occasions on which they manifest in-difference to the imminent death of friends and relatives, when paying attention to the critical state of these people would interfere with the social round. So, the Duc de Guermantes makes special ar-rangements not to be informed of the death of his cousin Amanien, which would prevent him from going to a masked ball and, the same evening, both he and the Duchesse ignore Swann's statement that he will be dead in three or four months. As Brée has pointed out,[6] there is a deliberate parallel here with the behavior of the Verdurins, who refuse to allow the deaths of Dechambre and the Princesse Sherbatoff to interfere with their entertainments and even go so far as to claim that reports of the death of these persons are "exaggerated." Whatever the modifications which the narrator has imposed on the sexual and social standards of Combray, it is clear that, as Moss observes,[7] society is, in these instances, being judged by the standards of "la bonté" which the narrator has acquired from his mother and grandmother. By these standards, it is found want-ing.

Just as deadly in its effect as actual cruelty, as Brée remarks,[8] is the frivolity of society, which nullifies any attempt to go at all deeply into ideas or feelings. Society has no use for great talent or deep thought, as Mme de Villeparisis's gentle mockery of the literary men she has known, such as Chateaubriand, makes apparent. It oc-curs to the narrator that Chateaubriand and his contemporaries must have made much the same impression on society as the insuf-ferably tactless Bloch:

Apres le dîner, quand j'étais remonté avec ma grand'mère, je lui disais que les qualités qui nous charmaient chez Mme de Villeparisis, le tact, la finesse, la discrétion, l'effacement de soi-même n'étaient peut-être pas bien précieuses, puisque ceux qui les possédèrent au plus haut degré ne furent que des Molé et des Loménie et que, si leur absence peut rendre les rela-

[6] Brée, pp. 105–110.
[7] Moss, pp. 99–100.
[8] Brée, p. 104.

tions quotidiennes désagréable, elle n'a pas empêché de devenir Chateaubriand, Vigny, Hugo, Balzac, des vaniteux qui n'avaient pas de jugement, qu'il était facile de railler, comme Bloch . . . [I, 726–727].

Mme de Villeparisis herself has too much literary talent to make her socially acceptable, and it is this talent which probably accounts for her downfall, as much as her scandalous past:

Ce que les artistes appellent intelligence semble prétention pure à la société élégante qui, incapable de se placer au seul point de vue d'où ils jugent tout, ne comprenant jamais l'attrait particulier auquel ils cèdent en choisissant une expression ou en faisant un rapprochement, éprouve auprès d'eux une fatigue, une irritation d'où naît très vite l'antipathie [II, 185].

Just as Mme de Villeparisis is annoying to members of fashionable society because of her talent, so Bergotte, because of his genius, is infinitely more so. He falls lamentably short of the standards of society as expounded by M. de Norpois who, however, is very well able to bear Mme de Villeparisis:

Ah! voilà quelqu'un qui donne raison à l'homme d'esprit qui prétendait qu'on ne doit connaître les écrivains que par leurs livres. Impossible de voir un individu qui réponde moins aux siens, plus prétentieux, plus solennel, moins homme de bonne compaignie. Vulgaire par moments, parlant à d'autres comme un livre, et même pas comme un livre de lui, mais comme un livre ennuyeux, ce qu'au moins ne sont pas les siens, tel est ce Bergotte. C'est un esprit des plus confus, alambiqué, ce que nos pères appelaient un diseur de phébus et qui rend encore plus déplaisantes, par sa façon de les énoncer, les choses qu'il dit [I, 474].

This is not just a prejudice on M. de Norpois's part, since the narrator has the same impression when he meets Bergotte, at a dinner given by Mme Swann. Bergotte certainly does talk in a way which has no obvious connection with his written style, and his enunciation is very strange. But Bergotte's manner of speaking is more intimately connected with his writing than the narrator, at this point, realizes:

Dans certains passages de la conversation où Bergotte avait l'habitude de se mettre à parler d'une façon qui ne paraissait pas affectée et déplaisante qu'à M. de Norpois, j'ai été long à découvrir une exacte correspondance avec les parties de ses livres où sa forme devenait si poétique et musicale. Alors il voyait dans ce qu'il disait une beauté plastique indépendante de la signification de ses phrases et, comme la parole humaine est en rapport avec l'âme, mais sans l'exprimer comme fait le style, Bergotte avait l'air de parler presque à contresens, psalmodiant certains mots et, s'il poursuivait au-dessous d'eux une seule image, les filant sans intervalle comme un même son, avec une fatigante monotonie. De sorte qu'un débit prétentieux, emphatique et monotone était le signe de la qualité esthétique de ses propos et l'effet, dans sa conversation, de ce même pouvoir qui produisait dans ses livres la la suite des images et l'harmonie [I, 550].

Bergotte's conversation is unsuitable for a drawing room or a dinner table because he is always approaching topics from a novel point of view, in his search for "quelque élément précieux et vrai, caché au cœur de chaque chose" (I, 550). The novelty of his approach is fatiguing for his audience, which wants only what it is accustomed to. Even the narrator is annoyed by the unexpectedness of Bergotte's remarks, although he ought to be more open to literary novelties, especially considering the source from which they come.

Whatever the requirements of society, Bergotte is enough of a man of genius to remain unaffected by them, although he is not above intriguing for a place in the Academy. He does not become fashionable until his talent has dried up and he is close to death, when Mme Swann constructs a salon around him. He also remains unaffected by the requirements of morality, so that people are struck by the discrepancy betwen his works and his life: "Ses derniers romans [étaient] pleins d'un souci si scrupuleux, si douloureux, du bien, que les moindres joies de leurs héros en étaient empoisonnées et que pour le lecteur même il s'en dégageait un sentiment d'angoisse à travers lequel l'existence la plus douce semblait difficile à supporter" (I, 558). But in spite of the moralizing tone of his books, Bergotte behaves cruelly toward his wife and is involved in a half-incestuous love affair which, according to some accounts, is complicated by unscrupulousness in money matters. There is a contradiction here which, according to Proust, may not be a real one. Bergotte may be leading a vicious life out of a hypersensibility which, in turn, leads to the tone of moral anguish which is so typical of Bergotte's works: "Peut-être n'est-ce que dans des vies réellement vicieuses que le problème moral peut se poser avec toute sa force d'anxiété" (I, 558). Anxiety, since it provides Bergotte with a theme for his books, is useful to him. Consequently, his life, which seems to be so much at variance with his work, is a source of inspiration for it.

Generally speaking, Bergotte acts in the most contradictory manner, being capable of extreme harshness and extraordinary kindness. But at least he is never cruel out of a lack of comprehension. He has an ability to enter into the feelings of others which is intimately linked with his talent for creating imaginary characters:

Parce qu'il imaginait les sentiments des autres aussi bien que s'ils avaient été les siens, quand l'occasion faisait qu'il avait à s'adresser à un malheureux, au moins d'une façon passagère, il le faisait en se plaçant non à son point de vue personnel, mais à celui même de l'être qui souffrait, point de vue d'où lui aurait fait horreur le langage de ceux qui continuent à penser à leurs petits intérêts devant la douleur d'autrui. De sorte qu'il a excité autour de lui des rancunes justifiées et des gratitudes ineffaçables [I, 559].

His behavior is the result of subordinating his life to his work:

Peut-être, plus le grand écrivain se développa en Bergotte aux dépens de l'homme à barbiche, plus sa vie individuelle se noya dans le flot de toutes les vies qu'il imaginait et ne lui parut plus l'obliger à des devoirs effectifs, lesquels étaient remplacés pour lui par le devoir d'imaginer ces autres vies [I, 559].

He arranges his life for the sake of his writing, having affairs with little girls to whom he pays large sums because he knows that the emotional effect they have on him is a source of inspiration. Being consciously aware of the mechanism by which love opens the door to art, by detaching the lover from every frivolous and material consideration, a mechanism which we have seen operating upon the life of the unconscious and unwilling Swann, Bergotte deliberately seeks the occasion of falling in love. And if love brings suffering, then that too, he knows, will help his artistic production by setting his soul in movement:

Il s'excusait à ses propres yeux parce qu'il savait ne pouvoir jamais si bien produire que dans l'atmosphère de se sentir amoureux. L'amour, c'est trop dire, le plaisir un peu enfoncé dans la chair aide au travail des lettres parce qu'il anéantit les autres plaisirs, par exemple les plaisirs de la société, ceux qui sont les mêmes pour tout le monde. Et même si cet amour amène des désillusions, du moins agite-t-il de cette façon-là aussi la surface de l'âme, qui sans cela risquerait de devenir stagnante [III, 183].

The disappointments which these girls bring him are instructive:

On n'arrive pas à être heureux mais on fait des remarques sur les raisons qui empêchent de l'être et qui nous fussent restées invisibles sans ces brusques percées de la déception. Les rêves ne sont pas réalisables, nous le savons; nous n'en formerions peut-être pas sans le désir, et il est utile d'en former pour les voir échouer et que leur échec instruise [III, 183].

The suffering which love brings is a source of inspiration because it destroys habit, detaches the sufferer from the world, and teaches general truths which can be used in works of literature. Consequently, by seeking occasions for suffering, Bergotte is doing what will be best for his work. Proust is so convinced of the truth of this axiom that he causes his narrator to express regret that the Baron de Charlus has no talent as a writer, since his homosexuality puts him in a position where anxiety and suffering are the constant and necessary companions of love:

Et en écoutant Jupien, je me disais "Quel malheur que M. de Charlus ne soit pas romancier ou poète! Non pas pour décrire ce qu'il verrait, mais le point où se trouve un Charlus par rapport au désir fait naître autour de lui les scandales, le force à prendre la vie sérieusement, à mettre des émotions dans le plaisir, l'empêche de s'arrêter, de s'immobiliser dans une vue ironique et extérieure des choses, rouvre sans cesse en lui un courant douloureux. Presque chaque fois qu'il adresse une déclaration, il essuie une avanie, s'il ne risque pas même la prison." Ce n'est pas que l'éducation des enfants, c'est celle des poètes qui se fait à coups de gifles [III, 831].

The refinements of a Baudelaire or a Rimbaud, which the narrator's grandmother so tardily began to dread for her grandson, seem to be exercising more and more of a fascination over him. These remarks about Bergotte and the Baron de Charlus shed increased light on the conflict between life and art and show that, in the narrator's opinion, life should be subordinated to art.

Bergotte subordinates life to art in more ways than in the conduct of his love affairs. If he can use love to the advantage of his art, with a deliberateness which seems positively cynical, he is also incapable of using his intelligence for any purpose but an artistic one, and so is liable to neglect his material advantage in a way which would not be possible in any nonartist but a convinced and extreme altruist:

C'était surtout un homme qui au fond n'aimait vraiment que certaines images et (comme une miniature au fond d'un coffret) que les composer et les peindre sous les mots. Pour un rien qu'en lui avait envoyé, si ce rien lui était l'occasion d'en entrelacer quelques-unes, il se montrait prodigue dans l'expression de sa reconnaissance, alors qu'il n'en témoignait aucune pour un riche présent. Et s'il avait eu à se défendre devant un tribunal, malgré lui il aurait choisi ses paroles, non selon l'effet qu' elles pouvaient produire sur le juge, mais en vue d'images que le juge n'aurait certainement pas aperçues [I, 559–560].

His work is even the last thing in his mind at the moment of his death. Having gone to see Vermeer's *View of Delft*, he is, as we have seen, deeply struck by the way in which a particular part of the picture has been painted, and begins to think that he should have lavished the same care and attention on his most recent books, which now seem to him to be too dry. He fixes his attention on the picture, even though he is, at the same time, undergoing dizzy spells which are the warning signal of the attack which is to carry him off. Just before he dies, he becomes aware that he has imprudently given up his life for Vermeer's painting. Monnin-Hornung disapproves of Bergotte for being able to think of his life at this moment, and takes particular exception to the fact that Bergotte thinks of the exchange of his life for this painting as imprudent.[9] Her criticism seems too harsh: that Bergotte is able to concentrate on a picture at all at the moment of his death, let alone draw conclusions from it about his own work, shows a truly remarkable devotion to art. For him to be able to regard the picture, at this moment, as more important than his life, he would have to be a kind of aesthetic superman. And although Proust regards his artists as superior to other men in the act of their artistic production, he makes it clear that in the conduct of their lives they are no more than human.

Proust follows up the description of Bergotte's death with a kind of sermon, in which he suggests that the duty felt by the artist to produce works of art is a kind of moral duty; that, at any rate, the aesthetic duty is as mysterious as the ethical one, and the two may be connected in origin. At the same time, by his talk of another world from which these values come, Proust sets up religious echoes in his reader's mind which suggest that producing works of art is a religious duty, whether the artist is consciously religious or not, for which the artist may be rewarded in an afterlife:

Ce qu'on peut dire, c'est que tout se passe dans notre vie comme si nous y entrions avec le faix d'obligations contractées dans une vie antérieure; il n'y a aucune raison dans nos conditions de vie sur cette terre pour que nous nous croyions obligés à faire le bien, à être délicats, même à être polis, ni pour l'artiste athée à ce qu'il se croie obligé de recommencer vingt fois un morceau dont l'admiration qu'il excitera importera peu à son corps mangé par les vers, comme le pan de mur jaune que peignit avec tant de science et de raffinement un artiste à jamais inconnu, à peine identifié sous le nom de Ver Meer. Toutes ces obligations, qui n'ont pas leur sanction dans la vie présente, semblent appartenir à un monde différent, fondé sur la bonté, le scrupule, le sacrifice, un monde entièrement différent de celui-ci, et dont nous sortons pour naître à cette terre, avant peut-être d'y retourner revivre sous l'empire de ces lois inconnues auxquelles nous avons obéi parce que nous en portions l'enseignement en nous, sans savoir qui les y avait tracées — ces lois dont tout travail profond de l'intelligence nous rapproche et qui sont invisibles seulement — et encore! — pour les sots [III, 187–188].

Art is linked, by the terms in which Proust speaks of it, to the values of goodness, scrupulosity, self-abnegation, and self-sacrifice. However much Bergotte may have offended against the moral law in his private life, he has obeyed it in his works, by his obedience to the obligations imposed upon him by his aesthetic instinct. And, in

[9] Monnin-Hornung, pp. 60–61.

spite of all his sins, he may be reaping the reward for this obedience in some future life.

At the time when the narrator meets him, Elstir is free from the moral flaws of Bergotte. But he once was the ridiculous and pretentious "M. Biche," an habitué of the Verdurins who was something of an amateur procurer. The narrator, deeply impressed by the famous and dignified Elstir, is astonished to think that the two men can be the same: "Serait-il possible que cet homme de génie, ce sage, ce solitaire, ce philosophe à la conversation magnifique et qui dominait toutes choses, fût le peintre ridicule et pervers adopté jadis par les Verdurin?" (I, 863). Elstir sees the astonishment and disappointment which the narrator feels at this realization, and goes out of his way to give him a lesson on the development of a great man. Even the wisest men, Elstir tells the narrator, have, in their youth, said or done things which they must blush for later on. But such episodes have to be gone through before maturity is reached. These young men who have been taught "la noblesse d'esprit et l'élégance morale" (I, 864) by their preceptors have a merely negative and sterile wisdom. True wisdom represents a combat and a victory over evil and banality, but this evil and banality have to be encountered to be overcome. Elstir is a generous teacher for the narrator, on whom he not only lavishes this moral teaching, but whom he allows to inspect his studio and whom he instructs in the symbolism of Gothic architecture. He loves to give of himself, and lives in isolation only for lack of people to understand him. This isolation is good for his art, since it allows him to devote his time entirely to painting, but his generosity of spirit and his wish to teach are less good, because they distract him from his art. Consequently, it is just as well that few disciples come to him. His choice of solitude, a choice which is widely misunderstood, being attributed to a variety of bad motives, sets him far from the lure of society. He has no wish to continue frequenting the Verdurins, who feel somewhat resentful at his departure. There is no suffering in his life (unless he suffers at being misunderstood — but we are not told that this is the case), but only a love which makes his solitude all the more welcome. Detached from the world as he is, he has no need of suffering to detach him still further, so he may indulge in nobility of soul to his heart's content, without resorting to the morally dubious artistic aids of Bergotte.

Vinteuil, as we have already seen, has no lack of suffering in his life, which is full of the vicarious guilt brought to him by his daughter. Just as in Catholicism the merits of the saints flow over onto those who are not leading a saintly life, so in the Proustian religion of art the ultimately beneficial effects of the suffering brought by sexual indulgence may operate even on those who have done nothing to bring this suffering on themselves. As an obscure and impecunious piano teacher, Vinteuil also has no temptation to go into society. Consequently, all the best part of himself goes into his work which, as we have seen in the previous chapter, is marked at its finest moments by a triumphant joy which is the result of complete detachment.

For a long time, the narrator is far from finding this detachment. He wastes his time with the aristocratic companions to whom his grandmother, ironically enough, has introduced him. Even as he does this, he feels guilt at following the frivolous pleasures of society. At the same time, he feels guilty at the distress he causes his mother by keeping Albertine, whom he has no serious intention of marrying, in their Paris apartment. Suffering and increased guilt come to him from the disappearance and death of Albertine, whom with his relentless inquiries he has hounded into the grave. But his deepest sense of guilt comes from his continual postponement of the act of writing. His parents and his grandmother would love to see him produce something, not so much because they regard the work of a writer as having an overriding value as because it seems to be the only kind of work for which the narrator is suited, and they are anxious to see him work at something. The standards of Combray, which set devotion to a recognized calling above visiting duchesses, are active in the narrator to make him feel guilty at putting off his act of literary production.[10] One of the thoughts which come to his mind, when he finally receives the inspiration which will allow him to start writing, is that his grandmother would have been so happy to know that he is about to start work at last: "Et ma seule consolation qu'elle ne sût pas que je me mettais enfin à l'œuvre d'art était que (tel est le lot des morts) si elle ne pouvait pas jouir de mon progrès, elle avait cessé depuis longtemps d'avoir conscience de mon inaction, de ma vie manquée, qui avaient été une telle souffrance pour elle" (III, 903).

The narrator's pride and joy in the work he is about to begin are inextricably mingled with guilt feelings. Not only does he feel

[10] Cf. Brée, p. 114.

guilty at having delayed for so long a labor which he feels to be of the greatest importance, but he also feels guilty at the fact that he is going to use, as material for his book, people who have been dear to him and who have died. He feels that they have died for his sake:

J'avais beau croire que la vérité suprême de la vie est dans l'art, j'avais beau, d'autre part, n'être pas plus capable de l'effort de souvenir qu'il m'eût fallu pour aimer encore Albertine que pour pleurer encore ma grand'mère, je me demandais si tout de même une œuvre d'art dont elles ne seraient pas conscientes serait pour elles, pour le destin de ces pauvres mortes, un accomplissement. Ma grand'mère que j'avais, avec tant d'indifférence, vue agoniser et mourir près de moi! O puissé-je, en expiation, quand mon œuvre serait terminée, blessé sans remède, souffrir de longues heures, abandonné de tous, avant de mourir! D'ailleurs, j'avais une pitié infinie même d'êtres moins chers, même d'indifférents, et de tant de destinées dont ma pensée en essayant de les comprendre avait, en somme, utilisé la souffrance, ou même seulement les ridicules. Tous ces êtres qui m'avaient révélé des vérités et qui n'étaient plus, m'apparaissaient comme ayant vécu une vie qui n'avait profité qu'à moi, et comme s'ils étaient morts pour moi [III, 902].

By a fruitful paradox, the narrator, by putting off the act of writing and at the same time gathering impressions which will help him in that act, has accumulated a capital of guilt and suffering on which he can draw for artistic inspiration. By the same token, the act of writing will help to annul that guilt and suffering, even though the narrator feels that some additional act of expiation will be necessary. Although it may not completely placate their reproachful shades, his work will be an attempt at expiation toward those whom he has used, and will also insure them a continued existence in the minds of others: "[Ce livre] ferait de ceux qui ne sont plus, en leur essence la plus vraie, une acquisition perpétuelle pour toutes les âmes" (III, 903). A book, he says, is like a cemetery. But it is not only those whom he has known whose graves he disturbs. He himself has died many deaths, and so lies beside them. The various selves who have been himself and who have died in turn will all be used for his book, which will provide spiritual life for future generations: "Moi je dis que la loi cruelle de l'art est que les êtres meurent et que nous-memes mourions en épuisant toutes les souffrances, pour que pousse l'herbe non de l'oubli mais de la vie éternelle, l'herbe drue des oeuvres fécondes, sur laquelle les générations viendront faire gaiment, sans souci de ceux qui dorment en dessous, leur 'déjeuner sur l'herbe'" (III, 1038). At the heart of the Proustian religion of art, as of the Christian religion, lies a mystery of death and resurrection.

Not only is the art work like the grass of a cemetery on which future generations will come to picnic, but it is also itself a food. Just as Christ asked his followers to feed on his body and blood, so the readers of Proust's work feed on those lives which have been offered up for them. Proust compares the work of art to food on more than one occasion. Thus, he says that he does not have the presumption to compare his future novel to a cathedral; he would rather liken his creative activity to that of Françoise preparing a *bœuf mode* (III, 1035). Again, he speaks of aesthetes, themselves incapable of artistic production, as starving for works of art, from which they are incapable of extracting the truly nourishing element: "Et, en effet, comme ils n'assimilent pas ce qui dans l'art est vraiment nourricier, ils ont tout le temps besoin de joies artistiques, en proie à une boulimie qui ne les rassasie jamais" (III, 892). But even though aesthetes may be incapable of absorbing the truly nourishing part of an art work, it is the artist's duty to provide them with this spiritual food. In an answer to an inquiry made by Maurice Montabré, Proust expresses his awareness of this duty very clearly, giving it, at the same time, a religious connotation:

Que si le papier venait absolument à faire défaut, je me ferais, je crois, boulanger. Il est honorable de donner aux hommes leur pain quotidien. En attendant je confectionne de mon mieux ce "Pain des anges" dont Racine (que je cite de mémoire et sans doute avec bien des fautes) disait:

> Dieu lui-même le compose
> De la fleur de son froment
> C'est ce pain si délectable
> Que ne sert pas à sa table
> Le monde que vous suivez
> Je l'offre à qui veut me suivre
> Approchez: voulez-vous vivre?
> Prenez, mangez, et vivez.[11]

By the same token, one of the features of the experience of involuntary memory which prove that this experience is supremely suited to act as the basis for a novel is the fact that it comes in the form of spiritual food. The narrator expresses this idea three times. Thus, he says that in his being was a "personnage intermittent, ne reprenant vie que quand se manifestait quelque essence générale, commune à plusieurs choses, qui faisait sa nourriture et sa joie" (III, 718). Again, he says: "L'être qui était rené en moi quand, avec un tel frémissement de bonheur, j'avais entendu le bruit commun à

---

[11] Proust, *Lettres retrouvées*, présentées et annotées par Philip Kolb (Paris: Plon, 1966), p. 144.

la fois à la cuiller qui touche l'assiette et au marteau qui frappe sur la roue, à l'inégalité pour les pas des pavés de la cour Guermantes et du baptistère de Saint-Marc, etc., cet être-là ne se nourrit que de l'essence des choses, en elle seulement il trouve sa subsistance, ses délices" (III, 872). Shortly after this, he says that his true inner self wakes to life when two sensations are the same in the past and the present, and receives "la céleste nourriture qui lui est apportée" (III, 873). One might say that Proust's intention is to absorb external reality and present it, in a form which they, in turn, can absorb, to his readers. This is, basically, the intention at the back of the spiritualization of the material: the material world is transformed by the artist into spiritual food.

For Proust, the art work is the only means of entering into, and absorbing, the innermost nature of another being. We have seen him express, in "Du Côté de chez Swann," the conviction that one is inescapably contained within oneself. In "La Fugitive" he restates this conviction, more definitely and more gloomily: "Les liens entre un être et nous n'existent que dans notre pensée. La mémoire en s'affaiblissant les relâche, et, malgré l'illusion dont nous voudrions être dupes et dont, par amour, par amitié, par politesse, par respect humain, par devoir, nous dupons les autres, nous restons seuls. L'homme est l'être qui ne peut sortir de soi, qui ne connaît les autres qu'en soi, et, en disant le contraire, ment" (III, 450). Only art can convey to another mind the echo of the "vibration interne" (I, 87) of an individual personality. By conveying the innermost essence of an artist's mind, the art work provides spiritual nourishment and even rejuvenation for the person who receives it, a nourishment and rejuvenation which cannot be received in any other way:

N'est-ce pas que ces éléments, tout ce résidu réel que nous sommes obligés de garder pour nous-mêmes, que la causerie ne peut transmettre même de l'ami à l'ami, du maître au disciple, de l'amant à la maîtresse, cet ineffable qui différencie qualitativement ce que chacun a senti et qu'il est obligé de laisser au seuil des phrases où il ne peut communiquer avec autrui qu'en se limitant à des points extérieurs communs à tous et sans intérêt, l'art, l'art d'un Vinteuil comme celui d'un Elstir, le fait apparaître, extériorisant dans les couleurs du spectre la composition intime de ces mondes que nous appelons les individus et que sans l'art nous ne connaîtrions jamais? Des ailes, un autre appareil respiratoire, et qui nous permissent de traverser l'immensité, ne nous serviraient à rien, car si nous allions dans Mars et dans Vénus en gardant les mêmes sens, ils revêtiraient du meme aspect que les choses de la Terre tout ce que nous pourrions voir. Le seul véritable voyage, le seul bain de Jouvence, ce ne serait pas d'aller vers de nouveaux paysages, mais d'avoir d'autres yeux, de voir l'univers avec les yeux d'un autre, de cent autres, de voir les cent univers que chacun d'eux voit, que chacun d'eux est; et cela nous le pouvens avec un Elstir, avec un Vinteuil avec leurs pareils, nous volons vraiment d'étoiles en étoiles [III, 257–258].

Literature is life and, in fact, the only real life:

La vraie vie, la vie enfin découverte et éclaircie, la seule vie par conséquent réellement vécue, c'est la littérature; cette vie qui, en un sens, habite à chaque instant chez tous les hommes aussi bien que chez l'artiste. Mais ils ne la voient pas parce qu'ils ne cherchent pas à l'éclaircir [III, 895].

Style, for the writer, as color for the painter, is a matter of vision. The artist develops both his personal view of life and a means of conveying it to others. His is the only means of conveying this view to others:

Par l'art seulement nous pouvons sortir de nous, savoir ce que voit un autre de cet univers qui n'est pas le même que le nôtre, et dont les pay-sages nous seraient restés aussi inconnus que ceux qu'il peut y avoir dans la lune. Grâce à l'art, au lieu de voir un seul monde, le nôtre, nous le voyons se multiplier, et, autant qu'il y a d'artistes originaux, autant nous avons de mondes à notre disposition, plus différents les uns des autres que ceux qui roulent dans l'infini et, bien des siècles après qu'est éteint le foyer dont il émanait, qu'il s'appelât Rembrandt ou Ver Meer, nous en-voient encore leur rayon spécial [III, 895–896].

The artist who brings a gift of such price is immeasurably superior to those who merely accept the gift. A good reader absorbs the spiritual life of a writer and profits by doing so, but the writer who offers him that life is far above him:

Et quant à la jouissance que donne à un esprit parfaitement juste, à un cœur vraiment vivant, la belle pensée d'un maître, elle est sans doute entièrement saine, mais, si précieux que soient les hommes qui la goûtent vraiment (combien y en a-t-il en vingt ans?), elle les réduit tout de même à n'être que la pleine conscience d'un autre [III, 894].

The artist is, on a superior scale, an exponent of "la bonté," since he devotes himself to producing something which is essential to the spiritual well-being of others. Consequently he is, to a large extent, free from the moral obligations which are incumbent on other men. As we already noticed, the moral dilemmas in the lives of Bergotte and Vinteuil are positively beneficial from an aesthetic standpoint, because they detach them from the world and provide inspiration for their work. The guilt of the narrator is also good, in that it pro-vides him with a stimulus to get on with his work. His egoism, again, is beneficial, since it is "un égoisme utilisable pour autrui" (III, 1036). The author ought to be selfish, for the sake of his work. The narrator realized this long before he became convinced of his

vocation: "Les êtres qui en ont la possibilité — il est vrai que ce sont
les artistes et j'étais convaincu depuis longtemps que je ne le serais
jamais — ont aussi le devoir de vivre pour eux-mêmes . . . (I, 906).
He is forcibly reminded of this necessary selfishness at the moment
of his realization of his vocation, when he takes time from his work
to write a couple of letters, one in reply to an invitation from Mme
Molé and the other a letter of condolence on the death of Mme
Sazerat's son. He is punished for these acts of politeness by falling
into a state of complete exhaustion, in which he is unable to get on
with his work. By writing these letters, he has sacrificed a real duty
to the unreal obligation of showing himself to be polite and sympathetic. The act of "bonté" which consists of writing his book is
superior to all other acts of personal "bonté."

Even when he neglects the rules of "la bonté" in personal matters,
the artist is superior to the nonartist who neglects the same rules,
but without performing any superior act of "bonté" in compensation. Only the narrator's mother and grandmother live up to the
requirements of "la bonté" in their life to the same degree as the
artist does in his work. Brée maintains that the nonartistic characters in Proust's work are judged for the lack of awareness which they
show by performing kind and unkind acts alike, without thinking
about what they are doing. Because the artist is the only one to be
fully aware of what he is doing, then the artist, with the exception
of the narrator's mother and grandmother, is the only truly moral
being. For her, the artist's morality is the only one which the narrator recognizes.[12] But this opinion can be disputed. It can be maintained that it is not so much their lack of awareness with which
Proust is reproaching the nonartistic characters as their lack of altruism. And if he castigates them for their failure to live up to a
high standard of altruism, this surely means that he insists on this
standard, rather than that he fails to recognize it. But the artist's
morality is of particular interest to him, partly because of the special
importance of the artist and partly because he is an artist himself.

In this connection, it is interesting to see how Proust's attitude
compares with that of a Catholic philosopher who has made a special study of the respective claims of morality and art. In his work
La Responsabilité de l'artiste,[13] Jacques Maritain says that art and
morality constitute two autonomous worlds, each with its own spe-

[12] Brée, p. 244.

[13] Jacques Maritain, *La Responsabilité de l'artiste*, traduction de l'anglais par
Georges et Christiane Brazzola, revue par l'auteur (Paris: A. Fayard, 1961).

cific virtues, within the human personality. To morality belong the virtues of the practical intellect, while to art belong the virtues of the speculative intellect. Morality has nothing to do with the act by which a work of art is produced, but it does have to do with the artist as a human being. Beauty is an absolute and makes demands like a god, but it is subordinate to and dependent on the Absolute which is God. Within its sphere, the artistic consciousness is as absolute in its demands as the moral conscience in its. In fact, the two are sufficiently closely connected for the artist to be unable to go against his artistic conscience without, at the same time, going against his moral conscience. In the last analysis, art is subordinate to ethics. But in its turn, ethics is ruled by love, so that prudence (the virtue of the practical intellect) is subordinate to charity. The prudent man and the artist have difficulty understanding each other, but the contemplative and the artist are close. Maritain goes on to say that, while the artist (like Pater and Wilde) may be tempted to develop his ethical life for the good of his art, having certain virtues only in the creation of the art work and not in his life at all, he is liable to have these virtues (specifically integrity, courage, and honesty) in this special, restricted area to a very marked degree. But whether he subordinates his life to his work or not, the artist, for his production of the work of art, must have humility, magnanimity, prudence, integrity, strength, temperance, simplicity, and candor, even if he does not have them in his private life. If man were not divided against himself, Maritain feels, the aesthetic virtues would act as an introduction to the moral ones. In the same way, there is an affinity between aesthetic experience and mysticism. The former can lead to the latter or else away from it, to a magical substitute, as in the case of Mallarmé and the Symbolists.

Twice in the same work Maritain suggests that the artist and the contemplative mystics have much in common. Schopenhauer, again, would say the same thing, although for different reasons. For Maritain, the artist is a man who is capable of exercising certain virtues and of attaining a state of contemplation in his work, although these virtues and this mystical state may be totally absent from his life. In contrast to Proust, Maritain feels that the artist should not be excused from being virtuous in his life and that, in the end, he will be judged as a man by his entire life, not simply by his work. Obviously, Maritain is replying to the whole complex of late nineteenth-century attitudes which Proust has summed up in his work. For Schopenhauer, from whom these attitudes largely sprang, there is one single important virtue, from which all the others arise, and that is selfless detachment. This detachment is present in both the saint and the artist to a very much more marked degree than in other men who are, for the most part, mere unconscious puppets of the striving will. A person in whom selfless detachment is strongly developed has a particular aptitude for contemplation. So far as my understanding of Schopenhauer extends, he makes no distinction in kind between the contemplation of the artist and that of the mystic. Insofar as there is a distinction, it appears to be one of duration. The artist keeps slipping back from his contemplation of the Ideas (or eternal essences) into daily life, whereas the mystic remains in a more or less permanent state of contemplation.[14]

In this connection, one particularly striking similarity between Schopenhauer and Proust may be found in their taste for Dutch paintings. As we have seen, a study of Vermeer was the specific aesthetic task which Swann neglected in favor of society, and which he took up again when love had (temporarily) detached him from society; a painting by Vermeer is the last object seen by Bergotte; Vermeer is discussed by the narrator and Albertine; and, finally, Vermeer is one of the artists invoked by Proust in "Le Temps retrouvé" to prove that the influence of an artist's special vision extends far beyond his mortal existence. What is the importance of Dutch painting for Schopenhauer? Simply, the evidence it provides that the artists who produced it were in a state of blessed detachment:

Inward disposition, the predominance of knowing over willing, can produce this state [of contemplation] under any circumstances. This is shown by those admirable Dutch artists who directed this purely objective perception to the most insignificant objects, and established a lasting monument of their objectivity and spiritual peace in their pictures of *still life*, which the aesthetic beholder does not look on without emotion; for they present to him the peaceful, still frame of mind of the artist, free from will, which was needed to contemplate such insignificant things so objectively, to observe them so attentively, and to repeat this perception so intelligently; and as the picture enables the onlooker to participate in this state, his emotion is often increased by the contrast between it and the unquiet frame of mind, disturbed by vehement willing, in which he finds himself.[15]

Vermeer's paintings are not exactly still lifes, since figures rather than fruit and flowers appear in them. But these figures are represented as so still and serene that what Schopenhauer says of still life

[14] Schopenhauer, I, 346, 405.
[15] Ibid., p. 255.

can equally well be applied to them. It can hardly be an accident that Proust, who was so deeply marked by his early experiences and who read Schopenhauer as a schoolboy, in the class of his admired teacher Alphonse Darlu,[16] should four times have used pictures of this type as a counterweight to those manifestations of the cosmic will, an individual love and an individual life.

The question of the connection between the artist and the mystic, as it appears to have existed for Proust, is one of considerable interest. I propose to discuss this topic at greater length in the next three chapters, particularly Chapter Eight.

[16] André Ferré, *Les Années de collège de Marcel Proust* (Paris: Gallimard, 1959), p. 214.

CHAPTER SIX

CHRISTIAN LANGUAGE
AND CHRISTIAN BELIEF

In the last chapter, we found that Proust advocated a system of morality founded on altruism and involving a kind of double standard. Nonartists should practice "la bonté" toward each other and are judged wanting if they do not; artists practice "la bonté" by producing works of art and are exonerated from performing acts of kindness which might interfere with their devotion to the work of art. The narrator's mother and grandmother are the only perfect exponents of "la bonté" among the nonartists. Are they Christians? François Mauriac thinks not, for they attain perfection too easily. For Mauriac, God is terribly absent from Proust's work; there is no such thing for any one of Proust's characters as a struggle against original sin toward goodness or any divine assistance in such a combat.[1]

It is certainly true that the narrator's mother and grandmother do not go through any apparent struggles to reach their peak of kindness, self-forgetfulness, and consideration for others. Neither do they appear outstandingly devout. They go to mass, certainly, but one has the impression that this is rather because they would consider it extraordinary not to go than because their church attendance represents anything special for them. Piroué suggests that their reading of Mme de Sévigné serves to impress Christian values upon them. Linking Vinteuil with the narrator's mother and grandmother, he says that these three people have managed to combine

---

[1] François Mauriac, *Du Côte de chez Proust* (Paris: Éditions de la Table Ronde, 1947), pp. 66–67.

obedience to God and to the World, to Christianity and civilization, for they have holiness as their goal and Mme de Sévigné as their example. Their scruples, kindness, and spirit of self-sacrifice are not only Christian virtues, but virtues of tact and *savoir-vivre*.[2] It is true that the narrator's mother and grandmother quote continually from Mme de Sévigné. As we have seen, the narrator's grandmother was favorably impressed by Jupien because he made a remark which would have been worthy of Mme de Sévigné; she wants her grandson to cultivate a "Sévigné" attitude to life; and she is delighted with the Baron de Charlus bcause he talks of Mme de Sévigné exactly as she would do. She takes a volume of Mme de Sévigné with her on every journey she makes, and both she and her daughter quote frequently from this author in their own letters. On several occasions, the narrator's mother rebukes him for some failure of delicacy or principle by quoting Mme de Sévigné. Once, the rebuke is directed at him because he called his grandmother "your mother," instead of "my grandmother," in a letter; at other times, because he is wasting his money, like Charles de Sévigné; and, on another occasion, because, again like Charles de Sévigné, he is taking up Albertine's time and attention without any serious intention of marrying her. So we see that the narrator's mother and grandmother use Mme de Sévigné as a standard for judging questions of sensibility and conduct and as a pattern for their own letters. But their sympathy with Mme de Sévigné does not lead them to the point where they refer to any of those passages in her letters which have a direct bearing on Catholicism. Like the Baron de Charlus, although from a very less special point of view, they appreciate Mme de Sévigné because she expresses feelings which were already valuable to them before they started reading her. And there is no evidence that Vinteuil ever read Mme de Sévigné at all, still less that he was inspired by her to seek holiness as his goal.

The most ostensibly devout characters in Proust's work are Tante Léonie and the Baron de Charlus. Neither is an example of those Christian virtues which are also virtues of tact and *savoir-vivre*. Tante Léonie's devoutness, we are given to understand, is part of her neurasthenia, since she is "toujours couchée dans un état incertain de chagrin, de débilité physique, de maladie, d'idée fixe et de dévotion" (I, 49). Her prescriptions are mixed in with her prayer books, in such a way that the reader has the impression that the two

---

[2] Georges Piroué, *Par les chemins de Marcel Proust: essai de critique descriptive* (Neuchâtel: A la Baconnière, 1955), p. 26.

groups of things belong to the same category, both being used to combat an imaginery illness:

D'un côté de son lit était une grande commode jaune en bois de citronnier et une table qui tenait à la fois de l'officine et du maître-autel, où, au-dessous d'une statuette de la Vierge et d'une bouteille de Vichy-Célestins, on trouvait des livres de messe et des ordonnances de médicaments, tout ce qu'il fallait pour suivre de son lit les offices et son régime, pour ne manquer l'heure ni de la pepsine ni des vêpres [I, 52].

Religion, for Tante Léonie, is simply a way of occupying herself with her own condition and getting through the day in a reassuringly regular fashion. It has no effect on her conduct which, as we saw in the previous chapter, can be at times half crazy, and even positively cruel. But if Tante Léonie is half crazy, there are times when the Baron de Charlus appears entirely so. As the narrator remarks, the Baron's insolence and noisiness were accepted by society, but a stranger, hearing him shout, might well have taken him for a mad-man. If the Baron's social conduct is extraordinary and his private behavior abnormal, his religious beliefs are equally unusual, being those of the Middle Ages:

Le baron était non seulement chrétien, comme on le sait, mais pieux à la façon du Moyen Age. Pour lui, comme pour les sculpteurs du XIIIe siècle, l'Église chrétienne était, au sens vivant du mot, peuplée d'une foule d'êtres, crus parfaitement réels: prophètes, apôtres, anges, saints personnages de toute sorte, entourant le Verbe incarné, sa mère et son époux, le Père Eternel, tous les martyrs et docteurs, tels que leur peuple en plein relief se presse au porche ou remplit le vaisseau des cathédrales. Entre eux tous, M. de Charlus avait choisi comme patrons intercesseurs les archanges Michel, Gabriel et Raphaël, avec lesquels il avait de fréquents entretiens pour qu'ils communiquassent ses prières au Père Eternel, devant le trône de qui ils se tiennent [II, 1040].

His Christianity reaches its peak during an almost fatal illness, when he edifies those around him by an eloquence which is as mildly Christian as his former tirades were violent. However, mixed in with his saintly conversation were "des pensées qui n'avaient de chrétien que l'apparence":

Il implorait l'archange Gabriel de venir lui annoncer, comme au prophète, dans combien de temps viendrait le Messie. Et s'interrompant d'un doux sourire douleureux, il ajoutait: "Mais il ne faudrait pas que l'Archange me demandât comme à Daniel de patienter 'sept semaines et soixante-deux semaines,' car je serai mort avant." Celui qu'il attendait ainsi était Morel. Aussi demandaitil il aussi à l'Archange Raphaël de le lui ramener comme le jeune Tobie. Et, mêlant des moyens plus humains (comme les Papes mala-des qui, tout en faisant dire des messes, ne négligent pas de faire appeler leur médecin), il insinuait à ses visiteurs que si Brichot lui ramenait rapidement son jeune Tobie, peut-être l'Archange Raphaël consentirait-il à lui rendre la vue comme au père de Tobie ou dans la piscine probatique de Bethsaïde [III, 323-324].

There seems to be something crazy about the Baron's religiosity, as about his other preoccupations and interests. In Proust's opinion, religious belief has very little influence on conduct. Rather, it is modified to suit the character of the believer.

The priesthood appears but little in Proust's narrative. We meet the parish priest of Combray, who suffers from neurasthenia and whose chief preoccupations are the state of his church (which, with mistaken zeal, he would like to see restored) and etymologies (mostly false). We have no evidence that, in his visits to Tante Léonie, he ever talks to her about spiritual matters. In addition to the parish priest, we get a brief glimpse of a monk who is a brother-in-law of the narrator's grandmother. He comes to grieve over the grandmother's deathbed, and is observed with sympathy by the narrator. Prompted by a professional suspicion of human nature, the monk puts his hands over his eyes and spies on the narrator through his fingers, to see if his sympathy is genuine. That is all we see of him. Finally, in Jupien's brothel, we meet "cette chose si rare, et en France absolument exceptionnelle, qu'est un mauvais prêtre" (III, 829). These examples all suggest that, while Proust feels no antagonism to the clergy, he feels no particular reverence for it either. In spite of his implied amusement at Saint-Loup's babblings about Rachel being a kind of poet-priest, Proust would obviously be inclined to accept Bergotte, Vinteuil, or Elstir as a spiritual guide rather than a priest.

To return to Mauriac's charge that God is terribly absent from Proust's work, it is true that there are very few allusions to God in *A la Recherche du temps perdu*. The steeple of Saint-Hilaire provides us with one of Proust's few direct references to the Deity. After saying that the steeple summed up the church, expressing what one might call its consciousness, and that it gave a form, a coronation, and a consecration to every hour and aspect of Combray, the narrator goes on to compare it to other steeples seen in his later life, and to say that this one steeple is the one which has most importance for him, for it appeared raised before him like the finger of God. But it seems permissible to presume that the special importance which this one steeple holds for the narrator is due to the fact that he beheld it at a time in his life when he possessed "le sentiment qui nous fait non pas considérer une chose comme un spectacle, mais y croire comme en un être sans équivalent" (I, 66). The church itself is described in terms which attribute its prestige quite as much to the art works with which it is filled and to the historical associations which carry it so far back in time as to the presence of God. The narrator finds something supernatural about the church because of its stained glass windows, its tapestries, and its yet more ancient treasures:

Tout cela, et plus encore les objets précieux venus à l'église de personnages de légende (la croix d'or travaillée, disait-on, par saint Éloi et donnée par Dagobert, le tombeau des fils de Louis le Germanique, en porphyre et en cuivre émaillé), à cause de quoi je m'avançais dans l'église, quand nous gagnions nos chaises, comme dans une vallée visitée des fées, où le paysan s'émerveille de voir dans un rocher, dans un arbre, dans une mare, la trace palpable de leur passage surnaturel; tout cela faisait d'elle pour moi quelque chose d'entièrement différent du reste de la ville . . . [I, 61].

However, the church does have enough of a religious atmosphere to confer a special value on the hawthorns which are placed on the altar for the month of Mary celebrations:

N'étant pas seulement dans l'église, si sainte, mais où nous avions le droit d'entrer, posées sur l'autel même, inséparables des mystères à la célébration desquels elles prenaient part, elles faisaient courir au milieu des flambeaux et des vases sacrés leurs branches attachées horizontalement les unes aux autres en un apprêt de fête, et qu'enjolivaient encore les festons de leur feuillage sur lequel étaient semés à profusion, comme sur une traîne de mariée, de petits bouquets de boutons d'une blancheur éclatante. Mais, sans oser les regarder qu'à la dérobée, je sentais que ces apprêts pompeux étaient vivants et que c'était la nature elle-même qui, en creusant ces découpures dans les feuilles, en ajoutant l'ornement suprême de ces blancs boutons, avait rendu cette décoration digne de ce qui était à la fois une réjouissance populaire et une solennité mystique [I, 112].

The hawthorns, being like young girls dressed in white, being decorated like a bridal train and bearing their clusters of stamens like bouquets, take on the aspect of brides in general and of Mary, the bride of God, in particular. The religious associations of the altar and of the month of Mary celebrations are carried over onto the hawthorns to give them a special prestige. When the narrator comes to see the hawthorns again, in the hedge outside Swann's park, the flowers will continue to have religious associations for him:

La haie formait comme une suite de chapelles qui disparaissaient sous la jonchée de leurs fleurs amoncelées en reposoir; au-dessous d'elles, le soleil posait à terre un quadrillage de clarté, comme s'il venait de traverser une verrière; leur parfum s'étendait aussi onctueux, aussi délimité en sa forme que si j'eusse été devant l'autel de la Vierge, et les fleurs, aussi parées, tenaient chacune d'un air distrait son étincelant bouquet d'étamines, fines et rayonnantes nervures de style flamboyant comme celles qui à l'église ajouraient la rampe du jubé ou les meneaux du vitrail et qui s'épanouissaient en blanche chair de fleur de fraisier [I, 138].

From being contained in the church, the hawthorns have come to form a church of their own, with chapels, stained glass windows, ribs and vaulting. After the white hawthorns comes a pink one, decked in "une parure de fête — de ces seules vraies fêtes que sont les fêtes religieuses" (I, 139). The narrator explains that the connection between the "parure de fête" of the flower and the religious festivity which it adorns is an essential one, because the flower and the festivity both recur at fixed points in the year, according to the sequence of the church calendar and the seasons, and not at purely arbitrary moments like "les fêtes mondaines." The pink hawthorn has been decorated by Nature in the taste of a village woman decorating a portable altar for a procession:

Et certes, je l'avais tout de suite senti, comme devant les épines blanches mais avec plus d'émerveillement, que ce n'était pas facticement, par un artifice de fabrication humaine, qu'était traduite l'intention de festivité dans les fleurs, mais que c'était la nature qui, spontanément, l'avait exprimée avec la naïveté d'une commerçante de village travaillant pour un reposoir, en surchargeant l'arbuste de ces rosettes d'un ton trop tendre et d'un pompadour provincial. Au haut des branches, comme autant de ces petits rosiers aux pots cachés dans des papiers en dentelles dont aux grandes fêtes on faisait rayonner sur l'autel les minces fusées, pullulaient mille petits boutons d'une teinte plus pâle qui, en s'entrouvrant, laissaient voir, comme au fond d'une coupe de marbre rose, de rouges sanguines, et trahissaient, plus encore que les fleurs, l'essence particuliere de l'épine, qui, partout où elle bourgeonnait, où elle allait fleurir, ne le pouvait qu'en rose [I, 140].

Not only is the bush like a portable altar, but parts of it may be seen as decorations upon the altar. The hawthorn bush has undergone a transformation. From being a decoration for the altar, it has become itself a decorated altar, but without ceasing to be associated with young girls:

Intercalé dans la haie, mais aussi différent d'elle qu'une jeune fille en robe de fête au milieu de personnes en négligé qui resteront à la maison, tout prêt pour le mois de Marie, dont il semblait faire partie déjà, tel brillait en souriant dans sa fraîche toilette rose l'arbuste catholique et délicieux [I, 140].

The connection between the hawthorn and church festivities is not a temporary one, for it recurs later in the book, when the narrator is at Balbec. Leaving Albertine and her friends playing games, he goes for a walk with Andrée and comes across a hawthorn bush, which is not in flower at that moment. He stops to question the bush about its blossoms, and is informed that he will find them in the parish church the following May. He will easily recognize them, for "ces demoiselles sont si gaies, elles ne s'interrompent de rire que pour chanter des cantiques" (I, 922). As well as being connected with the seasons and with religious festivals, the hawthorn bush is now connected with the narrator's lost childhood: "Auteur de moi flottait une atmosphère d'anciens mois de Marie, d'après-midi du dimanche, de croyances, d'erreurs oubliées" (I, 922). Doubtless because he had believed in it "comme en un être sans équivalent," it is able to resurrect the past, and so claim a place in that religion of art which is based on resurrection of the past as well as in Catholicism.

The hawthorns are not the only flowering trees to have a religious value in the eyes of the narrator. Later again, he will accompany Saint-Loup on a visit to Rachel, who is staying in a suburb of Paris. The pear and cherry trees flowering in the gardens look like altars and give a first-communion air to the suburb:

Ayant quitté Paris où, malgré le printemps commençant, les arbres des boulevards étaient à peine pourvus de leurs premières feuilles, quand le train de ceinture nous arrêta, Saint-Loup et moi, dans le village de ban-lieue où habitait sa maîtresse, ce fut un émerveillement de voir chaque jardinet pavoisé par les immenses reposoirs blancs des arbres fruitiers en fleurs. C'était comme une de ces fêtes singulières, poétiques, éphémères et locales qu'on vient de très loin contempler à époques fixes, mais celle-là donnée par la nature. Les fleurs des cerisiers sont si étroitement collées aux branches, comme un blanc fourreau, que de loin, parmi les arbres qui n'étaient presque ni fleuris, ni feuillus, on aurait pu croire, par ce jour de soleil encore si froid, voir de la neige, fondue ailleurs, et qui était encore restée là, après les arbustes. Mais les grands poiriers enveloppaient chaque maison, chaque modeste cour d'une blancheur plus vaste, plus unie, plus éclatante, comme si tous les logis, tous les enclos du village fussent en train de faire, à la même date, leur première communion [II, 154–155].

Other pear trees, in an orchard and before the town hall, are then described, but without religious allusions. Saint-Loup talks to the narrator about his feeling for Rachel and then goes to fetch her, leaving the narrator to his contemplation of lilacs, which bring back memories of Combray, and yet another pear tree. Saint-Loup returns with Rachel, in whom the narrator recognizes a woman who was once offered to him in a house of prostitution. In this shock of recognition, the narrator experiences with great intensity the contrast between the extremely high value which Saint-Loup places on her (a value which approaches religious veneration, since her personality is, for him, enclosed within her body as within a tabernacle) and the complete indifference which he himself feels towards her, knowing that she would be ready to do anything he wanted for twenty francs. This contrast causes the narrator to embark on a meditation on the importance of imagination and illusion in love, a meditation which moves him so much that, in order to hide his feelings, he turns his eyes towards the pear and cherry trees in the next garden. He feels that there is a link between Robert de Saint-Loup's love for Rachel and his own emotion before the flowering trees. Both feelings belong to a realm of realities which are invisible for the eyes but which are felt by the heart. Suddenly, he hails the pear trees in religious terms. They appear before him like angels or even, he suggests, like the risen Christ:

Ces arbustes que j'avais vus dans le jardin, en les prenant pour des dieux étrangers, ne m'étais-je pas trompé comme Madeleine quand, dans un autre jardin, un jour dont l'anniversaire allait bientôt venir, elle vit une forme humaine et "crut que c'était le jardinier"? Gardiens des souvenirs de l'âge d'or, garants de la promesse que la réalité n'est pas ce qu'on croit, que la splendeur de la poésie, que l'éclat merveilleux de l'innocence peuvent y resplendir et pourront être la récompense que nous nous efforcerons de mériter, les grandes créatures blanches merveilleusement penchées au-dessus de l'ombre propice à la sieste, à la pêche, à la lecture, n'était-ce pas plutôt des anges? [II, 160–161].

In this passage Proust is combining three themes. At one and the same time he is hymning the power of imagination, which can bestow value on anything; he is welcoming memories of his childhood in Combray, which now seems to him like a golden age, precisely because the value-giving power of his imagination was then so strong; and he is continuing the association of religious values with flowering trees. This association has been carried beyond the linking of the hawthorns with the church and the altar; the pear trees, because of their connection with childhood innocence, are angels in their own right. This idea is continued in a passage which makes the suburb appear like a new Sodom or Gomorrah: "Nous coupâmes par le village. Les maisons en étaient sordides. Mais à côté des plus misérables, de celles qui avaient l'air d'avoir été brulées par une pluie de salpêtre, un mystérieux voyageur, arrêté pour un jour dans la cité maudite, un ange resplendissant se tenait debout, étendant largement sur elle l'éblouissante protection de ses ailes d'innocence: c'était un poirier en fleurs" (II, 161). One could understand this passage in two ways. On the one hand, it constitutes a metaphor for Saint-Loup's love for Rachel. Because she is so venal, she is rightly

housed in a village which looks as if it had been burned with fire
and brimstone. But Saint-Loup's idealistic love for her spreads an
innocent, imaginative, protective screen before her. At the same
time the passage is equally applicable to the narrator's feelings,
since, in the midst of sordid surroundings, among the shocks, disappointments, and disillusionments of his adult life, he is able to
regain contact with the enchanted world of his childhood, through
the intercession of those flowering trees on whom, as a child, he had
bestowed a religious value.

That religious value had originally come from the church of Combray, but the narrator has left Saint-Hilaire behind him, together
with his vanished childhood. In his maturity, churches have become
places to be visited for their aesthetic or historic interest. Thus, on
his arrival at Balbec, he hastens to visit the church in order to admire the statues of the Virgin and the Apostles, of which he has
already seen reproductions in a museum. He is disappointed at first
by the way in which the church simply forms a part of the town,
but then he eliminates the town from his consciousness by concentrating his attention upon the statues: "Mais je ne voulus plus penser
qu'à la signification éternelle des sculptures, quand je reconnus les
Apôtres dont j'avais vu les statues moulées au musée du Trocadéro
et qui, des deux côtés de la Vierge, devant la baie profonde du
porche, m'attendaient, comme pour me faire honneur. La figure
bienveillante, camuse et douce, le dos voûté, ils semblaient s'avancer
d'un air de bienvenue en chantant l'*Alleluia* d'un beau jour" (I,
659). This passage gave Mauriac some hope that Proust might turn
out to be a Christian after all. In his pious hope that Proust found
grace *in articulo mortis*, Mauriac expresses the belief that Proust today sees smiling and living the procession which he had admired
so much in the porch of the church of Balbec.[3] But Mauriac seems
to be overlooking the fact that the "signification éternelle" of these
sculptures seems for Proust to be that of the work of art rather than
that of the religious artifact, while the "*Alleluia* d'un beau jour"
seems to refer to the sunshine of that particular day rather than to
the gospel which the apostles originally announced. As Proust remarks, in "Le Temps retrouvé," a taste for religious art or even
religious literature is no proof of orthodoxy: "Ce ne sont pas forcé-
ment les dévots, ni même les catholiques, qui sont les plus savants
concernant la Légende Doré ou les vitraux du XIIIe siècle" (III,

---

[3] Mauriac, p. 70.

962). Some time after his visit to the church of Balbec, the narrator will tour Normandy with Albertine, looking for churches for her to sketch. Later again, he will find in Venice an anologue of Combray, as the golden angel of St. Mark's comes to represent for him the same central point, the same indicator of the weather and the time of day, as the steeple of the parish church of Combray. But, unlike the steeple of Saint-Hilaire, the angel of St. Mark's will not appear like the finger of God raised above the crowd. It brings to him nothing more than a promise of fine weather — a promise which is explicitly compared by the narrator to the Gospel message, to the latter's detriment: "Quand à dix heures du matin on venait ouvrir mes volets, je voyais flamboyer, au lieu du marbre noir que devenaient en resplendissant les ardoises de Saint-Hilaire, l'Ange d'or du campanile de Saint-Marc. Rutilant d'un soleil qui le rendait presque impossible à fixer, il me faisait avec ses bras grands ouverts, pour quand je serais une demi-heure plus tard sur la Piazzetta, une promesse de joie plus certaine que celle qu'il pût être jadis chargé d'annoncer aux hommes de bonne volonté" (III, 623).

Religious value appears to have been taken out of the church of Combray and bestowed, on the one hand, upon the hawthorns which stood on its altar and, on the other hand, upon the sunlight which shone upon its floor and made the stained glass windows sparkle. It is difficult to know how else to interpret a passage describing the sun and the sea, seen from a hotel window at Balbec. Proust begins playfully enough by describing a house, seen from the corridor window, which has received a patina of light from the setting sun, so that it appears like a reliquary. The narrator makes a "station" before the window to make his "devotions" to the view. But his moment of "adoration" does not last long, for a valet who looks like a sacristan comes to close the window as if he were closing the doors of a shrine (I, 802). This use of religious language seems so "precious" and so decorative that one does not react to it as one would to a serious piece of nature mysticism. This seems to be one of the times when Proust is indulging in a joke at the expense of the "religious" nature of his own aestheticism. As he remarked of the use of Catholic phraseology by certain Jewish journalists, it is quite possible to use religious language "sans ombre de tartuferie, mais avec une pointe de cabotinage" (III, 211–212). But when the narrator goes on to apply religious terms to the sun and the sea, as seen from his hotel room, in a way which is equally elaborate but which appears, because of its insistence, to be more serious. The sea, observed through the divisions of the window, looks like stained glass; the sky is stigmatized by "la figure raide, géométrique, passagère et fulgurante du soleil (pareille à la représentation de quelque signe miraculeux, de quelque apparition mystique)"; the sky itself inclines toward the hinge of the horizon like a religious picture before the main altar, while the different sections of the sunset reflected in the bookcase are like panels of a reliquary, separately exhibited in a museum (I, 802–803).

In connection with this description, it is interesting to observe that when Proust is speaking of religious works of art, he has a strong tendency to speak of these objects as being found in a museum. As we noticed in the case of the sculptures of the church of Balbec, this approach takes the stress off the specifically religious purport of the object and reminds us that it is, primarily, a work of art. But when Proust wishes to confer a special value on a beautiful natural object or a secular work of art, by comparing it with a religious work of art, then the religious art work is allowed to have a religious value which it can bestow upon the object to which it is being compared. We have seen this process at work in the case of the church of Saint-Hilaire and the hawthorns; another example comes to mind in the case of the painted angels to which we have seen the music of Vinteuil compared. Again, Proust is liable to diminish the purely religious significance of the religious art work by a certain irony, as when he reminds us of the destructibility of the Virgin of Balbec, or when he describes the *Virtues* and *Vices* of Giotto in terms which bring out strongly their somewhat ludicrous side.

The mixture of admiration and irony with which Proust regards Giotto's religious paintings is particularly marked in his description of Giotto's *Charity*. The impetus for this description comes from a passage by Ruskin which we know Proust knew and admired, since he quotes it twice in his translation, *La Bible d'Amiens*.[4] Ruskin's phrase runs as follows: "While the ideal Charity of Giotto at Padua presents her heart in her hands to God, and tramples at the same instant on bags of gold, the treasures of the world, and gives only corn and flowers; that on the west porch of Amiens is content to clothe a beggar with a piece of the staple manufacture of the town."[5] Proust repeats Ruskin's observations about this virtue's at-

[4] Ruskin, *La Bible d'Amiens*, pp. 62, 303, fn.
[5] Ruskin, *The Art of England and the Pleasures of England: Lectures given in Oxford in 1883–1885* (London: G. Allen, 1904), p. 373.

titude, but with comic interjections which make one think of the
giggles of a choirboy who has seen something funny in one of the
hymns: "Par une belle invention du peintre elle foule aux pieds
les trésors de la terre, mais absolument comme si elle piétinait des
raisins pour en extraire le jus ou plutôt comme elle aurait monté
sur des sacs pour se hausser; et elle tend à Dieu son coeur enflammé,
disons mieux, elle le lui 'passe,' comme une cuisinière passe un tire-
bouchon par le soupirail de son sous-sol à quelqu'un qui le lui de-
mande à la fenêtre du rez-de-chaussée" (I, 81). The comparison of
Giotto's *Charity* to the pregnant kitchen maid does nothing to increase the dignity of the kitchen maid; it rather decreases the dignity of the painting by emphasizing its air of vulgarity and unawareness. Only after the narrator has acknowledged that he later came
to find a symbolic value and a kind of special reality in this picture
does he concede a likeness between *Charity*'s expression and that of
certain nuns who were "des incarnations vraiment saintes de la
charité active" (I, 82). Once the religious message of the picture has
been made fun of and quite nonreligious values have been found in
it, then a connection between it and religious feeling becomes al-
lowable.

It is interesting to compare this treatment of a religious painting
with the way in which Proust describes the longing of the narrator
to see the acting of La Berma. To hear this actress in a leading role
in a great play takes on the dimensions of a spiritual duty which one
has to be scrupulous in performing: "Car quand c'est dans l'espoir
d'une découverte précieuse que nous désirons recevoir certaines impressions de nature ou d'art, nous avons quelque scrupule à laisser
notre âme accueillir à leur place des impressions moindres qui pour-
raient nous tromper sur la valeur exacte du Beau" (I, 440). The
narrator's excitement over this prospect makes his doctor feel that
he should not go, for the trip to the theater will make him ill, bringing him in the long run more suffering than pleasure. But the narrator feels that the revelation which this visit will bring him will be
worth the suffering it may induce: "Ce que je demandais à cette
matinée, c'était tout autre chose qu'un plaisir: des vérités appartenant à un autre monde plus réel que celui où je vivais, et desquel-
les l'acquisition une fois faite ne pourrait pas m'être enlevée par des
incidents insignifiants, fussent-ils douloureux à mon corps, de mon
oiseuse existence" (I, 442). The metaphysical nature of his expectation is expressed in terms which are strongly religious: "Caché comme le Saint des Saints sous le rideau qui me la dérobait et derrière

lequel je lui prêtais à chaque instant un aspect nouveau, . . . la
divine Beauté que devait me révéler le jeu de la Berma, nuit et jour,
sur un autel perpétuellement allumé, trônait au fond de mon esprit,
de mon esprit dont mes parents sévères et légers allaient décider s'il
enfermerait ou non, et pour jamais, les perfections de la Déesse
dévoilée à cette même place où se dressait sa forme invisible" (I,
443). That the boy finds the production, in reality, disappointing
does not alter the fact that his longing for beauty is such that it is
appropriate to use religious terms to describe it. The religious meaning of a work of art must be subordinated to its aesthetic value; but
aesthetic values are worthy of religious terminology. The fact that
religious terminology is at this point used in a faintly ironic way
reflects only on the adolescent's fever of ignorant excitement; I do
not think that Proust intends us to understand that the aesthetic
experience is not, in itself, worthy of this language.

     Thus far, we have seen how religious language, in Proust's work,
has a distinct tendency to appear at a certain distance from subjects
and attitudes which are traditionally religious. The best people in
A la Recherche du temps perdu are not pious; the most pious people are not the best ones; and religious values seem to have faded
out of traditionally religious objects to pass into surrounding areas,
like the colors of the tapestry or the outlines of the memorial tablets
in Saint-Hilaire. There is yet another way in which Proust uses religious language, and that is to parody the seriousness with which
people take each other and themselves. It is surprising how often
Proust describes snobs, social climbers, and people of some social
rank in religious terms.

     We are struck, first of all, by the way in which such terms are ap-
plied to the Verdurins. Thus, the Verdurins exclude female guests
because they are less willing than the men to accept without question the dogma of the prestige of the Verdurin circle, and "cet esprit
d'examen et ce démon de frivolité pouvait par contagion devenir
fatal à l'orthodoxie de la petite église" (I, 188). Mme Verdurin's
attitude toward the behavior of her guests is almost that of a pope:
"Comme tout pouvoir ecclésiastique, [Mme Verdurin] jugeait les
faiblesses humaines moins graves que ce qui pouvait affaiblir le
principe d'autorité, nuire à l'orthodoxie, modifier l'antique credo,
dans sa petite Église" (III, 244). Brichot, again, speaks of Mme Verdurin's salon in a way which the narrator interprets in ecclesiastical
terms: "Certes, je comprenais bien que par 'salon' Brichot entendait —

comme le mot église ne signifie pas seulement l'édifice religieux mais la communauté des fidèles — non pas seulement l'entresol, mais les gens qui le fréquentaient . . ." (III, 203). But this metaphor is not limited to the Verdurins. It is applied in an identical fashion to the Guermantes circle: "Comme l'église ne signifie pas seulement le temple mais aussi l'assemblée des fidèles, cet hôtel de Guermantes comprenait tous ceux qui partageaient la vie de la duchesse . . ." (II, 15). Perhaps the most elaborate sequence of religious metaphors applied to the exercise of a social function appears in the description of the older Mme de Cambremer, arrayed for her visits in a set of ornaments chosen not for their decorative but for their hieratic value: "Malgré la chaleur, la bonne dame avait revêtu un mantelet de jais pareil à une dalmatique, et par-dessus lequel pendait une étole d'hermine dont le port semblait en relation non avec la température de la saison, mais avec le caractère de la cérémonie. Et sur la poitrine de Mme de Cambremer un tortil de baronne relié à une chaînette pendait à la façon d'une croix pectorale" (II, 806). Proust continues this analogy over several pages. The umbrella, purses, and handkerchief carried by Mme de Cambremer become "les ornements de sa tournée pastorale et de son sacerdoce mondain" (II, 808). Later on, as she climbs into her carriage, she looks like an old bishop: "Puis elle monta en voiture, balançant la tête, levant la crosse de son ombrelle, et repartit par les rues de Balbec, surchargée des ornements de son sacerdoce, comme un vieil évêque en tournée de confirmation" (III, 824).

One cannot help smiling at these metaphors, but are they only humorous? René Girard does not think so. The narrator, he points out, longs continually for "a kind of mystical communion, with an individual, or with a group, dwelling, he believes, in a superior realm of existence and entirely separated from the vulgar herd." [6] When the narrator is a child, he looks for this superior group among the adults who surround him and among the authors of his favorite books; later, as he succumbs to snobbery, he seeks it in the world of the salons. The members of the salons do everything they can to encourage this attitude, by their exclusiveness, which suggests that the salon is "a temple of esoteric mysteries of which the snobs constitute the initiates, mysteries which would be diluted and lost if they were imparted to the unworthy." [7] Most of the characters in the

---

[6] René Girard, ed., *Proust: A Collection of Critical Essays* (Englewood Cliffs, N.J.: Prentice-Hall, 1962), p. 2.

[7] Ibid., p. 4.

novel, says René Girard, "are constantly seeking mystical union with a pseudo divinity and must therefore be, at least subconsciously, committed to self divinization" [8] — a self-divinization which they secretly know to be a sham.

Most of Proust's characters seem to be afflicted with a religious impulse which finds its object anywhere but in religion. For the ordinary snob, the aristocrat alone is divine. The younger Mme de Cambremer idolizes modern art and music as well as the aristocracy. Saint-Loup (as we have already noticed) regards Rachel as something holy. The narrator himself, once he has left Combray, seems to have a greater capacity than anyone else in the book for finding fragments of the divine everywhere except in the church. It is common enough for the lover to regard his beloved as divine, and, although the narrator avoids Swann's type of idolatry, Albertine is the idol of the narrator's heart in just as real a sense as Manon was that of Des Grieux. Both women represent an inferior good on which the lover squanders the emotional energy and the devotion which he ought to have reserved for the superior good of his true god. (Of course, in Des Grieux's case, this god is God, and in the narrator's case it is art, but the parallel is still valid.) It is only fitting that, in her character as an idol, Albertine should appear to the narrator in the guise of a painted wooden angel, as she plays to him in their Paris apartment:

Les yeux (comme, dans un minerai d'opale où elle est encore engainée, les deux plaques seules polies encore) devenus plus résistants que du métal tout en restant plus brillants que de la lumière, faisaient apparaître, au milieu de la matière aveugle qui les surplombe, comme les ailes de soie mauve d'un papillon qu'on aurait mis sous verre; et les cheveux, noirs et crespelés, montrant d'autres ensembles selon qu'elle se tournait vers moi pour me demander ce qu'elle devait jouer, tantôt une aile magnifique, aiguë à sa pointe, large à sa base, noire, empennée et triangulaire, tantôt massant le relief de leurs boucles en une chaîne puissante et variée, pleine de crêtes, de lignes de partage, de précipices, avec leur fouetté si riche et si multiple semblant dépasser la variété que réalise habituellement la nature, et répondre plutôt au désir d'un sculpteur qui accumule les difficultés pour faire valoir la souplesse, la fougue, le fondu, la vie de son exécution, faisaient ressortir davantage, en l'interrompant pour la recouvrir, la courbe animée et comme la rotation du visage lisse et rose, du mat verni d'un bois peint. Et aussi par contraste avec tant de relief, par l'harmonie aussi qui les unissait à elle, qui avait adapté son attitude à leur forme et à leur utilisation, le pianola qui la cachait à demi comme un buffet d'orgue, la bibliothèque, tout ce coin de la chambre semblait réduit à

[8] Ibid., p. 5.

n'être plus que le sanctuaire éclairé, la crèche de cet ange musicien, œuvre d'art qui, tout à l'heure, par une douce magie, allait se détacher de sa niche et offrir à mes baisers sa substance précieuse et rose [III, 383].

The insistence on the mineral quality of her eyes, the sculptured appearance of her hair, and the painted wooden appearance of her complexion makes of Albertine a strikingly static, artificial creation. One cannot help wondering if a contrast is intended between the idolized wooden angel, Albertine, and the angel who appeared in the form of a pear tree, pointing the narrator toward his lost age of faith and the poetic use of the imagination, away from the squandering of faith and imagination on romantic love.

The narrator had attributed a kind of supernatural quality to Albertine and her companions long before this episode, and that supernatural charm still continues to cast a special aura about them, even after his feeling for them has sobered down: "Les créatures surnaturelles qu'elles avaient été un instant pour moi, mettaient encore, même à mon insu, quelque merveilleux dans les rapports les plus banals que j'avais avec elles, ou plutôt préservaient ces rapports d'avoir jamais rien de banal" (I, 950). Albertine is not only vaguely supernatural; she even takes the place of Christ for the narrator, as his mother had done in his childhood. Her goodnight kiss has the calming effect of that of his mother when he was a child — and we remember that his mother's kiss was compared to a viaticum. In a passage which was retained in the earlier editions but which the Pléiade edition has relegated to the "Notes et variantes," the narrator repeats the idea of the viaticum and makes it even more explicit by saying that Albertine slips her tongue between his lips like a communion wafer.[9]

But if Albertine is a supernatural being, an (artificial) angel, and a (substitute) Christ figure, she is one who can bring no redemption to her lover, being in need of redemption herself. In a passage describing the street cries outside their window in liturgical terms (III, 127, 136–137), Leo Spitzer finds evidence of the narrator's wish to rescue Albertine from the debauchery to which she is naturally prone. He sees in the religious allusions of this passage a vindication of the rights of the supraterrestrial, in the name of which the nar-

[9] In earlier editions, this passage occurs between the passage ending ". . . quelque bonté loyale chez Albertine" and the one beginning "— Viendrez-vous avec nous demain, grand méchant?" (III, 78). In the 1954 Pléiade edition, it has been placed in the "Notes et variantes" (III, 1070).

rator wishes to keep Albertine from the edge of the precipice of sensuality.[10] There is no denying the continuity of religious terms in this passage; and the narrator certainly wishes to keep Albertine to himself, away from the opportunities she might have for affairs with others. But why should he be supposed to have a purely religious concern for keeping Albertine away from the edge of the "precipice"? He himself is not slow to indulge in fancies for shopgirls and to attempt to lure them into the apartment, in Albertine's absence. There seems to be something playful and decorative about Proust's drawing of an analogy between the cries of the street vendors and the strains of the Catholic liturgy. It certainly is difficult to take as genuinely religious in an orthodox sense a passage which occurs a little further on, in which he compares a butcher's boy weighing meat to "un bel ange qui, au jour du Jugement dernier, préparera pour Dieu, selon leur qualité, la séparation des Bons et des Méchants et la pesée des âmes" (III, 138). The motivating force behind this comparison seems to be an appreciation of the solemn, statuesque attitude of the butcher's boy as he performs a primordial gesture which finds its equivalent in ecclesiastical art, because it was on observation of such a gesture that the mediæval artists based their idea of what an angel separating souls would be like. The way in which Proust compares a sculptured saint in the porch of Saint-André-des-Champs to a peasant girl who has sought shelter beneath that porch (I, 151, 152), a comparison which is intended not to bestow saintly qualities on the living girl but to show how far the sculptor was influenced in his portrayal by observation of contemporary peasants, seems to support this contention. The impression which one is intended to receive from the passage on the street may well be, as Leo Spitzer claims, of the importance of ritual as it has spilled over from a centuries-old religious tradition into daily life.[11] On the other hand, Proust may be suggesting that the forms of the religious ritual were an elaboration of vocal patterns which are natural to the French people. This interpretation would make of this passage, in spite of its religious overtones, an expression of interest in philological and sociological rather than religious factors. The difficulty of interpretation with which we find ourselves confronted should put us on our guard against responding to a religious stimulus, as used by Proust, with a uniformly traditional religious

[10] Leo Spitzer, "L'Étymologie d'un 'Cri de Paris,'" *Romanic Review*, XXV, No. 3 (October, 1944), 244.

[11] Ibid., pp. 249–250.

reaction. And yet Proust is using that stimulus with a full awareness of what his readers' reaction is likely to be.

There is yet another use of religious expressions by Proust in which his nonreligious purpose is so blatant that we are not likely to go astray. It is a fact that Proust had a highly developed taste for the incongruous use of religious allusions — a taste which, more than once, leads him into a type of humorous blasphemy, not unlike that of his friend and mentor, Anatole France. Thus, he takes an obvious pleasure in applying to young homosexuals desired by older ones verses which were originally applied, in the tragedies of Racine, to young Jews and Jewesses saved from the enemies of their faith. So, M. de Vaugoubert, hearing from the Baron de Charlus that all the secretaries of a particular embassy are homosexual, experiences emotions which the narrator compares to those of Élise, in *Esther*, on discovering that the queen is surrounded by Jewish maidens (II, 665). *Athalie* is quoted in connection with M. Nissim Bernard's fancy for a young waiter (II, 843), while M. de Charlus quotes a verse from *Esther*, "Prospérez, cher espoir d'une nation sainte" (II, 987), on viewing the waiters and attendants at the Balbec hotel. These passages seem to combine humorous blasphemy with Proust's quite serious notion of a similarity between the fate of homosexuals and that of the Jews, together with the idea, which we have seen used in a normal sexual context, of the tendency of the lover to apply feelings which are properly religious to the object of his love.

Perhaps the most striking of the passages in which Proust mixes religious language with distinctly irreligious preoccupations appears in "Sodome et Gomorrhe," in his fantastic re-creation of the legend of the destruction of Sodom. According to Proust, the angels who were sent by God to discover whether the inhabitants of Sodom had done all the things of which they had been accused were easily deceived by those Sodomites who were ashamed of their tendencies. Consequently, the present race of homosexuals is descended from those who escaped from Sodom. Proust's sympathies seem to be entirely with those who succeeded in making their escape: "Car les deux anges qui avaient été placés aux portes de Sodome pour savoir si les habitants, dit la Genèse, avaient entièrement fait toutes ces choses dont le cri était monté jusqu'à l'Éternel, avaient été, on ne peut que s'en réjouir, très mal choisis par le Seigneur, lequel n'eût dû confier la tâche qu'à un Sodomiste" (II, 631). That "on ne peut que s'en réjouir" expresses an undeniable satisfaction. Proust's satisfaction is understandable enough, in view of the circumstances of his own life, but it is certainly the reverse of scriptural. Edmund Wilson may have been taking Proust's scriptural allusions too seriously when he wrote that Proust in his delineation of the characters in "Sodome et Gomorrhe" gives us a conviction of their damnation, a conviction which is reinforced by the scriptural nature of his title. Wilson introduces this statement by expressing the belief that Proust inherited from his mother "the capacity for apocalyptic moral indignation of the classical Jewish prophet." [12] But if Proust makes his appearance as a Jewish prophet, it is by no means always as a genuine one. There are times when it seems as if he had made himself up to figure as a prophet in one of those operas on Jewish themes which the narrator's grandfather is so fond of humming. And sometimes the opera is a comic one.

Edmund Wilson finds in the delineation of the narrator's mother and grandmother not Christian standards, but rather Jewish ones.[13] It certainly seems to be true that the narrator's mother and grandmother were based on Proust's own mother and grandmother, for whose adherence to the Jewish faith he had a deep respect, but his feeling for Judaism does not seem to have extended beyond his sentiments of filial duty. He himself was brought up as a Catholic, but what faith he had as a child seems to have ebbed away as he grew up. He was left, as an adult, with a longing for faith but without the ability to believe, as one can see from a letter he wrote to his friend Georges de Lauris in 1904:

Je ne suis pas comme vous, je ne trouve pas la vie trop difficile à remplir et quelle folie, quelle ivresse si la vie immortelle m'était assurée! Comment pouvez-vous vraiment, je ne dis pas, ne pas croire, car de ce qu'une chose soit souhaitable cela ne fait pas qu'on y croie — au contraire, hélas! — mais en être satisfait (non la satisfaction intellectuelle de préférer la vérité triste au doux mensonge); tous ceux qu'on a quittés, qu'on quittera, ne serait-il pas doux de les retrouver sous un autre ciel dans les vallées vainement promises et inutilement attendues! Et se réaliser enfin! [14]

Proust's longing for faith did not necessarily make him very respectful of those who have it, however. In the same letter, he speaks of the true believer in terms which, although they show a lively interest in the attitude of a fervent Catholic, would not strike the believer himself as at all flattering:

[12] Edmund Wilson, *Axel's Castle: A Study in the Imaginative Literature of 1870–1930* (New York: Charles Scribner's Sons, 1931), pp. 159, 144.

[13] Ibid., p. 145.

[14] Proust, *A un ami*, p. 75.

Ce sont les vilains dévots qui sont incapables d'esthétique, les vrais, les derniers catholiques ceux qui disparaîtront un jour, les pithécanthropes de Java qu'on envoie des savants examiner dans leur forêt et rapportés pendant qu'il y en a encore au Jardin des Plantes, qu'il est passionnant et mélancolique de voir se livrer naïvement à leurs ébats caractéristiques dans ces édifices mystérieux où ils trempent les doigts dans des bénitiers et qui ont eux-mêmes la forme de l'instrument de supplice de celui qu'ils pleurent, qu'ils implorent et qu'ils glorifient.[15]

In view of this letter, Proust's request that François Mauriac should ask Francis Jammes to recommend him to his favorite saint [16] seems to have been nothing but a piece of politeness — rather overdone, as so many of Proust's gentillesses were.

It is true that the letter to Georges de Lauris does not constitute the only statement of Marcel Proust's attitude toward the average Catholic. In the third part of "En Mémoire des églises assassinées," which was published under the title "La Mort des cathédrales" in the same year as Proust addressed this letter to Georges de Lauris, we find an expression of sympathy with the practices of the Catholic faith which, unlike the above passage, was pondered over at length and intended for the general public. In this article, we find a deep feeling for the wealth of symbolism and the profound spiritual life which are represented by a solemn mass, together with the assertion that "Quand le sacrifice de la chair et du sang du Christ ne sera plus célébré dans les églises, il n'y aura plus de vie en elles." [17] If we put these two expressions of opinion side by side, we find that they represent an attitude of mind, not at all uncommon among those who have been taught in their youth to love a religion which in their maturity they have left behind, composed of a mixture of exasperation and affection. The exasperation is directed toward the rigidity of the true believer, while the affection is directed toward the cult which he celebrates. If we could resurrect Proust today, by means of one of those mediums in whom his narrator was sometimes tempted to believe, I think he would tell us that, while he did not regard the spiritual life of a Catholic as the only valid one, he regarded it as certainly more valuable, and infinitely more poetic, than no spiritual life at all.

Finally, if we continue to search through Proust's correspondence for indications of his religious attitude, we shall find plenty of evidence that he had a taste for using religious expressions incon-

---

[15] Ibid., p. 74.
[16] Mauriac, p. 33.
[17] Proust, *Pastiches et mélanges*, p. 201.

gruously. Thus, we find him writing to Mme de Noailles to compare her to Christ crucified between two thieves (in 1902, when two other poets shared a prize with her); to assure her (in 1903) that she is a new and better Virgin Mary, or else, if she does not care to be considered so virginal, a Carthaginian goddess; and to inform her (in a letter which may have been written in 1907) that, since she is at once the greatest poet and the most beautiful woman of her time, she could be the object of a new religion based on a miracle of incarnation.[18] In 1913 he also compares the praise which critics are compelled to lavish on her to the praises which the angels sing before the throne of God.[19] When he is confronted with the vanity of Montesquiou, he feels inspired to nourish it with similar hyperboles. Thus, in (perhaps) 1896, Proust tells Montesquiou, in a metaphor whose implications are rather involved, that his sensibility is usually hidden from men as Christ was hidden from the eyes of the disciples at Emmaus.[20] In another letter, written in 1907, Proust refers to his reading of Montesquiou's latest work in terms appropriate to taking communion.[21] In 1903, 1904, and 1905, striking a lower note, he compares Montesquiou's lecture trips and speeches to selected groups to the journeys which the Apostles made to evangelize the heathen and the discourses which they made to selected churches.[22] He must have been very fond of this metaphor to repeat it so often, or else very gratified by its reception. Certainly Proust knew that this use of religious language to flatter his correspondents would please them, and he does not seem to have entertained any doubts as to its being appropriate. If we are to look for any serious intention at all in these compliments, then we have to find it in the cult of the religion of art, of which both Montesquiou and Mme de Noailles may be considered adherents.

On the basis of the passages we have considered so far, we see Proust as an agnostic who mixes a respect and longing for religious things with a tendency to make fun of the devout and to parody scripture. He uses religious language most seriously when describing objects which are not usually thought of as religious, these objects being scenes of natural beauty and works of art. In the next chapter we shall consider more fully the use of religious language both in this connection and in the description of the narrator's experiences of involuntary memory.

[18] Proust, *Correspondance générale*, II, 34, 47, 148.
[19] Ibid., p. 196.   [21] Ibid., p. 200.
[20] Ibid., I, 30.   [22] Ibid., pp. 84–85, 180, 216–217.

CHAPTER SEVEN

CHRISTIAN STRUCTURE

In the previous chapter, we saw how Proust bestowed a religious value on flowering trees. By the way in which I discussed this, I suggested that this was, to a large extent, a question of a simple association of ideas. Because the narrator had already seen hawthorns on the altar of the parish church, he thought of an altar when he looked at the hawthorns in Swann's park. Then, later on, the religious associations which the hawthorns had acquired became extended to flowering trees in general.

This is a simple, easy explanation. It accounts in terms of well-known psychological mechanisms for a certain part of Proust's displacement of religious values. As far as it goes, it is true enough. But as a total explanation it is somewhat superficial. To consider the matter more deeply, we need to take into account the explanation given by Curtius. For this critic, there is something religious, not merely in the vocabulary selected to describe the hawthorns, but also, and more essentially, in the way in which the narrator looks at them. In his analysis of this passage, Curtius points out that the narrator gazes upon the hawthorns in Swann's park with a peculiar intensity, the object of which is to unite himself mentally with them by entering into "leur secret" (I, 138–139). This manner of observing an object Curtius equates with the technique of contemplation, as practiced by the mystics. He explains that it is a question of a type of perception which seldom or never occurs in daily life, and which is at the limit of the normal waking state. It coincides with what the mystics call contemplation, a term defining the way in which a real relationship is set up between a subject and an object.

According to Evelyn Underhill, he goes on, contemplation consists of an extreme application of the attention, in the course of which the ego forgets itself entirely in its profound union with the object. Curtius corroborates this description of contemplation by pointing out that one has only to concentrate one's attention on an object — it hardly matters what object — while avoiding all excitement or conscious thought, to become aware, first of an extraordinary calm within oneself, and then of an intense increase in reality and importance on the part of the object. Our own spiritual energy encounters a current of life which seems to spring from the object, and we acquire a notion of the object's innermost essence.[1] This description of contemplation is applicable to the way in which Proust's narrator observes the hawthorns. At the same time, it is at the opposite pole from the superficial observation of the Realist, a type of observation which we have seen Proust eschew in his criticism of the Goncourts. Yet, as Curtius acknowledges, Proust's method of observation is like that of the mystic without being entirely the same. The religious mystic sinks his faculties of perception into a natural object in order to arrive at a state of union with God. Concentration on the object becomes a means of getting rid of that consciousness of the self which is an impediment to union with God. Evelyn Underhill, to whom Curtius refers us, gives several examples of this technique and its results. The Indian mystics, she points out, frequently hynotize themselves into a state of ecstasy by repeating a sacred word or by focusing their attention on a nearby object. By this means, "the pull of the phenomenal world is diminished and the mind is placed at the disposal of the subconscious powers." [2] Occidental mystics are less prone to induce ecstasy deliberately, but "here and there among them also we find instances in which ecstatic trance or lucidity, the liberation of the 'transcendental sense', was inadvertently produced by purely physical means." [3] The examples she gives are those of Jacob Boehme falling into a state of ecstasy as he gazed upon a burnished pewter dish, St. Ignatius Loyola attaining a state of profound spiritual insight as he watched the surface of a stream, and Emmanuel Kant collecting his thoughts by gazing steadily at a neighboring church steeple.[4] Yet, however much

---

[1] Curtius, pp. 94–95.

[2] Evelyn Underhill, *Mysticism: A Study in the Nature and Development of Man's Spiritual Consciousness* (New York: E. P. Dutton, 1911), p. 69.

[3] Ibid.

[4] Ibid.. pp. 69–70.

Proust's narrator may resemble a mystic in his contemplation of the hawthorns, he differs from the mystic in that this contemplation does not lead, in his case, to union with God or even to transcendental insights. The narrator is attempting to enter into closer contact with the hawthorns themselves, not (at this stage, at any rate) with some reality beyond them. Curtius acknowledges this distinction. In his opinion, the narrator is entering into communion with universal life.[5] This would make Proust an incipient nature-mystic, since his technique of contemplation is, for Curtius, on the threshold of mysticism as of all other forms of spirituality.[6] However, Proust, for this critic, does not cross the threshold of mysticism, since his technique of contemplative observation is, above all, an aesthetic method.

In Proust, Curtius finds signs not only of a tendency toward nature mysticism but, in his search for eternal essences and spiritual values enclosed in matter or hovering beyond it, of a kind of Platonism. He points to the passage describing the death of Bergotte for evidence of this. It is here that Proust alludes most clearly to an afterlife and a spiritual world of ideal values, although these allusions are made with a reserve which Curtius attributes to a kind of modesty.[7] Not every critic, however, is so charitable as to attribute Proust's hesitation solely to modesty and discretion. Robert Champigny, for instance, in his comment on this appraisal by Curtius, calls Proust's attitude pseudo-Platonist.[8] It is certainly true that, for a Platonist, Proust is exceptionally hesitant in his references to an afterlife and a spiritual world of idea values. Is Bergotte permanently dead? he asks, and is unable to give a definite answer: "Certes, les expériences spirites pas plus que les dogmes religieux n'apportent de preuve que l'âme subsiste" (III, 187), he replies. The most we can say, Proust continues, is that everything in our life happens *as if* we entered it with a load of obligations contracted in a former life — obligations both ethical and aesthetic in nature — and that *perhaps* we shall return to the world from which these obligations are derived. Consequently, the idea that Bergotte will not remain dead forever is not unlikely. In the meantime, it is his books which keep his vigil, like angels with outspread wings, and which

[5] Curtius, p. 96.

[6] Ibid.

[7] Ibid., p. 150.

[8] Robert Champigny, "Temps et reconnaissance chez Proust et quelques philosophes," *PMLA*, LXXIII (March, 1958), 133.

appear as the symbols of his resurrection. Leaving the question of
Platonism aside for the moment, it is interesting to see how angels
are invoked once more, in a semi-religious context, and yet at a
certain distance from the angels of orthodox Christianity. The
angels who watch over Bergotte are not spiritual entities exterior
to himself, but the externalized products of his own mind. No
sooner has an autonomous world of spiritual values been, however
hesitantly, invoked, than those beings who are traditionally seen as
intermediaries between the spiritual realm and mankind are identified with the products of man's mind.

As Curtius observes, there is a considerable degree of reserve in
the allusions which Proust makes to spiritual matters. At one moment like a nature mystic and at another like a Platonist, he nevertheless evades definition as either of these things. From a certain
point of view, this is hardly surprising. *A la Recherche du temps
perdu* is a novel, after all, rather than a philosophical treatise or a
religious apology. But even as I make this statement, I remember
the wealth of philosophical and religious meanings which appear
below the surface of this novel and which tantalize us with the
promise of some total message. Like the narrator striving to recall
a memory which lies just beyond the threshold of consciousness,
Proust's reader finds himself stretching out again and again to reach
some portion of a religious or philosophical system, which nevertheless eludes his grasp. It is true that there are philosophical ideas in
Proust's work. Otherwise it would have been impossible for me to
talk about a struggle between spirit and matter in my opening
chapters. And yet, Proust's utterances on the subject of spirit and
matter could not easily be restated in philosophical terms, although
they may remind us, at moments, of some particular philosopher.
Again, while I believe in the presence in Proust's work of a religion
of art, that religion of art appears to me to take the form of a set of
emotionally colored attitudes rather than of a systematic theology.
One reason for this is that Proust, as a good novelist, relies on suggestion rather than assertion. As we have seen, the suggestion is
continually made, in the episode of the narrator and the hawthorns,
that a mystical experience is just around the corner. This suggestion
is not explicit, but it is all the more potent in that it is embedded
in the actual structure of the experience described.

Similar structures can be found in other passages, specifically
those having to do with moments of involuntary memory and changing perspective. Let us first examine the passage in which the

steeples of Vieuxvicq and Martinville are described. The terms of
the description, we notice at once, are not ostensibly religious. But
there may be some implicit analogy between the narrator's view of
the steeples and his contemplation of the hawthorns, since the
steeples seem at one moment to resemble flowers and at another to
resemble girls, while their surface seems like a kind of bark which
the narrator's mind tears back to discover what is hidden beneath
it. There may be a discreet religious suggestion conveyed by the
fact that the steeples are three in number and merge, from one point
of view, into one. It has been suggested that an allusion to the Trinity is intended both here and in the description of the trees of Hudimesnil.[9] But, in my opinion, if Proust is alluding to the Trinity, it
is in such a distant way that the reader must take full responsibility
for making the connection.

In the episode of the three trees of Hudimesnil, the references
which Proust makes to the supernatural are, to begin with, of a
mythological rather than a religious nature. The trees are like norns
or witches: "Cependant ils venaient vers moi; peut-être apparition
mythique, ronde de sorcières ou de nornes qui me proposaient des
oracles" (I, 719). Then they appear to him as ghosts demanding
resurrection: "Je crus plutôt que c'étaient des fantômes du passé, de
chers compagnons de mon enfance, des amis disparus qui invoquai-
ent nos communs souvenirs. Comme des ombres ils semblaient me
demander de les emmener avec moi, de les rendre à la vie. Dans
leur gesticulation naïve et passionnée, je reconnaissais le regret im-
puissant d'un être aimée qui a perdu l'usage de la parole, sent qu'il
ne pourra nous dire ce qu'il veut et que nous ne savons pas deviner"
(I, 719). Not only are the trees demanding resurrection for themselves, but a part of the narrator is to be resurrected also by his
recognition of what they have to tell him: "Je vis les arbres s'éloigner
en agitant leurs bras désespérés, semblant me dire: Ce que tu n'ap-
prends pas de nous aujourd'hui, tu ne le sauras jamais. Si tu nous
laisses retomber au fond de ce chemin d'où nous cherchions à nous
hisser jusqu'à toi, toute une partie de toi-même que nous t'appor-
tions tombera pour jamais au néant" (I, 719). In fact, the narrator
is unable to decipher the message which the trees are trying to convey to him, and a feeling of deep sadness descends on him in consequence: "Et quand, la voiture ayant bifurqué, je leur tournai le
dos et cessai de les voir, tandis que Mme de Villeparisis me deman-

[9] Elliott Coleman, *The Golden Angel: Papers on Proust* (New York: Coley
Taylor, 1954), p. 26.

dait pourquoi j'avais l'air rêveur, j'étais triste comme si je venais
de perdre un ami, de mourir à moi-même, de renier un mort ou de
méconnaître un dieu" (I, 719). The narrator's sadness combines the
themes, already indicated, of the trees as old friends, as fragments
of his own being demanding to return to consciousness, and as
ghosts wishing to return to life by means of his sympathetic understanding. At the very end of the passage the suggestion is slipped in
that in them he has also failed to recognize a god. It is probable
that Proust intended a parallel between this and the passage in
which the narrator compares his initial failure to recognize the pear
trees as angels with the Magdalene's failure to recognize the risen
Christ. Proust seems to be suggesting that the idea conveyed by the
trees has something divine about it. He does not say that this divinity is the God of the Christian or any other currently accepted religion. He could have been thinking, for instance, of the disguises of
Athena in the *Odyssey*. C. K. Scott Moncrieff, apparently dissatisfied
with the ambiguity of this passage, makes it more explicit by trans-
lating it as follows: "And when, the road having forked and the
carriage with it, I turned my back on them and ceased to see them,
with Mme de Villeparisis asking me what I was dreaming about, I
was as wretched as though I had just lost a friend, had died myself,
had broken faith with the dead or had denied my God." [10] Some
critics, who rely on the English translation rather than on the
original text, have been led astray by this.

Now let us consider the moments of involuntary memory to see
how much religious suggestion can be found in them, if one is
really determined to look. The *madeleine* episode begins with the
subject of death — one that can be guaranteed to put Proust's reader
in a serious, reflective state of mind, more open to philosophical and
religious suggestion than might be the case in other moods. All his
memories of Combray have been blotted out, the narrator says, by
the one overpowering memory of the *drame du coucher* and are, in
fact, dead. They might have remained dead for him until the day
of his own death, if it had not been for a certain chance. Leaving
the reader in suspense, the narrator goes on to speak of a Celtic belief that the souls of those we have lost are imprisoned in inanimate
objects and can be released by our recognition. Then he repeats his
statement that we must depend on chance for a resurrection of the
past, since the efforts of our intelligence are useless. As in the case

[10] Proust, *Remembrance of Things Past*, trans. C. K. Scott Moncrieff, 2 vols.
(New York: Random House, 1934), I, 545.

of the episode of the trees of Hudimesnil, there is a curious mixture of religious suggestions linked to the theme of death and resurrection. The inevitability of death and the possibility of resurrection are basic ingredients of every religion; the Celtic belief to which Proust alludes carries us away from Christianity into the realm of myth (like the norns and witches to which the trees of Hudimesnil are compared); while our dependence on chance and the futility of the efforts of our intelligence are faintly, but distinctly, reminiscent of Christian teaching about the futility of human effort and the gratuitousness of divine grace.

The introductory comment on the resurrected memory here comes to an end, and the physical circumstances of the resurrection are evoked. On the narrator's return to his home, one cold and gloomy day of his adult life, his mother offers him some tea, although he is not in the habit of drinking it. He refuses and then, he does not know why, changes his mind and accepts. The very banality of these details, combined with the tone of awed attention in which they are narrated, gives to this episode something of the character of a conversion narrative. It is not uncommon for the convert, describing his decisive moment of spiritual enlightenment, to say something like this: "It was a normal day like any other; I was, if anything, rather more tired and depressed than usual. But, without paying attention to what I was doing (yet at the prompting of God, all unaware and undeserving as I was), I performed a particular action which fell a little outside my normal routine, and suddenly my heart was flooded with divine grace." [11]

To go with his tea, his mother sends for "un de ces gâteaux courts et dodus appelés Petites Madeleines qui semblent avoir été moulés dans la valve rainurée d'une coquille de Saint-Jacques" (I, 45). As Philip Kolb has pointed out, [12] two religious associations are conveyed by the name and shape of the *madeleine*: Mary Magdalene is the type both of the repentant sinner and of the contemplative mystic, while the St. James cockleshell is the emblem of the pilgrim.

On tasting the crumbs of the *madeleine* in a spoonful of tea, the narrator is invaded by a powerful joy. This emotion has the most

[11] Underhill, pp. 219, 222–223, 223–224, 226; William James, *The Varieties of Religious Experience: A Study in Human Nature, Being the Gifford Lectures on Natural Religion, Delivered at Edinburgh in 1901–1902* (New York: Longmans, Green and Co., 1915), pp. 191, 213, 221, 224–225.

[12] Philip Kolb, "Some Proustian Enigmas," a paper delivered at the seventy-sixth annual meeting of the Modern Language Association of America, before the Romance section, in Chicago, December 27, 1961.

extraordinary effect on him, for he ceases, quite suddenly, to feel contingent, mediocre, and mortal:

Un plaisir délicieux m'avait envahi, isolé, sans la notion de sa cause. Il m'avait aussitôt rendu les vicissitudes de la vie indifférentes, ses désastres inoffensifs, sa brièveté illusoire, de la même façon qu'opère l'amour, en me remplissant d'une essence précieuse: ou plutôt cette essence n'était pas en moi, elle était moi. J'avais cessé de me sentir médiocre, contingent, mortel. D'où avait pu me venir cette puissante joie? Je sentais qu'elle était liée au goût du thé et du gâteau, mais qu'elle le dépassait infiniment, ne devait pas être de même nature [I, 45].

This rapture might be compared, if one wished, to that of a saint taking communion. The *madeleine* resembles the Host, in that a metaphysical ecstasy has been induced as a result of the physical act of eating, without that ecstasy's being limited to the taste of the food or of the same nature as that taste. We could say that like the ecstatic who goes so far as to doubt whether God is in him or whether he is not himself God, the narrator feels that the precious essence with which he has been filled is actually himself. But again, it might be safer to understand this statement about the "precious essence" with which the narrator has been filled as a warning not to confuse that essence with God or the Infinite or any transcendental entity. Proust goes on, after this, to speak of the tea as a "breuvage" whose "vertu" is diminishing. No longer would the reader be justified in thinking of the tea as a communion cup: these are rather the terms in which one speaks of a magic potion whose effects can wear off, like the love philter of Tristan and Yseult. Then the narrator says that the answer is not in the cup but in his mind: what he seeks is something, as yet undiscovered, within his mind, which his mind, to discover, will have to create. This is a fairly rationalistic statement, but, at this very point, religious terms creep in again: "Et je recommence à me demander quel pouvait être cet état inconnu, qui n'apportait aucune preuve logique, mais l'évidence, de sa félicité, de sa réalité devant laquelle les autres s'évanouissaient" (I, 45). We find ourselves confronted with a special experience which can be neither explained nor explained away by logic, but whose reality is proved by the overwhelming joy it brings. It seems natural to be reminded, at this point, of Pascal's famous maxim, "Le coeur a ses raisons que la raison ne connaît point" [13] and of the "certitude" and "joie" which, according to the *Mémo-*

---

[13] Blaise Pascal, *Pensées et opuscules*, publiés . . . par Léon Brunschvicg (Paris: Hachette, 1951), p. 458 (no. 277).

rial [14] he made for himself, were the distinguishing marks of his ecstatic experience, an experience which owed nothing to the arguments of the philosophers.

A tremendous effort is needed for the narrator to arrive at the degree of introspection needed for him to identify and decode the obscure message within. It is an effort in which (like the efforts of a Christian to lead a devout life) he fails, again and again, renewing the struggle each time, in spite of the temptation to give it up and think of worldly things. The temptation (again, as in the Christian experience) is at its height just before the moment when help arrives and the victory is finally won. The visual memory connected with the tea and *madeleine* suddenly rises to the surface of the narrator's sconsciousness, and grateful tribute is paid by him to the senses of smell and taste which have preserved it:

La vue de la petite madeleine ne m'avait rien rappelé avant que je n'y eusse goûté; peut-être parce que, en ayant souvent aperçu depuis, sans en manger, sur les tablettes des pâtissiers, leur image avait quitté ces jours de Combray pour se lier à d'autres plus récents; peut-être parce que, de ces souvenirs abandonnés si longtemps hors de la mémoire, rien ne survivait, tout s'était désagrégé; les formes — et celle aussi du petit coquillage de pâtisserie, si grassement sensuel sous son plissage sévère et dévot — s'étaient abolies, ou, ensommeillées, avaient perdu la force d'expansion qui leur eût permis de rejoindre la conscience. Mais, quand d'un passé ancien rien ne subsiste, après la mort des êtres, après la destruction des choses, seules, plus frêles mais plus vivaces, plus immatérielles, plus persistantes, plus fidèles, l'odeur et la saveur restent encore longtemps, comme des âmes, à se rappeler, à attendre, à espérer, sur la ruine de tout le reste, à porter sans fléchir, sur leur gouttelette presque impalpable, l'édifice immense du souvenir [I, 47].

These senses are small weak things, which nevertheless survive the ruin of everything more substantial. In this (although Proust does not actually say so) they may be understood to resemble the poor, weak, and foolish whom God chose to be the founders of His Church instead of the rich, wise, and mighty. Strong in the Christian virtues of faith, hope, and fortitude (one might well continue), they bear up the whole structure of memory, as the spiritual power of the leaven of saints gives strength to the whole mass of careless, superficial, or downright sinful Christians. But now the memory of Combray is recalled and religious suggestion is, for the time being, abandoned.

I have made this analysis of the *madeleine* passage not because

[14] Ibid., pp. 142–143.

I am convinced that Proust intended it to bear the weight of all the implications I have chosen to find in it, but because I wished to demonstrate how Proust appeals to the suggestive power of religious associations, without actually making any direct and explicit religious claims. The reader is given the elements of a religious structure and left to put them together at his own discretion. The same will hold true of the narrator's moments of involuntary memory at the Guermantes reception, in "Le Temps retrouvé." The narrator is in a despondent mood. He enters the courtyard of the Hôtel de Guermantes while ruminating gloomy thoughts about his lack of talent and the fallaciousness of literature. But as soon as he puts his foot on the uneven paving stones, his discouragement vanishes before the same felicity which he had felt on the previous occasions of his perceptions of spatial perspective and involuntary memory. "Felicity," it should be noted, is a term which is most properly applied to the joy of the ecstatic or of the saints in paradise. His doubts vanish; no logical argument has been brought against them, but suddenly they are without importance. The experience brings him joy and certitude (two more words with religious implications, as we noted above) and makes death a matter of indifference to him. "Felicity" is once more the word which Proust applies to the involuntary memory stimulated by the sound of a spoon chinking against a plate. The various experiences of involuntary memory which press upon the narrator are identified as signs which have come to him of their own accord and which are destined to restore his faith in literature: "Alors on eût dit que les signes qui devaient, ce jour-là, me tirer de mon découragement et me rendre la foi dans les lettres, avaient à cœur de se multiplier . . ." (III, 868). After making use of these religious expressions, Proust proceeds to counteract them by bringing in magic. The involuntary memory which results from the narrator's use of a starched napkin to wipe his lips transports him, like a genie of the *Arabian Nights*, to Balbec. Then these impressions are followed by a rational explanation of the joy he feels in his resurrected memories. To explain the nature of this joy, Proust invokes paradise, while denying its real existence:

Oui, si le souvenir, grâce à l'oubli, n'a pu contracter aucun lien, jeter aucun chaînon entre lui et la minute présente, s'il est resté à sa place, à sa date, s'il a gardé ses distances, son isolement dans le creux d'une vallée ou à la pointe, d'un sommet, il nous fait tout à coup respirer un air nouveau, précisément parce que c'est un air qu'on a respiré autrefois, cet air plus pur que les poètes ont vainement essayé de faire régner dans le Paradis et qui ne pourrait donner cette sensation profonde de renouvellement que s'il avait été respiré déjà, car les vrais paradis sont les paradis qu'on a perdus [III, 870].

The past is identified as the real paradise — apparently because Proust wishes to make it clear that he is not looking for a paradise in the next world. Having established this, he uses the words "certitude" and "felicity" once more to characterize his narrator's sensations. His memories had transformed him into an extratemporal being, the narrator says, and that is why his fear of death had been dissipated, as if by a miracle: "Cet être-là n'était jamais venu à moi, ne s'était jamais manifesté, qu'en dehors de l'action de la jouissance immédiate, chaque fois que le miracle d'une analogie m'avait fait échapper au présent" (III, 871). There is in him, the narrator says, a being which feeds only on the essence of things. This being is his real self, a self which is normally quiescent, but which wakes to life when memory causes a moment to live simultaneously in the past and in the present. Then it receives the celestial nourishment which is being brought to it. (Here we may point out that there are many references to spiritual food both in the Bible and in the *Confessions* of St. Augustine,[15] to name one famous religious writer with whom Proust was familiar,[16] so Proust is again using a religious allusion to emphasize the importance of the narrator's spiritual experience.) It finds itself in a state of contemplation which is brief in duration but which belongs by its nature to eternity. All other pleasures — those of love, society and friendship — are unreal. He concludes that what he has to do with his memories is to preserve them in a book.

The rest of "Le Temps retrouvé" forms a meditation on literature in general, the book he intends to write in particular, and the vanity and mutability of human existence when compared to the extratemporality (which Proust seems to equate with eternity) of involuntary memory and works of art. Religious language reappears in his speculations on the nature of the book he intends to write:

Que celui qui pourrait écrire un tel livre serait heureux, pensais-je, quel labeur devant lui! Pour en donner une idée, c'est aux arts les plus élevés et les plus différents qu'il faudrait emprunter des comparaisons; car cet écrivain, qui d'ailleurs pour chaque caractère en ferait apparaître les faces opposées pour montrer son volume, devrait préparer son livre minutieusement, avec de perpétuels regroupements de forces, comme une offensive, le supporter comme une fatigue, l'accepter comme une règle, le construire

---

[15] St. Augustine, *Confessions*, translated, with an introduction, by R. S. Pine-Coffin (Harmondsworth: Penguin Books, 1961), pp. 61, 147, 197, 252, 211.

[16] There is a quotation from St. Augustine in Proust, *Lettres à Reynaldo Hahn*, présentées, datées et annotées par Philippe Kolb; préface d'Émmanuel Berl (Paris: Gallimard, 1956), pp. 81–82.

comme une église, le suivre comme un régime, le vaincre comme un obstacle, le conquérir comme une amitié, le suralimenter comme un enfant,
le créer comme un monde, sans laisser de côté ces mystères qui n'ont
probablement leur explication que dans d'autres mondes et dont le pres-
sentiment est ce qui nous émeut le plus dans la vie et dans l'art [III, 1032–
1033].

The narrator will construct his book like (among other things) a
church. Does he intend it to take the place of a church? He speaks
of the great literary works of the nineteenth century as cathedrals,
but says that he is not so ambitious as to call his own work a cathedral. He seems to think of his work as a church, but entertains some
doubts as to whether that church will find a congregation: "Je ne
savais pas si ce serait une église où des fidèles sauraient peu à peu
apprendre des vérités et découvrir des harmonies, le grand plan
d'ensemble, ou si cela resterait, comme un monument druidique au
sommet d'une île, quelque chose d'infréquenté à jamais" (III, 1040).
His work will certainly be a temple for him, if for no one else, since
he goes on to speak of "des vérités que je voulais ensuite graver dans
le temple." [17]

It is in tones of genuine contrition that the narrator speaks of his
past carelessness and sloth. Daunted at the thought of the labor
which lies ahead of him, he considers how he may conserve his
health and strength to undertake it, and deplores the lack of prudence which, in moments of drunken euphoria, had made him completely careless of the fact that his precious thoughts could be lost
with his body. This idea sounds vaguely Christian: a truly devout
person is unmindful for the safety of his body, except insofar as he
wishes to preserve it in order to carry out the work which God has
assigned to him, so that he may be a minister of grace for others.
In this task, prudence is a necessary virtue. Constant activity in
God's work is also a necessary virtue, and the narrator laments his
past sloth in accents of real distress: "Mais au lieu de travailler,
j'avais vécu dans la paresse, dans la dissipation, dans la maladie, les
soins, les manies, et j'entreprenais mon ouvrage à la veille de mourir,
sans rien savoir de mon métier" (III, 1041). Making an explicit religious comparison, he renders thanks for the service his illness has
done in detaching him from the world, at the same time as he expresses the fear that it has used up his strength:

La maladie qui, en me faisant, comme un rude directeur de conscience,
mourir au monde, m'avait rendu service ("car si le grain de froment ne

[17] III, 1041.

meurt après qu'on l'a semé, il restera seul, mais s'il meurt, il portera beaucoup de fruits"), la maladie qui, après que la paresse m'avait protégé contre la facilité, allait peut-être me garder contre la paresse, la maladie avait usé mes forces et, comme je l'avais remarqué depuis longtemps, notamment au moment où j'avais cessé d'aimer Albertine, les forces de ma mémoire [III, 1044].

This passage makes one think of Mauriac's comment that Proust may be compared to Pascal in his concern for "le bon usage des maladies." [18] It also makes one think of Proust's comment on Elstir's withdrawal from the Verdurin circle: "C'est avec le salon Verdurin qu'Elstir avait rompu; et il s'en félicitait comme les convertis bénissent la maladie ou le revers qui les a jetés dans la retraite et leur a fait connaître la voie du salut" (II, 940). Proust is using the language and expressing the attitudes of a religious convert, as he very well knows.

It is interesting to see how closely the phenomenon of involuntary memory, as described by Proust, fits into the pattern of conversion, as defined by Underhill:

It is a disturbance of the equilibrium of the self, which results in the shifting of the field of consciousness from lower to higher levels, with a consequent removal of the centre of interest from the subject to an object now brought into view: the necessary beginning of any process of transcendence. It must not, however, be confused or identified with religious conversion as ordinarily understood: the sudden and emotional acceptance of theological beliefs which the self had previously either rejected or treated as conventions dwelling upon the margin of consciousness and having no meaning for her actual life. The mechanical process may be much the same; but the material involved, the results attained, belong to a higher order of reality.[19]

This disturbance of the equilibrium of the self seems to be abrupt, but it is actually "the sequel and the result of a long period of restlessness, uncertainty and mental stress." [20] As examples of such apparently sudden conversions, Underhill cites, among others, St. Francis of Assisi and St. Catherine of Genoa. In both cases, the moment of enlightenment had followed on a long period of despondency or abstractedness, in which the pleasures of the world were sought, but less and less enjoyed. Then enlightenment came in a blinding flash and entirely changed the course of their lives.[21]

William James gives additional details on the phenomenon of

[18] Mauriac, pp. 60–61.
[19] Underhill, pp. 213–214.
[20] Ibid., p. 216.
[21] Ibid., pp. 217–220.

conversion. It is marked, he says, by a preliminary stage in which the individual, in a state of anxiety and despondency, realizes the futility of his personal efforts and simply lets go, committing himself to God. This self-abandonment is followed by a state of gladness which is experienced as a gift of grace coming from without: "In this state of mind, what we most dreaded has become the habitation of our safety, and the hour of our moral death has turned into our spiritual birthday. The time for tension in our soul is over, and that of happy relaxation, with no discordant future to be anxious about, has arrived. Fear is not held in abeyance, as it is by mere morality, it is positively expunged and washed away." [22] The potential convert supposes that his conscious strivings away from evil and toward good are getting him nowhere. In fact, while his conscious efforts hinder him, if anything, from reaching his goal, unconscious forces are at work within him to bring him toward it. But his attitude at the crucial moment must be one of complete passivity, or he will not be able to allow these unconscious forces to help him to take the last necessary step.[23] Once this step has been taken, a feeling of joy, illumination, and warmth floods his being, and, in certain cases, quite ordinary objects will appear bathed in a kind of celestial light.[24]

One can certainly see the parallel between the phenomenon of conversion and that of involuntary memory, as described by Proust, especially when one considers that the narrator's last burst of involuntary memory follows on a period when he had become progressively more and more disenchanted with the world and the flesh and completely discouraged about his own abilities. Of course, the narrator does not have just one experience leading to conversion, but several, in the sequence of his involuntary memories, and his "conversion" does not lead to union with God, any more than did his "mystic contemplation" of the hawthorns, but to a realization of the "essence" which constituted his real being and which provided him with the inspiration which he needed for artistic creation. His experience is one of integration with a lost part of himself, not of union with a transcendental entity; but the experience, involving as it does his total outlook on life, is felt by him as religious. As William James says: "Religion, whatever it is, is a man's total reaction upon life, so why not say that any total reaction upon life

[22] James, p. 47.
[23] Ibid., pp. 208–209.
[24] Ibid., p. 253.

is a religion?" [25] Because the experience which the narrator describes is felt by him to be, in this sense, religious, he uses to convey it language and experiential patterns which are connected with religious experience of a more traditional Western type — that is, union with a transcendental Being — and yet, in such a way that the experience he describes cannot be confused with this more traditional type, except by those who are determined to think of the religious experience as having one form only. Proust's wish to differentiate between the two types of experience would explain the references to Celtic beliefs and to norns, ghosts, witches, genies, and magic philters, together with the purely rational explanations of these sensations, which we have seen scattered throughout the passages describing the narrator's "mystical" experiences. Without these additions, they might conceivably be mistaken for expressions of orthodox religion (and, in fact, even with these additions, they sometimes are). As we have already seen, Proust wants to be sure that the artistic impulse receives from religion all the prestige which religion can bestow, without giving any of that prestige back again.

There is agreement among several modern critics that Proust is using Christian experiences as a stylistic means of explaining and giving value to his cult of art. Girard finds a definite Christian structure in *A la Recherche du temps perdu*, but he points out that Proust's "Christianity" is not to be taken literally.[26] Poulet, while avoiding speculation about Proust's personal beliefs, sees a striking analogy between the function of memory in Proust's work and that of divine grace in Christian belief. For him, Proustian memory is like divine grace in that it is an inexplicable phenomenon which descends upon a fallen nature, not to restore it to its first condition, but to give it the help it needs in order to find the way of salvation. It is at the same time something added to a being and the most essential, most personal act of that being. And just as there are some graces to which one responds and others to which one does not respond, so it is with memories.[27] In order to deserve the final, irresistible surge of memories which overwhelm him at the matinee of the Princesse de Guermantes, the narrator has had to make an effort to respond to quite resistible intimations of memory or spatial perspective earlier in his life. At the same time, he has had to seek after all manner of false gods, in the shape of society, friendship,

[25] Ibid., p. 35.
[26] Girard, p. 11.
[27] Poulet, pp. 372–373.

and love, in order to recognize their vanity; and he has had to go through a period of sterility, in which he became aware of the futility of his conscious efforts, in order to experience his moments of involuntary memory as a grace from on high. Parallel to the story of the success of the narrator in finding integration and inspiration is the story of Swann who, as we have already seen, comes close to finding illumination through art, but then falls away from it again. As Cocking remarks:

> The reader has been prepared long for the idea of this spiritual wasting, for it figures largely in the explanation of Swann's artistic infertility in the first two volumes, and it was perhaps with the introduction of this scheme of decline, death and resurrection that Proust came to see how certain religious notions could be adapted to his purpose and how some ready-made patterns of emotional response which, in so many contemporary minds, were inhibited by the intellectual refusal of religious experience could be released in the more acceptable context of the religion of art.[28]

Proust's insistence on the extratemporal nature of his narrator's experience also fits into the religious framework, even while rational explanations are given for this extratemporality. As Cocking also says: "The meticulous detail could be fitted (though not without a certain amount of intellectual evasion) into the grand pattern, richly related to a traditional religious patterns, of spiritual destiny conceived in terms of the gulf between the eternal and the temporal and culminating in the redemption of the temporal through art."[29]

As we have seen Cocking observe, a large part of the reader's acceptance of Proust's "religion of art" depends on that reader's denial of traditional Christianity, together with his retention of a conditioned response to religious language. Proust's indications of agnosticism play an important part in winning the reader's sympathy and making him ready to respond to those suggestions of religious value which Proust places in traditionally nonreligious areas. We have already seen how Proust makes fun of the devout while retaining certain Christian (or more than Christian) ethical standards in a form which detaches them from the system which first gave them root. To feel that one should be kind, sympathetic, and hardworking, willing to dedicate one's life and even to die in the service of an ideal; to feel an intense emotional allegiance to anything which is presented as both spiritual and a duty; to attend spiritualistic séances while doubting the reality of an afterlife; to visit

[28] Cocking, p. 34.
[29] Ibid., p. 35.

churches for their artistic rather than their religious associations; to feel bitter disappointment at the failure of physical union to lead to the interpenetration of souls; and, finally, to remain in doubt as to whether this set of values actually corresponds to anything real: all this is both true of Proust's narrator and typically modern. The reader of *A la Recherche du temps perdu*, seeing in the narrator a pilgrim as bewildered and doubting as himself, is all the more inclined to accept as valid those messages which the narrator hesitantly imparts. If, in spite of the doubts which he openly avows, Proust can still contrive to believe in something, then that something must really exist (or so the reader tends to feel). Alternatively, Proust's reader may not be an agnostic. He may be that type of modern Christian who has flung so much doctrine overboard (as incompatible with advanced ideas) that he is untroubled by the absence of that doctrine in a work with religious pretensions and is willing to accept any use of religious language as evidence of an unambiguously religious intention on the part of the author. This being given, he will embrace the religion of art in the name of that Christianity to which he adheres, without more than a faint, confused idea of the difference between them. Again, a very fervent conservative Christian (such as Mauriac) might be willing to overlook Proust's intimations of agnosticism in favor of what looks like a movement toward Christianity, and so regard the religion of art as acceptable insofar as it is at least a beginning of religious belief. It is not impossible that Proust deliberately allowed for these varied reactions. In his own way, and for his own purposes, Proust may have been imitating St. Paul's ability to be all things to all men.

Proust is intensely ironic about the narrator's illusions and about the vain hopes and smug self-satisfaction of the characters he describes in general. But the two topics about which he is never ironic are, first, the narrator's aesthetic experiences, and second, the moments of his perception of spatial perspective and involuntary memory. Irony may be applied to the narrator's mistaken conceptions of what the aesthetic experience should be like, but not to the experience itself, when it is genuine. The tone of high seriousness which he then adopts may be traced to Ruskin, whom Proust admired deeply, although not blindly. The narrator's determination to consecrate his life to the work of art may be compared to what Proust says of Ruskin, in his preface to his translation, *La Bible d'Amiens*:

[Le critique] essayerait de reconstituer ce que pouvait être la singulière vie spirituelle d'un écrivain hanté de réalités si spéciales, son inspiration étant la mesure dans laquelle il avait la vision de ces réalités, son talent la mesure dans laquelle il pouvait les recréer dans son oeuvre, sa moralité enfin, l'instinct qui, les lui faisant considérer sous un aspect d'éternité (quelque particulières que ces réalités nous paraissent), le poussait à sacrifier au besoin de les apercevoir et à la nécessité de les reproduire pour en assurer une vision durable et claire, tous ses plaisirs, tous ses devoirs et jusqu'à sa propre vie, laquelle n'avait de raison d'être que comme étant la seule manière possible d'entrer en contact avec ces réalités, de valeur que celle que peut avoir pour un physicien un instrument indispensable à ses expériences.[30]

Ruskin, as Proust recognizes, was a genuinely religious man. In *"En mémoire des églises assassinées"* and in the *Bible d'Amiens*, Proust quotes a statement by Ruskin to the effect that his habit of reading the Bible with the respectful conviction that it was directly inspired by God made even his secular reading profoundly serious for him.[31] The religious habit of mind was carried over by him to nonreligious works. In the same way, Ruskin's religious feelings found an object in all beauty, whether that of nature or of the art work. Proust is careful to point out that this attitude is very different from that of an aesthetic dilettante:

Non seulement la principale religion de Ruskin fut la religion tout court et je reviendrai sur ce point tout à l'heure, car il domine et caractérise son esthétique), mais, pour nous en tenir à ce moment à la "Religion de la Beauté", il faudrait avertir notre temps qu'il ne peut prononcer ces mots, s'il veut faire une allusion juste à Ruskin, qu'en redressant le sens que son dilettantisme esthétique est trop porté à leur donner. Pour un âge, en effet, de dilettantes et d'esthètes, un adorateur de la Beauté, c'est un homme qui, ne pratiquant pas d'autre culte que le sien et ne reconnaissant pas d'autre dieu qu'elle, passerait sa vie dans la contemplation voluptueuse des œuvres d'art. . . .

Très loin d'avoir été un dilettante ou un esthète, Ruskin fut précisément le contraire, un de ces hommes à la Carlyle, avertis par leur génie de la vanité de tout plaisir et, en même temps, de la présence auprès d'eux d'une réalité éternelle, intuitivement perçue par l'inspiration. Le talent leur est donné comme un pouvoir de fixer cette réalité à la toute-puissance et à l'éternité de laquelle, avec enthousiasme et comme obéissant à un commandement de la conscience, ils consacrent, pour lui donner quelque valeur, leur vie éphémère. De tels hommes, attentifs et anxieux devant l'univers à déchiffrer, sont avertis des parties de la réalité sur lesquelles leurs dons spéciaux leur départissent une lumière particulière, par une sorte de démon qui les guide, de voix qu'ils entendent, l'éternelle inspiration des

[30] Ruskin, *La Bible d'Amiens*, p. 11.
[31] Proust, *Pastiches et mélanges*, pp. 130–131; Ruskin, *La Bible d'Amiens*, p. 34.

êtres géniaux. Le don spécial, pour Ruskin, c'était le sentiment de la beauté, dans la nature comme dans l'art. Ce fut dans la Beauté que son tempérament le conduisit à chercher la réalité, et sa vie toute religieuse en reçut un emploi tout esthétique. Mais cette Beauté à laquelle il se trouva ainsi consacrer sa vie ne fut pas conçue par lui comme un objet de jouissance fait pour la charmer, mais comme une réalité infiniment plus importante que la vie, pour laquelle il aurait donné la sienne.[32]

This application of religious feeling to everything beautiful affected Ruskin's language: "Il pourra parler des années où le gothique lui apparut avec la même gravité, le même retour ému, la même sérénité qu'un chrétien parle du jour où la vérité lui fut révélée." [33] Those qualities, described by the terms "gravité," "retour ému," and "sérénité," which Proust so well discerned in Ruskin, reappear, as we have seen, in "Le Temps retrouvé."

In the previous chapter, we saw how Proust may be considered as an agnostic whose lack of faith was considered by him as a positive lack, not as an advantage. Combray is a paradise for his narrator, looking back on it, not so much because it was peopled by superior beings (for it was not), as because it represents for him a time when he had faith in things. It is Ruskin's attitude of faith which makes a particular impression on Proust. Through his faith in the artists of the Middle Ages, who themselves were drawing on their faith in the Scriptures, Ruskin, Proust says, has produced a work in which we too can have faith: "Car Ruskin, pour avoir cru en ces hommes d'autrefois, parce qu'en eux étaient la foi et la beauté, s'était trouvé écrire aussi sa Bible, comme eux pour avoir cru aux prophètes et aux apôtres avaient écrit la leur. . . . Avant que nous arrivions à la cathédrale, n'était-elle pas pour nous surtout celle qu'il avait aimée? et ne sentions-nous pas qu'il y avait encore des Saintes Écritures, puisque nous cherchions pieusement la Vérité dans ses livres." [34] The reader, Proust seems to be saying, can find himself linked, in spite of his agnosticism, in a chain of faith, through the art work. The men of the Middle Ages produced their works in a spirit of faith; these works were then expounded by Ruskin, a man of the nineteenth century who combined faith in the art work with faith in "la religion tout court"; then, because of Ruskin's double faith in religion and the art work, the modern reader is

---

[32] Proust, *Pastiches et mélanges*, pp. 157–158; Ruskin, *La Bible d'Amiens*, pp. 54–55.
[33] Proust, *Pastiches et mélanges*, p. 158; Ruskin, *La Bible d'Amiens*, pp. 55–56.
[34] Proust, *Pastiches et mélanges*, p. 148; Ruskin, *La Bible d'Amiens*, p. 46.

enabled to find a religious satisfaction (otherwise denied to him) by having faith in Ruskin and in the works of art which Ruskin valued. This passage provides us with a striking example of the displacement of religious value from Christianity to the work of art, especially since Proust seems perfectly conscious of what he is about. Proust's attitude comes out even more clearly in another passage, in which he praises Ruskin with a profusion of religious terms which might very well have distressed Ruskin himself, since they would have appeared to him to be blasphemous:

Comprenant mal jusque-là la portée de l'art religieux au moyen âge, je m'étais dit, dans ma ferveur pour Ruskin: Il m'apprendra, car lui aussi, en quelques parcelles du moins, n'est-il pas la vérité? Il fera entrer mon esprit là où il n'avait pas accès, car son inspiration est comme le lys de la vallée. Il m'enivrera et me vivifiera, car il est la vigne et la vie. Et j'ai senti en effet que le parfum mystique des rosiers de Saron n'était pas à tout jamais évanoui, puisqu'on le respire encore, au moins dans ses paroles. Et voici qu'en effet les pierres d'Amiens ont pris pour moi la dignité des pierres de Venise, et comme la grandeur qu'avait la Bible, alors qu'elle était encore vérité dans le cœur les hommes et beauté grave dans leurs œuvres.[35]

The Bible is no longer a direct source of truth and beauty because we no longer have faith in it, Proust implies; and yet its language is sufficiently powerful to be an appropriate means of expressing appreciation for a purely human source of beauty and truth. This passage shows the same combination of religious doubt with the use of religious language which we observed in the passages describing the narrator's experiences of involuntary memory, with the exception that the repudiation of traditional Christian belief is here expressed more directly and clearly.

When one looks at *Jean Santeuil*, which Proust composed before his preoccupation with Ruskin, it seems all the more reasonable to suppose that it was after reading Ruskin that Proust perfected his use of the religious style. In *Jean Santeuil*, we find a tendency to apply religious terms to certain important themes, but the use of religious vocabulary and religious structure is far less developed than in *A la Recherche du temps perdu*. Thus, in *Jean Santeuil*, some effort is made to give a religious value to the moments of inspiration of the novelist C., which allow him to turn the humble surroundings of the village inn, in which he is composing, into something entirely different, by means of literature: "Pour ne pas le déranger, l'hôte, le pêcheur avaient cessé de parler et ils buvaient

---

[35] Proust, *Pastiches et mélanges*, p. 147; Ruskin, *La Bible d'Amiens*, p. 45.

en silence pendant que la petite fille continuait à terre à jouer avec le chien et Félicité à apporter les plats, comme dans le tableau de Rembrandt qui représente les pèlerins d'Emmaüs. Et à ce moment l'eau avait été changée sans qu'ils y eussent été pour rien." [36] Here we see already the taste which we have noticed in Proust for making a reference to a religious topic by means of a religious painting, and for applying religious language to an aesthetic occasion. But this is the only example in *Jean Santeuil* of such treatment of a work of art or of the aesthetic impulse, and it is comparatively undeveloped.

Further on, we find a description of a garden in terms of a painting of paradise, in which the flowers are compared to angels. Again, the angels figure in a painting: "[Elles sont] les innombrables anges d'une sorte de Jour, comme ceux qu'ont représentés les grands peintres de la Renaissance, des anges peints d'un rose, d'un bleu, d'un orangé aussi vifs. . . ." [37] A rather elaborate and not entirely clear picture of the garden is given, and then the religious metaphor is taken up again: "Et ces papillons, les petits oiseaux surtout qui s'ébattent en l'air, ou par groupes sont perchés dans les arbres, font penser aussi aux angelots ailés du tableau dont je parlais tandis que dans le ciel ouvert tout entier jusqu'au fond de son azur, le soleil trône comme Dieu le Père dans les rayons." [38] The impression which we receive is decorative, playful, and, in the totality of the passage, slightly confused. It does not have the intensity and the seriousness which lend such impact to Proust's later descriptions of hawthorns or pear trees in religious terms. The same holds true of a description of apple blossom, in which a very fleeting religious reference is made, in the midst of a fairly long description of the appearance of the flower. Its pistils are compared to "une sorte d'obscur et mysté-rieux chœur au sein d'une éclatante basilique." [39] But since this is the only religious allusion in the passage, it passes almost unnoticed. How much more suggestive is the passage describing the hawthorns on the altar of the parish church of Combray, where so many re-ligious allusions establish the intrinsic connection of the blossoms with the ceremony!

When Proust speaks of involuntary memories, in *Jean Santeuil*, he finds their value, as he will later, in their extratemporality, which he equates with eternity. He calls the reality perceived at such mo-

[36] Proust, *Jean Santeuil*, 3 vols. (Paris: Gallimard, 1952), I, 45.
[37] Ibid., I, 150.
[38] Ibid., p. 151.
[39] Ibid., p. 137.

ments by imagination "un objet éternel" and "une essence éternelle," and he attributes our pleasure in this experience to the fact
that we are separated momentarily from the present, "comme si
notre vraie nature était hors du temps, faite pour goûter l'éternel et
mécontente du présent, attristé du passé." [40] But instead of suggesting that there is something mystical about these extratemporal experiences, he attributes the perception of them solely to the
imagination. There is, however, a slight connection of this experience with religious feeling when Proust equates the physical occasion for the spiritual joy he feels in it with communion, using the
term "sous les espèces":

> Alors je sens sous les espèces du raisin dont dans le jardin je détachais une
> à une et goûtais les grappes blondes en commençant à travailler, sous les
> espèces de ces sombres et épicées compotes, rougeâtres, violacées ou marron
> qu'on me servait dans ma chambre . . . je sens la trame de ma vie d'autre-
> fois, senteur de wagons, hâte de l'heure, bruit des cloches boiteuses et re-
> tentissantes palpiter en moi, plus haut que la mémoire et que le présent,
> non point plates comme une image mais pleines comme une réalité et
> vagues comme un sentiment.[41]

This reference to communion is at once more explicit and less insidious than the veiled allusion to the eucharist which we found in
the *madeleine* episode. Perhaps Proust was the more hesitant in
using religious language, at this stage, to describe his experience of
creative art, natural beauty, and involuntary memory, in that God
is retained, in *Jean Santeuil*, as the ultimate giver of value, from
whom all other values are derived. So long as Proust still retained
certain religious beliefs, he may have felt some doubt as to the
propriety of using religious language, in a really extensive way, to
describe experiences which are not traditionally considered as religious. It seems paradoxical that it should take an unbeliever to
use a religious framework as fully and unhesitatingly as did Proust
in his maturity; and yet this was the case. It seems that he needed
the detachment of the agnostic to see in Ruskin's religious manner
a useful stylistic device, and to develop it, as such, for his own ends.

Another element which Proust found in Ruskin, and which he
proceeded to use and develop along his own lines, is a peculiarity
of the composition of the first part of *Sesame and Lilies*. In a footnote which extends over three pages, Proust comments on Ruskin's
method of stating a number of apparently disparate themes, at the

[40] Ibid., II, 232, 233.
[41] Ibid., 232.

beginning of his discourse, in order to unite them at the end, imposing a retrospective order on the whole. He concludes:

Je vois que dans la note placée à la fin de la conférence, j'ai cru pouvoir noter jusqu'à 7 thèmes dans la dernière phrase. En réalité Ruskin y range l'une à côté de l'autre, mêle, fait manœuvrer et resplendir ensemble toutes les principales idées — ou images — qui ont apparu avec quelque désordre au long de sa conférence. C'est son procédé. Il passe d'une idée à l'autre sans aucun ordre apparent. Mais en réalité la fantaisie qui le mène suit ses affinités profondes qui lui imposent malgré lui une logique supérieure. Si bien qu'à la fin il se trouve avoir obéi à une sorte de plan secret qui, dévoilé à la fin, impose retrospectivement à l'ensemble une sorte d'ordre et le fait apercevoir magnifiquement étagé jusqu'à cette apothéose finale.[42]

As Kolb has pointed out,[43] Proust had been looking, since his work on *Jean Santeuil*, for a means of bringing together and binding into a coherent pattern the disparate themes which he had a tendency to juxtapose without apparent connection. It seems very probable that he found the method for which he was looking in Ruskin, especially since this technique, as used by Ruskin, obviously made a deep impression on him.

Of course, we do not need to think of this stylistic technique as any the less Proust's own because he found it in Ruskin. As he said of his discipleship to Ruskin: "Il n'y a pas de meilleure manière d'arriver à prendre conscience de ce qu'on sent soi-même que d'essayer de de recréer en soi ce qu'a senti un maître. Dans cet effort profond, c'est notre pensée elle-même que nous mettons, avec la sienne, au jour." [44] At the same time, this need not invalidate the claim which has been made by several Proust critics that there is something Wagnerian about Proust's use of recurrent themes: Proust may perfectly well have been influenced by Ruskin and by Wagner at the same time. But there is another thing to be noticed about Proust's meandering structure, and that is that it corresponds to what Pascal called "l'ordre de la charité": "Cet ordre consiste principalement à la digression sur chaque point qu'on rapporte à la fin, pour la montrer toujours." [45] The structure which Proust found in *Sesame and Lilies* is, in fact, not simply Ruskin's invention

---

[42] Ruskin, *Sésame et les lys: des trésors des rois; des jardins des reines*, traduction, notes et préface par Marcel Proust (Paris: Mercure de France, 1935), pp. 62–63.

[43] Kolb, "Proust et Ruskin: nouvelles perspectives," *Cahiers de l'Association Internationale des Études Françaises*, No. 12 (juin, 1960), 259–273.

[44] Proust, *Pastiches et mélanges*, p. 197; Ruskin, *La Bible d'Amiens*, p. 93.

[45] Pascal, p. 461 (no. 283).

or the involuntary product of Ruskin's manic depression (as some maintain); it is traditionally typical of the religious mode of address.

Finally, there is yet another feature of Proust's style which fits into a religious context and which, for once, cannot be traced to Ruskin. This feature consists of the singularly indefinable character of the narrator. We are told many things about his character and reactions, but we do not obtain a direct impression of his character from his reactions. This is due to the fact that we see the world through his eyes, without any refraction through his personality or any rectification of that reality except from the point of view of his later discoveries. As Sartre points out,[46] we observe the narrator directly as a reflective consciousness whose experiences we share. As a result, the narrator represents a general human nature which allows every reader to identify with him. He becomes an Everyman passing through a series of experiences which may be understood as typical for everyone, just as Christian, in *The Pilgrim's Progress*, represents not an individual character but a generalization of a particular sort of human experience. The identification of the reader with the narrator also reduces the reader's resistance to the "mystical" episodes in *A la Recherche du temps perdu*: he accepts them as if they had happened to himself. Somehow, Proust has achieved, on the aesthetic plane, what Pascal attempted on the religious one: he has caused the reader to enter into his point of view so fully that the reader finds himself embarked on a kind of aesthetic *pari* before he has time to realize that this is the author's intent.

[46] Jean-Paul Sartre, *L'Être et le néant, essai d'ontologie phénoménologique* (Paris: Gallimard, 1949), p. 416.

CHAPTER EIGHT

MYSTICISM

In the last two chapters, we considered the ways in which Proust's language, attitudes, and use of situations fit into the main Western traditions of Platonism and Christianity. Less orthodox spiritual homes have, however, been found for him. It is these affiliations which we will consider in this final chapter.

Georges Cattaui, for instance, draws parallels between Proust and a very mixed group of mystics. For him, Proust resembles some oriental sage or Sufi poet[1] as much as a mystic of a Christian sort. Having said this, he goes on to call Proust an Albigensian, a Cathar, a Buddhist or a Sufi (he is not sure which), a Gnostic, an Orphic, a Neo-Pythagorean, a Cabbalist, and (in the sense in which this term may be applied to Romantic poets in general) a Dionysian.[2] Since he offers hardly any explanation of what he means, little of this seems very helpful.

A more profitable suggestion may be found in a letter by Marguerite Yourcenar which is quoted in Jean Mouton's recent study of Proust's religious attitudes.[3] Marguerite Yourcenar identifies as Buddhist Proust's awareness of the passage of time, the fragmentation of the external personality, and the vanity of desire. At the same time, she sees indications of a Christian attitude in Proust's

[1] Georges Cattaui, *Marcel Proust: Proust et son temps; Proust et le temps* (Paris: Julliard, 1952), p. 171.

[2] Ibid., pp. 250–251.

[3] Jean Mouton, *Proust* (Bruges: Desclée De Brouwer, 1968), p. 23. I should have liked to say more about this study, which is very subtle and suggestive, but it appeared just at the moment when I was preparing my manuscript for the printers.

sense of original sin and of the indignity of the flesh, in the mystical nature of his aesthetic contemplation, and in the charity with which he views his characters, in spite of their faults.

This is very interesting, but, even so, it is not as fully developed as R. C. Zaehner's very serious attempt to explain Proust's "message" in terms of Buddhist mysticism.[4] Basically, Zaehner, who is an orientalist and a student of comparative religion, divides mystical experience into three types. Into the first category fall Christian and Mohammedan (specifically, Sufi) mystics, who have a mystical experience of a theistic type. The Christian feels that he is united with God, while the Mohammedan feels annihilated in Him. Below this is a natural mystical experience, in which the mystic feels united either with some principle (not identified as God) underlying the universe, or with some basic, hitherto missing, part of himself. The nature mystic belongs to the first subdivision of the second category, while the Buddhist or the person who has achieved individuation (to quote the Jungian term) falls into the second. In the third category we find the person who thinks he is himself God. This belief may be explained either by Hindu monism or by acute mania (called by the Jungians inflation). It may also be induced by drugs. Zaehner, who makes a sharper distinction between Hindu and Buddhist views than would some scholars of oriental religion, is inclined to regard monism and mania as the same thing. His fourth chapter consists of an analysis of Proust and Rimbaud, in which he states that Rimbaud deliberately induced a mystical experience of the third type, of which he has left a record in *Une Saison en enfer*. He admires Rimbaud for having the grace to admit that this was a false mystical experience, which gave him no true insight and did him spiritual harm. Proust, on the other hand, seems to Zaehner to have had a natural mystical experience of a Buddhist type, in that he experienced within himself two levels of consciousness whose integration brought him joy and an increased ability to work. This very positive result of his mystical experience proves (according to the scriptural adage, "By their fruits ye shall know them") that it was good.

The assumption here, of course, is that the narrator is describing a mystical experience which Proust actually had. Zaehner shows that he believes this by consistently referring, in his analysis of the rele-

[4] Robert Charles Zaehner, *Mysticism, Sacred and Profane: An Inquiry into Some Varieties of Praeternatural Experience* (New York: Oxford University Press, 1961).

vant passages, to the protagonist as "Proust" instead of "the narrator." The matter, for lack of biographical record, is difficult to prove. The most one can say is that, however easy it may be to apply religious language to nonreligious experiences (and Proust, as we have seen, found it so easy that he frequently did so as a joke), an actual religious experience, for one who has never had one, is very difficult to invent. Zaehner, who seems well acquainted with mystical states, is convinced that Proust is describing, in the narrator's moments of involuntary memory, a mystical experience of an unusual but authentic type.

To prove his point, Zaehner begins by quoting a passage which we considered in Chapter Seven purely from the point of view of its Christian terms of reference:

Au vrai, l'être qui alors goûtait en moi cette impression la goûtait en ce qu'elle avait de commun dans un jour ancien et maintenant, dans ce qu'elle avait d'extratemporel, un être qui n'apparaissait que quand, par une de ces identités entre le présent et le passé, il pouvait se trouver dans le seul milieu où il pût vivre, jouir de l'essence des choses, c'est-à-dire en dehors du temps. Cela expliquait que mes inquiétudes au sujet de ma mort eussent cessé au moment où j'avais reconnu inconsciemment le goût de la petite madeleine, puisqu'à ce moment-là l'être que j'avais été était un être extra-temporel, par conséquent insoucieux des vicissitudes de l'avenir. Cet être-là n'était jamais venu à moi, ne s'était jamais manifesté, qu'en dehors de l'action, de la jouissance immédiate, chaque fois que le miracle d'une analogie m'avait fait échapper au présent [III, 871].

In his analysis of this passage, Zaehner lays stress on the intensity of the experience and on the sense of renewal and liberation which it brought. But the thing which interests him most is the fact that it is not clear whether it was "Proust" himself or another being who was experiencing this feeling of blessed release.[5] To elucidate the nature of this being, Zaehner goes on to quote the following passage:

L'être qui était rené en moi quand, avec un tel frémissement de bonheur, j'avais entendu le bruit commun à la fois à la cuiller qui touche l'assiette et au marteau qui frappe sur la roue, à l'inégalité pour les pas des pavés de la cour Guermantes et du baptistère de Saint-Marc, etc., cet être-là ne se nourrit que de l'essence des choses, en elle seulement il trouve sa substance, ses délices. . . . Mais qu'un bruit, qu'une odeur, déjà entendu ou respirée jadis, le soient de nouveau, à la fois dans le présent et dans le passé, réels sans être actuels, idéaux sans être abstraits, aussitôt l'essence permanente et habituellement cachée des choses se trouve libérée, et notre vrai moi qui, parfois depuis longtemps, semblait mort, mais ne l'était pas entièrement, s'éveille, s'anime en recevant la céleste nourriture qui lui est

[5] Ibid., p. 56.

apportée. Une minute affranchie de l'ordre du temps a recréé en nous, pour la sentir, l'homme affranchi de l'ordre du temps. Et celui-là, on comprend qu'il soit confiant dans sa joie, même si le simple goût d'une madeleine ne semble pas contenir logiquement les raisons de cette joie, on comprend que le mot de "mort" n'ait pas de sens pour lui; situé hors du temps, que pourrait-il craindre de l'avenir? [III, 872–873].

What makes the narrator's moment of illumination differ sharply from that of a Christian mystic, Zaehner points out, is that there is no suggestion of any union with God. On the contrary, it is with a deeper, underlying self, existing outside the categories of space and time and quite different from what we call the ego, that his mystic union takes place.[6] Zaehner considers this typically Buddhist. Another Buddhist feature may be found in the way in which the experience starts. For Zaehner, there is a parallel between the experience which Proust describes and that experience which the Zen Buddhists call satori. To achieve this state, a slight shock of an external nature, whether a sight or a sound or a tactile sensation, must be allowed to impinge on a mind emptied of conceptual thought and entertaining nothing more than free-flowing images. This requirement certainly seems to have been fulfilled by the narrator, in that he was thinking of nothing in particular when the various stimuli he mentions, none of which were important or out of the ordinary in themselves, brought him his moments of involuntary memory.[7] Furthermore, Proust's entire novel may be understood as conveying a Buddhist message — that of the transience and instability of everything in our daily lives and the futility of attaching ourselves to these transient, corrupt, and unstable things. The Buddhist attitude toward the world is one of disillusion and disgust, sentiments which Proust appears to echo. Moreover, Proust joins with the Buddhists in maintaining that there is a way out of this world of transience, corruption, and instability, into a state on the further side of space and time, a state which the Buddhists call nirvana. Zaehner concludes this comparison between Proust and a Buddhist by saying that the similarity is surprising, in view of the fact that Proust had, so far as we know, no knowledge of Buddhist writings.[8]

Since we started this chapter by referring to Cattaui's list of Proust's spiritual affinities, in which he twice compared Proust to a

[6] Ibid., pp. 57, 59.
[7] Ibid., p. 55.
[8] Ibid., p. 52.

Sufi, it is not irrelevant to point out that Zaehner (who has made a special study of the Sufis) does not consider Proust to be very like a Sufi at all, in view of the specifically theistic nature of the Sufi's mystical experiences. However, some of the Sufis were subject to Indian influences, which caused them to produce utterances of a vaguely Hindu-Buddhist kind.[9] This may explain why Cattaui thought of calling Proust a Sufi as well as a Buddhist: through Indian thought, the two systems meet.

Zaehner's theory is a very interesting one, and one which has all the charm of novelty. It is difficult to know whether we should welcome it or be on our guard against it on that account. The basic assumption on which he is proceeding is, of course, as we already observed, the assumption that Proust actually had a natural mystical experience of a Buddhist type. For those who believe that similarities can only be explained by influences, this assumption may seem to be ruined by Zaehner's frank admission that it is very doubtful that Proust was acquainted with Buddhist texts. But if we regard (as Zaehner does) religious states as having some kind of reality in the mind, independently of the efforts of religious organizers to put them there, then there is no reason why we should be surprised by such a phenomenon.

I find Zaehner's theory all the more interesting in that I had been reading books about Hinduism and Buddhism before I came across his book, in an effort to elucidate the remark made to me by an Indian friend, Ranganavan Iyer, that he found something very like an Indian outlook in the writings of Marcel Proust. (Zaehner, it is true, makes a sharp distinction between Hindu and Buddhist ideas, but it is a fact that they amalgamate in Mahayana Buddhism, a later development of original Buddhism, and so may be considered together.) I could not possibly claim that my reading has made me an authority on oriental religion, but at least it has taken me far enough for me to make some comments on Zaehner's theory, and even make some additions to it. There really do seem to be certain similarities between Buddhist and Hindu beliefs and certain basic attitudes in Proust, although it would be very dangerous to assume that Proust wished to present these attitudes in the form of an organized system. Specifically, I am thinking of his treatment of the themes of the nature of the self, introspection, enlightenment, compassion, and the interplay of truth and illusion. Of particular in-

[9] Ibid., pp. 161–164.

terest, in connection with this last, is the role played by sleep and
dreams in the mind and by appearance in the material world. The
one thread which holds the web of illusion together, for Proust as
for the Hindu or the Buddhist, is the sole connecting factor of relation, of which time, space, and causation are the most familiar, although not the only, forms. It should be interesting, and perhaps
rewarding, to follow these similarities through in some detail and
see whether they are really basic or only superficial.

I shall begin with a feature which Zaehner identified for us as
Buddhist, namely the narrator's division of himself, during his moments of involuntary memory, into two selves. As Christmas
Humphreys, a world authority on Buddhism, very clearly explains,
there are for the Buddhist three selves. The first is "Spirit or Ātman,
which is the 'common denominator' of all forms of life, and the
monopoly of none." [10] Something like this larger Spirit is mentioned
by Proust more than once. He speaks, for instance, of "la part de
l'Esprit éternel, laquelle est l'auteur des livres de Bergotte" (I, 557).
Again, at another point, he remarks: "Car mon intelligence devait
être une, et peut-être même n'en existe-t-il qu'une seule dont tout
le monde est co-locataire, une intelligence sur laquelle chacun, du
fonds de son corps particulier, porte ses regards, comme au théâtre
où, si chacun a sa place, en revanche, il n'y a qu'une seule scène"
(I, 568). The idea of the universal spirit in which we all participate
came to Proust from his philosophy teacher Darlu (who, I suppose,
derived it equally from Hegel and Hartmann). According to Henri
Bonnet, Darlu held that above individual minds is the universal
human mind (or spirit) which superimposes points of view and for
whom the different philosophical systems are the expression of an
ever-widening and ever-deepening truth.[11] However, the similarity
between Atman and this universal human spirit is only an external
and approximate once, since the Atman is that Spirit which works
through all human minds, not a composite of them. Continuing
with the Buddhist notion of Spirit, we find that Atman, the underlying, universal self, is (as one might expect) unaffected by time,
space, and mortality. The individual who can enter into contact
with it immediately ceases to feel the pressure of these three bonds.
Like the narrator tasting the *madeleine*, he ceases to feel con-

[10] Christmas Humphreys, *Buddhism* (Harmondsworth: Penguin Books, 1955),
p. 87. But many scholars consider this a Hindu concept.

[11] Henri Bonnet, *Alphonse Darlu (1849–1921), le maître de philosophie de
Marcel Proust* (Paris: Nizet, 1961), p. 36.

tingent, mediocre, and mortal. This seems to be what the Buddhists mean by enlightenment. But is the self with which Proust's narrator has come in contact really the Atman? And has he really achieved what a Buddhist would call enlightenment? After all, once he emerges from this extratemporal state, he is vividly, and even obsessively, concerned with death, and becomes very anxious to complete his work before death overtakes him. Strictly speaking, if I understand Buddhist thinking correctly, enlightenment should put a man completely beyond the thought of death.

To return to the Buddhist notion of the self, the Atman is obscured for most of us by the second self, which Humphreys calls "soul" and which he defines as "a growing, evolving bundle of attributes or characteristics, forming 'character.' This it is which passes, by a process of causal impulse, from life to life on the long road to perfection." [12] Rebirth is to be understood literally in Buddhism and metamorphically in Proust, although he does toy with the idea of reincarnation. He makes playful references to it in relation to dreaming and waking. For instance, in the opening pages of *A la Recherche du temps perdu*, Proust writes of a dream notion which continues after his awakening and then fades: "Puis elle commençait à me devenir inintelligible, comme après la métempsychose les pensées d'une existence antérieure . . ." (I, 3). Again, in a passage describing the narrator's troubled sleep at Balbec, Proust writes that sleep initiates us into (among other things) disincarnation, the transmigration of souls, reduction to the animal kingdom, destruction, and resurrection (I, 819–820). What Proust does appear to take rather more seriously, however, is the reincarnation of our ancestors in us. We have already noticed, in Chapter Two, the narrator's conviction that his ancestors in general and Tante Léonie in particular were reborn in him, in his maturity. In the noble, generous, and gentle Saint-Loup, a malicious, petty-minded ancestor also wakes, at long intervals and unexpectedly, to life. So we may suppose that what, for the Buddhist, is true of the individual is, for Proust, true of the race. Apart from this, Proust envisages reincarnation only in the form of the artist's rebirth in the minds of those who admire his work. In this form he welcomes it, although the Buddhist aspires to escape from reincarnation.

Finally, for the Buddhist, there is the third self, "body, here used in the sense of 'personality', composed of the lower attributes or

[12] Humphreys, p. 88.

skandhas. The point to be made clear is that there is nothing in man which entitles him to say 'I am this and you are that', throughout all eternity." [13] This last observation fits in very well with Proust's well-known decomposition of personality, which can be reduced to his conviction (which we observed in Chapter Five) that there is no deed for good or ill of which the same person may not be capable. Also fitting in with this concept is the narrator's analysis of himself at moments into, not two selves, as in his moments of involuntary memory, but multitudinous selves. This is expressed very clearly in the following passage:

Pendant quelques instants, et sachant qu'il me rendait plus heureux qu'elle [Albertine], je restais d'abord en tête à tête avec le petit personnage intérieur, saluer chantant du soleil, et dont j'ai déjà parlé. De ceux qui composent notre individu, ce ne sont pas les plus apparents qui nous sont le plus essentiels. En moi, quand la maladie aura fini de les jeter l'un après l'autre par terre, il en restera encore deux ou trois qui auront la vie plus dure que les autres, notamment un certain philosophe qui n'est heureux que quand il a découvert, entre deux œuvres, entre deux sensations, une partie commune. Mais le dernier de tous, je me suis quelquefois demandé si ce ne serait pas le petit bonhomme fort semblable à un autre que l'opticien de Combray avait placé derrière sa vitrine pour indiquer le temps qu'il faisait et qui, ôtant son capuchon dès qu'il y avait du soleil, le remettait s'il allait pleuvoir. Ce petit bonhomme-là, je connais son égoïsme: je peux souffrir d'une crise d'étouffements que la venue seule de la pluie calmerait, lui ne s'en soucie pas, et aux premières gouttes si impatiemment attendues, perdant sa gaîté, il rabat son capuchon avec mauvaise humeur. En revanche, je crois bien qu'à mon agonie, quand tous mes autres "moi" seront morts, s'il vient à briller un rayon de soleil tandis que je pousserai mes derniers soupirs, le petit personnage barométrique se sentira bien aise, et ôtera son capuchon pour chanter: "Ah! enfin, il fait beau" [III, 12].

Proust's awareness of changes in personality is based on the feeling that we have many selves. Thus, of the narrator's experience of one form of grief after another, at the death of Albertine, Proust writes: "Notre moi est fait de la superposition de nos états successifs. Mais cette superposition n'est pas immuable comme la stratification d'une montagne. Perpétuellement des soulèvements font affleurer à la surface des couches anciennes" (III, 544–545).

Introspection, which we have seen at work in the *madeleine* episode, is a fundamental virtue of Hindu-Buddhist practice, its most highly developed form being found in Yogic concentration. Humphreys explains that yoga is the concentration on a single point (it

[13] Ibid.

hardly matters what) to the exclusion of everything else, in order to overcome the natural diffuseness of the mind. The mind which can concentrate in this way actually forms itself into the shape of the object contemplated, and by so doing enters into a full understanding of its being.[14] In connection with this, we may recall Proust's remarks about music changing the shape of the listener's soul: "Mais la petite phrase, dès qu'il l'entendait, savait rendre libre en lui l'espace qui pour elle était nécessaire, les proportions de l'âme de Swann s'en trouvaient changées . . ." (I, 236). Even more striking, as an example of this type of concentration, is the episode in which the narrator gazes on the hawthorns. As we have already noticed in Chapter Seven, Underhill points out that this type of contemplation is really more typical of an Eastern than a Western mystic. There is one particularly oriental feature of the narrator's contemplation, and that is the way in which he attempts to copy mentally the gesture of the hawthorns: "En essayant de mimer au fond de moi le geste de leur efflorescence, je l'imaginais comme si ç'avait été le mouvement de tête étourdi et rapide, au regard coquet, aux pupilles diminuées, d'une blanche jeune fille distraite et vive" (I, 112). It is interesting to know (although we might have guessed) that this type of contemplation actually formed part of Proust's own experience. Evidence for this is supplied by Reynaldo Hahn, in his description of Proust gazing in complete absorption at a Bengal rose bush. To this description he adds the following commentary:

Que de fois, par la suite, j'ai assisté à des scènes similaires! Que de fois j'ai observé Marcel en ces moments mystérieux où il communiait totalement avec la nature, avec l'art, avec la vie, en ces "minutes profondes" où son être entier, concentré dans un travail transcendant de pénétration et d'aspiration alternées, entrait, pour ainsi dire, en état de transe, où son intelligence et sa sensibilité surhumaines, tantôt par une série de fulgurations suraiguës, tantôt par une lente et irrésistible infiltration, parvenaient jusqu'à la racine des choses et découvraient ce que personne ne pouvait voir — ce que personne, maintenant, ne verra jamais.[15]

For the Hindu, introspection is a duty which comes before all others, easily outweighing every other claim, including those of morality and even (according to Western views) of common decency. Heinrich Zimmer expresses this in the following terms:

The Self is not easily known. It cannot be realized except by the greatest effort. Every vestige of the normal waking attitude, which is appropriate

---

[14] Ibid., p. 116.
[15] Reynaldo Hahn, "Promenade," in *Hommage à Marcel Proust*, Les Cahiers Marcel Proust, I (Paris: Gallimard, 1927), p. 34.

and necessary for the daily struggle for existence (*artha*), pleasure (*kāma*), and the attainment of righteousness (*dharma*), must be abandoned. The really serious seeker of the Self has to become an introvert, disinterested absolutely in the pursuits of the world — disinterested even in the continuance of his individual existence; for the Self is beyond the sphere of the senses and intellect, beyond even the profundity of intuitive awareness (*buddhi*), which is the source of dreams and the fundamental support of the phenomenal personality.[16]

As we observed in Chapter Four, the narrator's ability to pursue an idea to its logical conclusion is what marks his superiority over Swann, making it possible for him to become a creative artist instead of a dilettante. And, as we saw in Chapter Five, the artist's dedication to creative introspection must outweigh for him every other claim, including those of morality as it is usually understood. The theme of the supreme importance of introspection is stated in an even clearer and more striking way in "Le Temps retrouvé," where the narrator decides to forsake the world and devote himself to the task of writing a book. He says that this is his only reason for wishing to continue to exist. In this, his attitude might conceivably be compared to that of a merciful Bodhisattva who, although he has attained enlightenment and is free to pass on into nirvana, chooses out of compassion to delay his escape from the bonds of existence, in order to help other beings to the "further shore" of enlightenment. Such an attitude lies at the base of much Buddhist art, especially in Japan; those charming views of mountains and clouds which we admire so much as art are intended to convey a message of detachment from one who has lived among those clouds and mountains long enough to be free of all human emotions save that of pity for the bewildered, toiling multitude. But the question must be raised whether compassion and the wish to spread enlightenment were Proust's only motives in writing a book, and whether the wish to survive in some form was not at least one of the considerations which influenced him.

Proust's conviction that it is a supremely important duty to write a great book, if one possibly can, is more understandable in a Hindu-Buddhist than in a Christian context. The Christian, of course, believes that he should make the most of his God-given talents; but Proust makes it clear that he considers writing a great book more valuable than any other use of one's abilities. In other words, if his attitude were really derived *in toto* from Christian belief, then, just

[16] Heinrich Zimmer, *Philosophies of India*, ed. Joseph Campbell (New York: Bollingen Foundation, 1951), p. 363.

as every Christian must wish that everyone else on earth should be a Christian, then it ought to follow that Proust should wish everyone else on earth to be a great author — which is manifestly absurd. But in Hindu-Buddhist terms, his attitude makes better sense, since only a few at any time are able to achieve enlightenment, while the rest continue with the world's work. The day when all mankind had achieved enlightenment would also be the day when all mankind had contrived to escape from the wheel of reincarnation and had consequently vanished from the earth. Proust actually envisages the advent of such a day (in his own terms) with a mixture of disappointed ambition and humorous resignation:

[Bergotte] allait ainsi se refroidissant progressivement, petite planète qui offrait une image anticipée de la grande quand, peu à peu, la chaleur se retirera de la terre, puis la vie. Alors la résurrection aura pris fin, car si avant dans les générations futuras que brillent les œuvres des hommes, encore faut-il qu'il y ait des hommes. Si certaines espèces d'animaux résistent plus longtemps au froid envahisseur, quand il n'y aura plus d'hommes, et à supposer que la gloire de Bergotte ait duré jusque-là, brusquement elle s'éteindra à tout jamais. Ce ne sont pas les derniers animaux qui le liront, car il est peu probable que, comme les apôtres à la Pentecôte, ils puissent comprendre le langage des divers peuples humains sans l'avoir appris [III, 184].

The idea that the world was generating its own destruction and would one day perish — whether of heat or of cold the scientists could not decide — was a commonplace of nineteenth-century thinking. But the idea of combining the scientific theory of the end of the world with the more fanciful notion of reading as a form of resurrection seems to be Proust's own. Although his idea of the way in which "la résurrection aura pris fin" is far from being the same as the Buddhist concept of universal escape from reincarnation, this passage demonstrates, I feel, yet another correspondence between Proust's imagination and that of a Buddhist — a correspondence which, for anyone interested in tracing the history of currents of thought and feeling, is intriguing. However, I have to admit that there is, at the same time, a sharp divergence of opinion between Proust and a typical Buddhist, as demonstrated by this passage, for Proust longs for eternal life (albeit in an aesthetic form) with all the tenacity of a Christian, and is not at all pleased at the prospect of the cessation of reincarnation, a cessation which must be the Buddhist's main goal.

Turning to the question of ethics, we find here what seems to be one of the closest parallels between Proust's attitude and that of a

Buddhist. The altruism of the narrator's mother and grandmother, because of its extreme nature, fits, at first sight, even better into a Buddhist than into a Christian context. The altruism of a truly detached Hindu or Buddhist goes far beyond anything which a Christian, however saintly, would consider reasonable or even right. Heinrich Zimmer gives many examples of this, one of the most striking being that of King Vessantara, who made a vow never to refuse what was demanded of him, no matter how unreasonable the request:

The tale is told, for example, in the popular story of the Children of King Vessantara, of how this pious monarch, who was an earlier incarnation of the Buddha, took a vow never to refuse anything demanded of him: "My heart and eye, my flesh and blood, my entire body — should anyone ask these of me, I would give them." Without a second thought he gave away a wonderful elephant on which the well-being of his kingdom depended, and was consequently driven into exile by his indignant people, together with his loyal queen and two little children. And when he was approached in the wilderness by an ugly old Brāhman who demanded the children as slaves, they were given without a qualm; the queen was demanded, and she too was given, But in the end, the Brāhman revealed that he was Indra, the king of the gods, and stated that he had descended to test the saintly human king, and so all ended well. In this case, the temptation of Indra having failed, the god was gracious in defeat.

Even the crudest, most elementary mind cannot but be amazed and outraged by such demonstrations of saintly indifference to the normal values of human welfare — particularly since nothing whatsoever is gained from them. For what does it really matter if a single dove is preserved from the talons of a hawk, a new born litter of tiger-kittens rescued from starvation, or a senile, nasty old Brāhman gratified in his greed and lust by the enslavement of a little prince and princess? . . .

In terms, however, of the basic problem and task of the Boddhisattva, it is precisely the apparent senselessness, even indecency, of the sacrifice that makes the difference; for to refuse a paradoxical surrender would be to subscribe (if only by negation) to the standards and world vision of the passion-bound, ego-ridden, common individual who has presented the demand.[17]

Zimmer's comments make it clear that Hindu or Buddhist altruism is of such an extreme sort that the other person's wishes are respected simply because they are the wishes of the other person and because it is, as a matter of principle, wrong to have wishes for oneself at all. It is true that Christianity also has a strong tendency in this direction, as instanced by Christ's injunction not only to give in to the person who wants to take our coat from us, but to

[17] Ibid., pp. 537–539.

give him our cloak as well, and to walk two miles with the person
who forces us to accompany him for one mile. But he did not tell us
to abandon innocent children to someone whose intention it would
be to deprave them. So the Hindu or the Buddhist goes beyond the
Christian, although in a way which the Christian would consider
wrong. But of course the altruism of the narrator's mother and
grandmother does not carry them into defiance of traditional morality, so this cannot apply to them. It might, however, apply to the
narrator, at least in the episode in which he feels that his compassion for the Baron de Charlus has involved him in a conflict with
traditional sexual morality. He explains, in this connection, that he
feels completely alienated from this morality when he is confronted
with an individual who has been made to suffer on moral grounds.
His sympathy with suffering then outweighs every other consideration, to the point where he feels that he has no moral sense at all
(III, 291).

Complete forgetfulness of self-interest, although motivated neither
by Christian nor by Hindu-Buddhist considerations, may be found
at moments, in the narrator. In a passage introducing a series of
introspective comments on the nature of his own "altruism," the
narrator represents himself as lingering politely by Elstir, when he
would much rather have been pursuing Albertine and her friends.
Quite unexpectedly, in view of the frivolous, mundane nature of
the immediate context, the narrator connects this with his readiness
to give up his life for his friends. He explains that, because he always looks at things from the point of view of those he happens to
be with, he puts whatever is important to them (including life itself)
before what is important to him. He does this, however, to win their
good opinion and not, as would his grandmother, out of the virtue
of complete altruism. On the contrary, he is a total egoist (I, 852–
854). So we find that the narrator's "altruism," at this point, springs
from a neurotic need for admiration, not from any principle at all.
Later, however, this characteristic bent of the narrator attains a
more refined form since, in "Le Temps retrouvé," he sacrifices his
life in a spirit of true altruism, by dedicating what is left of it to the
creation of a book. We have seen that this could be the attitude of
a merciful Bodhisattva. But, since Hindu-Buddhist and Christian
altruism are not always as easy to distinguish as in the fable of King
Vessantara, we might interpret this decision of the narrator's as an
imitation (in a purely aesthetic sense) of the supreme sacrifice of

Jesus Christ. (As we see from the epigraphs in *Les Plaisirs et les jours*, the *Imitatio Christi* was, at one time, one of Proust's favorite books.) Perhaps this is simply an example of the way in which Hindu-Buddhist and Christian attitudes occasionally overlap.

Fundamental as are the notions of Spirit, rebirth, enlightenment, Yogic concentration, and compassion in the Hindu-Buddhist scheme of things, the Hindu-Buddhist idea which was best known to the contemporaries and immediate predecessors of Proust was that of maya. The doctrine of maya is that of the illusory nature of the world of appearances, an idea which fascinated both Schopenhauer and Leconte de Lisle (although the latter misunderstood it by conceiving of it in an excessively absolute, because dualist, sense, as A. R. Chisholm explains in his *Towards "Hérodiade"*).[18] If we were to consider every example of illusion in *A la Recherche du temps perdu*, we should end by quoting almost the entire work. The presentation of character, for example, involves a continual interplay of truth and illusion with, as we observed in Chapter Three, truth turning out, as often as not, to be a modified form of what we originally took to be an illusion. The importance of optics in the Proustian presentation of reality seems to form an important part of this. But some of Proust's most striking presentations of the interplay of truth and illusion are not optical, but auditory. So, as Hindus points out in *The Proustian Vision*, we get a remarkable sequence of subsequently rectified auditory illusions in the passage describing the narrator's visit to Saint-Loup at Doncières.[19] The narrator thinks he hears someone moving around in the room, but discovers, on opening the door, that what he had heard was the movement of the logs of wood in the fire. Then he is unable to locate the ticking of a watch until he sees it. A person with cotton wadding in his ears, he goes on to remark, has a totally different impression of the world from one who does not. Hence (although Hindus makes no comment on this) he draws a conclusion which is quite unexpected in an occidental context but perfectly normal in an oriental one: that is, the lesson of total detachment:

Et à ce propos on peut se demander si pour l'Amour (ajoutons même à l'Amour l'amour de la vie, l'amour de la gloire, puisqu'il y a, paraît-il, des gens qui connaissent ces deux derniers sentiments) on ne devrait pas agir comme ceux qui, contre le bruit, au lieu d'implorer qu'il cesse, se bouchent

[18] Alan Rowland Chisholm, *Towards "Hérodiade": A Literary Genealogy* (Melbourne: Melbourne University Press, 1934), pp. 32–67.

[19] Hindus, pp. 113–114.

les oreilles; et, à leur imitation, reporter notre attention, notre défensive, en nous-même, leur donner comme objet à réduire, non pas l'être extérieur que nous aimons, mais notre capacité de souffrir par lui [II, 75].

However, although the world of appearance is illusory, for Hindu and Buddhist alike, when compared to the absolute reality of the Atman, for the Buddhist, or Brahman-Atman (i.e. God in the human soul), for the Hindu, it is not illusory in an absolute sense. This view was expressed in an authoritative manner by the ancient Hindu philosopher Śaṃkara:

While asserting the identity of the *Brahman* with the *Ātman*, and denying that the world was outside the Supreme, he did not accept the description of the world as a pure illusion. Waking experiences are different from dreams and external objects are not merely forms of personal consciousness. Śaṃkara explains the appearance of the world with an analogy. A person may mistake a rope for a serpent. The serpent is not there, but it is not entirely an illusion, for there is the rope. The appearance of the serpent lasts until the rope is closely examined. The world can be compared with the serpent and the *Brahman* with the rope. When we acquire true knowledge we recognise that the world is only a manifestation of the *Brahman*. The precise relationship between the *Brahman* and the world is inexpressible and is sometimes referred to as *māyā*.[20]

Humphreys expresses the same opinion more elliptically when he says that, for the Buddhist, phenomena are "unreal in a world of unreality, comparatively real in a world of comparative reality. Real in that each is part of an ultimate, unmanifest Reality." [21] In a way which is at least superficially similar, Proust insists that, however much our view may be obscured by the element of the relative and the subjective, certain truths do exist and may be ascertained. As Hindus points out, Proust demonstrably believes that the truth may be arrived at, albeit with great difficulty.[22] His interest in medical diagnoses is closely connected with this, since there may be many diagnoses, and yet, in any one patient, there is but one ailment and one cure.[23] Finally, Proust makes his belief in the reality of truth crystal clear when he says, of the German atrocities in Belgium, that, whether people wanted to believe in them or not, they were real.[24] But, in spite of the superficial similarity between Proust's attitude toward the interplay of truth and illusion and that of a Buddhist or Hindu, we cannot say that the two attitudes are

[20] Kshiti Mohan Sen, *Hinduism* (Baltimore: Penguin Books, 1961), p. 83.
[21] Humphreys, p. 15.
[22] Hindus, p. 115.
[23] Ibid., pp. 116–117.
[24] Ibid., p. 118.

identical unless we suppose that the truths at which Proust arrives are, for him, equivalent to transcendental Truth.

Sleep and dreams, which form an important part of the interplay of truth and illusion (since, in Proust's opinion, we may learn important truths under the illusory appearance of a dream) figure largely in Proust's work and, in fact, serve as an introduction to it. In the opening section of "Du Côté de chez Swann," the narrator drifts from one illusory state to another. From the borderland between sleeping and waking, he falls into dreaming, then into deep sleep, struggles from there into states of waking illusion, and finally arrives at true awareness with the dawning of day. This movement may be taken as an allegory of the novel as a whole. In "Le Temps retrouvé," the narrator says that dreams had always fascinated him, partly by the way in which they show up the completely subjective nature of our emotions, and partly by the tricks they play with time, tricks which had made him wrongly suppose, at one point, that they were one of the means of recovering lost time (III, 911–912). We see from this that we may obtain some truths from dreams, but that we are in the grip of an illusion if we suppose that they will give us the key to the most important truths. There is a considerable corpus of Hindu speculation about the exact relation to reality of various kinds of sleep and dreams.[25] The clearest example is to be found in a Hindu fable which is quoted by Aldous Huxley in his *The Perennial Philosophy*.[26] According to this fable, Indra, the representative of the gods, and Virochana, the representative of the Asuras (demons or titans), both went to a famous teacher to be taught the nature of the Self. In order to test their awareness of spiritual matters, the teacher gave them one incomplete and misleading answer after the other, in the hopes that they would realize that this was not the real truth and so request further enlightenment. He began by telling them that they would see the Self if they looked at their own reflections in a pool. This led Virochana to suppose that the Self was the physical body and consequently adopt a philosophy of material satisfaction, but Indra realized that this explanation of the Self was inadequate. Successively, his teacher suggested to Indra that the Self was the being which we are in dreams and the being which we are in deep sleep. But Indra saw the fallacies in both these explanations. Finally, his teacher, seeing that he was ready for the real answer,

---

[25] Zimmer, pp. 330, 353, 362, 377, 415, 452.

[26] Aldous Huxley, *The Perennial Philosophy* (London: Chatto and Windus, 1946), pp. 233–236.

explained to him the true nature of the Self. So it appears that, for the Hindu, dreams and deep sleep are unsatisfactory approximations of ultimate Reality, just as, for Proust, they are unsatisfactory approximations of the most important spiritual experience. Although they may provide some truths, there is too much illusion in them for them to open the door to Truth.

For the Hindu or the Buddhist, a thread of relation holds these truths, half-truths, real illusions, and apparent illusions together. Sometimes the relation is that of cause and effect, sometimes of space, sometimes of time. The sequence of cause and effect manifests itself as karma, on which Hindus comments with some eloquence. For him, Proust's morality is basically Judaeo-Christian. But something Hindu may be seen in it at the moment when the narrator's wrongdoing in watching the Lesbian scene at Montjouvain is both punished and made apparent for the first time by his suffering over Albertine's boast that Mlle Vinteuil is one of her dearest friends. Hindus sees in this event the operation of karma, that process by which everything we say, think, or do leads to an inevitable consequence, in one life or another. In passing, he remarks that Emerson had the notion of a similar moral force, and called it compensation.[27] Moving on from this to other forms of relation, we may observe that the interrelations of space are most strikingly demonstrated in the dance of the spires of Martinville, and those of time in the superimposition of the past and present, by means of the narrator's involuntary memories. The concept of relation is basic to Buddhist thought. Both it and maya are based on the concept of Mind-Only:

All manifested things, when analysed and taken to pieces, are found to lack continuous form or unchanging substance. As all is Mind, Mind-Only, all things, all compounds, are *Sunyata*, Void of ultimate content, a truth which has had profound effect on the finest of Buddhist art. All things are One and have no life apart from it; the One is all things and is incomplete without the least of them. Yet the parts are parts within the whole, not merged in it; they are interfused with Reality while retaining the full identity of the part, and the One is no less One for the fact that it is a million-million parts.[28]

Proust may not have meant something too different when he wrote: "Je m'étais rendu compte que seule la perception grossière et erronée place tout dans l'objet quand tout est dans l'esprit . . ." (III, 912). But in the case of this statement, the One is the individual

[27] Milton Hindus, *A Reader's Guide to Marcel Proust* (New York: Farrar, Straus and Cudahy, 1962), p. 123.
[28] Humphreys, p. 17.

mind with its value judgments, not the Whole. Because the individual's view of reality is essentially a construction of the mind, for the Buddhist, that mind also creates the relations between individual parts of material reality:

In the beginning is the One and only the One *is*. From the One comes Two, the innumerable Pairs of Opposites. But there is no such thing as two, for no two things can be conceived without their relationship, and this makes Three, the basic Trinity of all manifestation. From the three (or its six permutations and integrating seventh) come the manifold things of "usual life" which the Chinese call the Ten Thousand Things. These are unreal in a world of unreality, comparatively real in a world of comparative reality, Real in that each is part of an ultimate, unmanifest Reality. As Reality must be, if anything is, supremely Enlightened, this faculty of supreme Enlightenment informs all things, though none of them owns it. It alone is Real.[29]

In this connection, it may not be too fanciful to refer once more to the spires of Vieuxvicq and Martinville, as they move in their dance, appearing now as two spires followed by one, now as three together, and now as one in which the three have been absorbed. As we noticed in Chapter Seven, Elliott Coleman claims that a reference to the Trinity is meant. But it appears from the above quotation that a symbolism based on threes does not have to be Christian. (Neither does it have to be based on a Buddhist original, of course: three seems like a very natural symbol for relation.) It is not without interest to observe that there is also a progression in time from one to three as we move from the church at Combray, with its single spire, to that of Saint-André-des-Champs, with its twin spires, and finally to the three spires of Vieuxvicq and Martinville. The trees of Hudimesnil also fit into this symbolism, of course.

One cannot regard any form of relation as being more real than the rest. On this topic, Christmas Humphreys says: "The interrelation of all forms of life is absolute and intrinsic. Cause and effect are one, though we see the two sides of the coin in the relative illusion of time. For causation is only interrelation expanded into the 'past', 'present', and 'future' for convenience of our understanding and is only one mode of interrelation."[30] This casts an interesting light on the oft-quoted but seldom analyzed statement made by Proust about the importance of metaphor in his work:

Ce que nous appelons la réalité est un certain rapport entre ces sensations et ces souvenirs qui nous entourent simultanément — rapport que supprime

[29] Ibid., p. 16.
[30] Ibid., p. 19.

une simple vision cinématographique, laquelle s'éloigne par là d'autant plus du vrai qu'elle prétend se borner à lui — rapport unique que l'écrivain doit retrouver pour en enchaîner à jamais dans sa phrase les deux termes différents. On peut faire se succéder indéfiniment dans une description les objets qui figuraient dans un lieu décrit, la vérité ne commencera qu'au moment où l'ecrivain prendra deux objets différents, posera leur rapport, analogue dans le monde de l'art à celui qu'est le rapport unique de la loi causale dans le monde de la science, et les enfermera dans les anneaux nécessaires d'un beau style; même, ainsi que la vie, quand, en rapprochant une qualité commune à deux sensations, il dégagera leur essence commune en les réunissant l'une et l'autre pour les soustraire aux contingences du temps, dans une métaphore [III, 889].

In other words, the metaphor may be considered as a means of divesting causation of its unfounded claim to be the only real form of relation, by substituting for it another, more obviously mind-created form of relation.

Finally, two other of Proust's basic structural forms, the circle and the spiral, may be understood in a Buddhist sense: "The process of becoming is a circle; the process of becoming more, of growth, is a spiral, either up or down according as the growth is towards or away from wholeness." [31] Again, this is a natural metaphor; that is, one which could occur spontaneously in a mind with the poetic habit of thinking in symbols. That it is also Buddhist is an interesting coincidence.

Thus far, we have considered the ways in which Proust's way of thinking parallels Buddhism. But, striking as these similarities may be, there are equally striking differences. The most basic difference is the fact, with which we have found ourselves continually confronted, that, for Proust, the ultimate reality seems to be the human mind and spirit, whether taken individually or in a collective sense, and not something transcendental. Zaehner sees the integration of the two levels of the narrator's personality as Buddhist; but it would appear, from our quotations of Humphreys, that the Self — although the Buddhist refuses, unlike the Hindu, to talk about God — is something more transcendental than a part of the human psyche which can go missing or be recovered by the workings of the memory, whether voluntary or not. Perhaps the fact that Zaehner, as a Catholic and a student of Islam, is most frequently concerned in his studies and experience with a theistic version of Ultimate Reality, led him to develop a rather too prosaic, down-to-earth version of the Buddhist's experience. Because he saw that the Buddhist's

[31] Ibid., p. 23.

experience was not theistic, he was perhaps too ready to see it as simply natural. An equally serious impediment to regarding Proust's attitude as truly Hindu-Buddhist lies in the fact that, in the last resort, Proust is not entirely free of the illusions he denounces. He has conveyed their charm too well for that charm ever to be entirely broken. If the narrator retreats from the world and the flesh (a retreat which, of course, may be understood as Christian just as much as Buddhist), it is in disappointment and indignation that they have failed to keep their promises; not with the smiling irony of one who has gone so far in the way of detachment that he can hardly remember what those promises were. And no true ascetic, whether Buddhist or Hindu, would be capable of producing imagery of such voluptuousness (especially where food is concerned). What Proust says of the *madeleine* is also true of his style: it is "si grassement sensuel sous son plissage sévère et dévot" (I, 47). He is perhaps more like a Christian in this, in view of the fact that the Christian believes that the material world has been redeemed by the Incarnation, and that, while God is a Spirit and must be worshiped in the spirit, the conclusion that the spirit is the only good and that matter is wholly bad is heretical. But it is true, of course, that, as we have noticed again and again in this study, Proust's mind is characterized by a flight toward the spirit and away from material reality, matter being valued by him, in his more thoughtful moments, only insofar as it can be transformed into spirit. So the doctrine of the Incarnation appears to have influenced him far less than that of the Resurrection, insofar as his thinking is Christian.

Proust's Buddhism, like his Christianity, is in the last resort a metaphor. The two metaphors combine well enough, even to the point of overlapping, owing to similarities between the two religions. We have seen how completely the narrator's moments of involuntary memory may be interpreted in Christian terms and then, again, how they may equally well be explained by a natural mystical experience of a Buddhist (or semi-Buddhist) nature. In the end, since they form the basis for an art work which offers the only kind of escape from time seriously contemplated by Proust, they appear to be neither Christian nor Buddhist, but primarily aesthetic.

But in spite of all we can say to minimize them, Proust's Buddhist mannerisms do remain a fact, and one which is not easily explained away. Zaehner, not being a Proust critic, has every right to express surprise at Proust's Buddhist tendencies and leave the matter at that. As a student of religion, he is free to assume that Proust had a Buddhist experience which one does not have to invoke literary influences to explain. But in a study of this nature, some explanation, however inadequate, has to be attempted. To begin with, we can say that Proust does not appear to have been totally ignorant of Hindu-Buddhist concepts. For instance, his reference to reincarnation may be based on Hindu-Buddhist beliefs, although he may equally well have been thinking of the Pythagorean concept. Again, his reference to the Hindu caste system (I, 16) and his description of Albertine as a many-headed goddess of time (II, 365) (although in this second instance he may have been thinking of a Janus figure) indicate at least a superficial acquaintance with Hinduism. Furthermore, there is a very odd passage in which he describes Morel's state of near collapse, in his fright at being spied on by Charlus in a brothel, in terms which read like a parody of nirvana, that state which involves extinction without annihilation: "On avait l'impression de cette équivoque qui fait qu'une religion parle d'immortalité, mais entend par là quelque chose qui n'exclut pas le néant" (II, 1081).

These references are fleeting and far from respectful, but we do find some very respectful allusions, in "Combray," to certain lines in which Bergotte writes of the illusory nature of appearance (maya, in fact) in strongly Buddhist terms. Among other things, Bergotte is said to write of the "vain songe de la vie" and "l'inépuisable torrent des belles apparences" (I, 94). It is my impression that, at this moment, Bergotte represents Leconte de Lisle. These quotations rmind me strongly of the conclusion of Leconte de Lisle's poem *La Maya*:

La Vie antique est fait inépuisablement
Du tourbillon sans fin des apparences vaines.[32]

Most of the explicit references to Leconte de Lisle in *A la Recherche du temps perdu* are to that poet's Greek side, and most of these, again, are rather mischievously put into the mouth of the ridiculous Bloch. But it is demonstrably the Buddhist side of Leconte de Lisle which made the greatest impression on Proust as an adolescent. In *Jean Santeuil*, he wrote: "Les vastes poèmes de Leconte de Lisle, qui après avoir joué avec le Temps disaient avec une force éclatante le rêve de la vie et le néant des choses, étaient plus vivants, plus profonds, plus nourrissants pour lui que les œuvres classiques d'où

[32] Charles Leconte de Lisle, *Œuvres*, 4 vols. (Paris: A. Lemerre, 1881), III, 169.

cette inquiétude est absente." [33] On the following page, Jean Santeuil decides to quote the last two lines of *La Maya* as an epigraph
to his intended great work and append to it the following inscrip-
tion: "Celui qui a écrit ce livre sait que tout est vanité mais,
etc. . . ." [34] That is to say that, already as an adolescent, Proust was
deeply affected by the very special version of Buddhism evolved by
Leconte de Lisle, in which maya and the void confront each other
as opposite and equally valid absolutes, only to be reconciled in the
cult of beauty. As Irving Putter points out, Leconte de Lisle reacted
to the dissolving influence of the notion of the void by setting up
beauty as an absolute, by means of which one can enter into immortality.[35] As Leconte de Lisle says in *Hypatie*:

> Elle seule survit, immuable, éternelle,
> La mort peut disperser les univers tremblants,
> Mais la Beauté flamboie, et tout renaît en elle,
> Et les mondes encor roulent sous ses pieds blancs.[36]

The fact that Proust puckishly applied these lines to Odette (I, 639)
does not diminish the effect which Leconte de Lisle's advocacy of
beauty as the ultimate reality seems to have had on him. Rather it
suggests that, while Proust was fully aware of the stupidity and futility of Odette as an individual woman, he was willing to concede
a certain metaphysical value to her undeviating preoccupation with
her own appearance. As a woman who creates beauty, even if it is
only her own beauty, Odette is, to a certain extent, an artist. Again,
if one takes into account the fact that Proust, with all his irony and
cynicism, did not regard the world with quite the unrelieved gloom
of Leconte de Lisle, what Putter says about this poet finding
the religious values for which he sought, as a transcendental correc-
tive to his pessimism about life, in art,[37] may also be applied to
Proust.

Schopenhauer, again, whose influence on Proust we noted in
Chapters One and Five, is a source of Hindu-Buddhist ideas, not
only for Proust but for many of the writers whom Proust read. With
what may be interpreted as a delight in being deliberately misleading, but which may equally well be an indication of the extent

---

[33] Proust, *Jean Santeuil*, I, 124.

[34] Ibid., p. 125.

[35] Irving Putter, *The Pessimism of Leconte de Lisle: The Work and the Time*,
University of California Publications in Modern Philology, XLII, No. 2 (Berkeley
and Los Angeles: University of California Press, 1961), p. 383.

[36] Leconte de Lisle, II, 68.

[37] Putter, p. 384.

to which he had absorbed Schopenhauer's ideas wtihout retaining a conscious awareness of his debt to this philosopher, Proust makes only two direct allusions to Schopenhauer, both rather unimportant, while the two more important allusions which he makes (but without identifying the author he has in mind) are somewhat humorous. One of these is a reference to Schopenhauer's theory of love, in connection with the attraction of opposites,[38] while the other, put into Swann's mouth (where it may have, unknown to Swann, serious overtones, suggesting that Swann ought to have found something of the sort in music and is a mere blasphemer for claiming that he cannot find it), is a contradiction of Schopenhauer's belief that music is the direct expression of the Cosmic Will.[39] Nevertheless, Hindus' claim that Schopenhauer was one of the most important philosophical influences on Proust really seems justified.

Oddly enough, Hindus does not pay much attention to Schopenhauer's interest in Hindu-Buddhist ideas. He does use the word nirvana to characterize the chief lesson which Proust learned from Schopenhauer — that of the mystical value of artistic contemplation[40] — but otherwise he neglects this particular aspect, perhaps because he considers it self-evident. What is ironical, by the way, about this allusion to Buddhism, is that Schopenhauer's ideal of lucid, detached contemplation of the inner essence of the cosmic will would strike a true Buddhist as falling very far short of nirvana. Still, Schopenhauer tells us again and again how much he owed to the ancient Hindu texts (which later formed the basis for Buddhism). For instance, he calls the Vedas "the fruit of the highest human knowledge and wisdom, the kernel of which has at last reached us in the Upanishads as the greatest gift of this century." [41] Again, expressing the strongest admiration for Indian philosophy, he says: "In India our religions will never take rest. The ancient wisdom of the human race will never be displaced by what happened in Galilee. On the contrary, Indian philosophy streams back to Europe, and will produce a fundamental change in our knowledge and thought." [42]

In his opening paragraph, Schopenhauer informs us that his

---

[38] I, 727; cf. Schopenhauer, *The Metaphysics of the Love of the Sexes*, in *The Philosophy of Schopenhauer*, edited, with an introduction, by Irwin Edman (New York: Random House, 1956), pp. 337–376.
[39] I, 534; cf. Schopenhauer, *The World as Will and Idea*, I, 333.
[40] Hindus, *The Proustian Vision*, pp. 100–101.
[41] Schopenhauer, *The World as Will and Idea*, I, 458.
[42] Ibid., pp. 460–461.

basic doctrine, "The world is my idea," is confirmed by the Vedanta. The passage by Sir William Jones on the Vedanta which he cites expresses the doctrine of "Mind-Only." [43] The various forms of relation — time, space, and causation — have a purely relative value. This, he says, quoting the passage from Śaṃkara about the serpent and the rope, is explained by the Hindus in terms of maya.[44] Several times Schopenhauer refers to the phenomenal world and to the cosmic will which drives it on in terms of maya. For instance, he explains the special pleasure which we obtain from tragedy by saying that the tragic hero, shortly before his end, reaches a state of enlightenment which completely destroys the power of the cosmic will within him, and in which maya, as a consequence, no longer deceives him:

> In one individual it [the will] appears powerfully, in another more weakly; in one more subject to reason, and softened by the light of knowledge, in another less so, till at last, in some single case, this knowledge, purified and heightened by suffering itself, reaches the point at which the phenomenon, the veil of Maya, no longer deceives it. It sees through the form of the phenomenon, the *principium individuationis*. The egoism which rests on this perishes with it, so that now the motives which were so powerful before have lost their might, and instead of them the complete knowledge of the nature of the world, which has a *quieting* effect on the will, produces resignation, the surrender not merely of life, but of the very will to live. Thus we see in tragedies the noblest men, after long conflict and suffering, at last renounce the ends they have so keenly followed, and all the pleasures of life for ever, or else freely and joyfully surrender life itself.[45]

This interpretation of the attitude of the tragic hero is somewhat reminiscent of the attitude of the narrator in "Le Temps retrouvé," since the narrator has given up clinging to the pleasures of life. However, the parallel is not quite complete, since he does dread his approaching death. But there is at least one moment before that when he is so completely possessed by the cosmic will in the form of the sexual urge that he feels himself to be, as it were, its embodiment, and therefore immortal. Consequently he is in the grip of maya.

La mort eût dû me frapper en ce moment que cela m'eût paru indifférent ou plutôt impossible, car la vie n'était pas hors de moi, elle était en moi; j'aurais souri de pitié si un philosophe eût émis l'idée qu'un jour, même éloigné, j'aurais à mourir, que les forces éternelles de la nature me survivraient, les forces de cette nature sous les pieds divins de qui je n'étais

[43] Ibid., p. 4.
[44] Ibid., p. 9.
[45] Ibid., p. 327.

qu'un grain de poussière, qu'après moi il y aurait encore ces falaises arrondies et bombées, cette mer, ce clair de lune, ce ciel [I, 933].

Again, Schopenhauer says, as does Proust after him, that existence is constant sorrow and pain, especially if we regard the phenomenal world as real.[46] The particular ills of age and death, however bitter at the time, are the less a cause of constant pain in that they are universal. But minor ills are inescapable and deeply felt. We shake off one only to find ourselves in the grip of another, and, so long as we fail to achieve detachment, tedium is the only alternative to suffering.[47] (We may think here of the way in which the narrator divides his feelings toward Albertine between agonized suffering when she arouses his jealousy and ennui when he is sure of her possession). This deeply felt awareness of the universality of suffering (although Schopenhauer does not say so at this point) is at the root of Buddhism. In all the legends of Gautama Buddha, we hear how the young prince found his vocation through his discovery of old age, sickness, and death. The extinction of desire, he decided, was the only cure for the suffering arising from these ills.[48] Later on, however, Schopenhauer affirms that the Buddhist hope of nirvana is based on the wish to avoid birth, age, sickness, and death, since nirvana is the state in which these things no longer exist.[49] Schopenhauer also talks of the Hindu-Buddhist idea of reincarnation, although he refashions this idea in the special form of the survival of the individual in the species. This concept is very strikingly outlined at the beginning of the fourth book of *The World as Will and Idea*.[50] As we have seen, this is also one of the forms which the idea of reincarnation takes in *A la Recherche du temps perdu*.

In addition, we may say that it is possible that Proust found some of his Hindu-Buddhist ideas in Emerson, who was quite strongly influenced by the oriental scriptures. Although I have not discovered any references in Proust to this side of Emerson, I think the following quotation serves to indicate the admiration which Proust felt for this thinker and his conviction that allusions to Emerson's writings could only serve to elevate the tone of any conversation. In this passage, M. de Charlus is berating the narrator for giving moral support to Robert de Saint-Loup in his liaison with Rachel:

[46] cf. Hindus, *The Proustian Vision*, p. 88.
[47] Schopenhauer, *The World as Will and Idea*, I, 402.
[48] Humphreys, pp. 31–32.
[49] Schopenhauer, *The World as Will and Idea*, I, 460.
[50] Ibid., pp. 356–364.

"Allez auprès de Robert. Je sais que vous avez participé ce matin à un de ces déjeuners d'orgie qu'il a avec une femme qui le déshonore. Vous devriez bien user de votre influence sur lui pour lui faire comprendre le chagrin qu'il cause à sa pauvre mère et à nous tous en traînant notre nom dans la boue."

J'aurais voulu répondre qu'au déjeuner avilissant on n'avait parlé que d'Emerson, d'Ibsen, de Tolstoï, et que la jeune femme avait prêché Robert pour qu'il ne bût que de l'eau [II, 278].

Moreover, Henry Bonnet informs us of the admiration felt for Emerson by Alphonse Darlu.[51] Proust may very well have come across Emerson's idea of compensation which, as Milton Hindus remarks, is similar to the notion of karma. This would certainly explain how such a notion appeared in Proust's personal philosophy. Again, that there should be a parallel between compensation and karma is far from surprising, in view of Emerson's interest in oriental religion. Arthur Christy seems to think that Emerson formed this idea before hearing of the Hindu doctrine.[52] If his idea of compensation was not actually based on that of karma, then it was certainly reinforced by it. In addition, Emerson's concept of the Over-Soul, Christy points out, is close to the Hindu doctrine of Brahman-Ātman, while Emerson was also attracted by the notion of maya.[53]

Finally, we may point to two other possible sources of Buddhist ideas in Proust's work. Anatole France wrote a brief article on Buddhism which was included in *La Vie littéraire* (1888–92).[54] In this article, which Proust, with his youthful enthusiasm for the author, may very well have read, France speaks of Buddhism as constituting a system of ethics rather than a religion, since it has no gods. He praises this ethical system for its elevation, sweetness, and tolerance. Then he goes on to retell the story of Gautama Buddha and to give an account of his teaching of pity, resignation, humility, gentleness, and detachment. After saying that nirvana, which he defines as absolute repose, does not appeal to the average Westerner, he concludes by narrating a Buddhist legend which preaches detachment from desire. Proust may have acquired a favorable impression of Buddhism from this article, but it did not provide him with extensive information on Buddhist doctrine.

[51] Bonnet, p. 23.

[52] Arthur Christy, *The Orient in American Transcendentalism: A Study of Emerson, Thoreau and Alcott* (New York: Columbia University Press, 1932), pp. 11–12.

[53] Ibid., pp. 20, 86.

[54] Anatole France, *La Vie littéraire*, 3 vols. (Paris: Calmann-Lévy, 1919), III, 379–387.

A much more learned article, by Hippolyte Taine, based on *Die Religion des Buddha und ihre Entstehung* by M. Koeppen, appeared in the *Journal des Débats*, March, 1864, and was then included in *Nouveaux Essais de critique et d'histoire*,[55] which was first published in 1865 but was frequently reprinted after that. Taine gives an amount of information on the history and teachings of Buddhism which far exceeds that provided by Anatole France. This article may also be regarded as supplementing the account given by Schopenhauer, in that it includes a history of pre-Buddhist Indian religion, a less personal version of maya, a more accurate definition of nirvana, an account of Buddhist cosmology, and an allusion to the story of King Vessantara. It would be interesting to know if Proust ever read Taine's article, but unfortunately we have no evidence that he did.

Whatever his debt to France and Taine, it seems apparent that, in Leconte de Lisle, Schopenhauer, and Emerson, Proust may well have found an abundance of Hindu-Buddhist ideas — quite enough to account for his treatment of the themes of enlightenment, altruism (although this concept is also Christian), reincarnation, appearance, and relation. At the same time, the supposition that these ideas came to him through these secondary sources also accounts for the differences between his treatment of these themes and the significance which they have in real Buddhism. For instance, we may point to the precedent of Leconte de Lisle to explain Proust's decision to embody the fruits of his "enlightenment" in a novel instead of betaking himself to a life of pious asceticism. The only "Buddhist" element in Proust left completely unaccounted for is his concept of the nature of the self. For lack of evidence to the contrary, we have to suppose that this, insofar as it went beyond the idea of the universal mind or spirit, was Proust's own invention. The only way in which we can explain this parallel between Proust's thought and Buddhist belief is by saying that when Proust and the Buddhist philosophers analyzed themselves, what they saw was something very similar. This brings us back to the question whether Proust actually had a natural mystical experience. Doubtless we shall never know, for, in addition to our lack of evidence, the taste for the simulation of mysterious and "occult" experiences by two of those authors whom Proust names as his predecessors[56] must leave

---

[55] Hippolyte Taine, *Nouveaux Essais de critique et d'histoire* (Paris: Hachette, 1909), pp. 258–314.

[56] E.g., Nerval and Baudelaire (III, 919–920).

us permanently in doubt. To conclude this consideration of Hindu-Buddhist tendencies in Proust, we may add that much other evidence of Hindu-Buddhist influence (whether basic or superficial) on nineteenth-century German and French literature could be adduced. Readers who are interested in this subject may consult the works of A. R. Chisholm, P. Martino, Irving Putter, and S. Radhakrishnan.[57]

At this point, I feel I should make it clear that I do not believe for one moment that Proust wrote *A la Recherche du temps perdu* with the deliberate intention of propagating Hindu-Buddhist ideas or of demonstrating how much he owed to the philosophy of Schopenhauer. As he said in his youthful attack on the lesser Symbolists, a good author does not set out to illustrate a thesis; rather, because he has a particular feeling about life which he expresses in a very powerful way, he ends up by producing a kind of philosophy which owes nothing to the method of the philosophers:

Le romancier bourrant de philosophie un roman qui sera sans prix aux yeux du philosophe aussi bien que du littérateur, ne commet pas une erreur plus dangereuse que celle que je viens de prêter aux jeunes poètes et qu'ils ont non seulement mise en pratique mais érigée en théorie.

Ils oublient, comme ce romancier, que si le littérateur et le poète peuvent aller en effet aussi profond dans la réalité des choses que le métaphysicien même, c'est par un autre chemin, et que l'aide du raisonnement, loin de le fortifier, paralyse l'élan du sentiment qui seul peut les porter au cœur du monde. Ce n'est pas par une méthode philosophique, c'est par une sorte de puissance instinctive que *Macbeth* est, à sa manière, une philosophie.[58]

The allusion to Shakespeare is illuminating. Although Shakespeare did not set out to propound a philosophy, he did nevertheless express one, and one which was strongly colored by the form of Christianity which was current in Elizabethan England. In the same way as Shakespeare's mind was shaped by Christianity, Proust was marked emotionally by the "Buddhist" and "mystical" elements in his philosophical and literary reading. If we add to this the presence in Proust of an analytical, rationalistic, skeptical, agnostic mind which still (in true *fin-de-siècle* fashion) preserved a taste for religious things, and if we also consider the possibility (however remote) that he also had a natural mystical experience, then the fact

[57] Chisholm, pp. 15, 28–31, 33–61, 134–135; Pierre Martino, *Parnasse et Symbolisme (1850–1900)* (Paris: A. Colin, 1935), pp. 33–43; Putter, pp. 160–166; and Sarvepalli Radhakrishnan, *Eastern Religions and Western Thought* (New York: Oxford University Press, 1959), pp. 247–251 and *passim*.

[58] Proust, *Chroniques* (Paris: N.R.F., 1936), p. 154.

that his work seems somewhat Buddhist as well as semi-Christian (in view of the fact that Buddhism is the only religion to combine mysticism with a refusal to call upon the name of God) becomes less and less surprising.

Linked by its use of vocabulary and certain basic attitudes to two world religions, the Proustian religion of art still claims autonomy and awaits worshipers. Will it find them? Certainly, Proust's readers, to judge by the number of critical studies which appear on him, multiply daily. Even *Vogue* feels constrained to take note of his existence. But does this mean that all these readers bow the knee before Proust's central doctrine? Or do they read his work with other aims in view? Aldous Huxley, writing in the 1940s, scoffed at the prevalence among intellectuals of a religious attitude toward culture, an attitude which he thought a poor substitute for real religion.[59] This suggests that there were then many potential, if not always actual, adherents of Proust's religion of art. But in 1964 there appeared a book which attacked the religion of art quite as fervently as it attacked traditional Christianity, and for much the same reasons. This book was Sartre's autobiography, *Les Mots.*

In his autobiography, Sartre explains the adoration for literature which he first began to feel in early childhood by the influence of his grandfather's religious attitude toward belles-lettres, an attitude which was, at the same time, much more closely based on Christianity than Proust's religion of art and, according to Sartre, extremely common in the nineteenth century. In the opinion of Sartre's grandfather, beauty, whether it was found in works of literature or in Nature, brought men back to God. Operating in works of literature was the Spirit (that is, the Holy Spirit) which spoke to God of men and to men of God.[60] Although, in conformity with this view, he ought to have been overjoyed at the idea that his grandson had a literary vocation, Sartre's grandfather felt alarm at the idea that the boy might come to resemble Verlaine, whose poetry he appreciated but whose person he despised, a fear comparable to the grandmother's fear, in *A la Recherche du temps perdu,* that the narrator might come to emulate Baudelaire, Poe, Verlaine, and Rimbaud.[61] But, in spite of his grandfather's efforts to lead him toward a teaching career and away from full-time writing, the young Sartre was too deeply marked by the religion of art not to conceive

[59] Huxley, p. 127.
[60] Sartre, *Les Mots* (Paris: Gallimard, 1964), pp. 46, 147.
[61] Ibid., p. 129.

the idea that the material world was in the grip of Evil and that what he had to do was to seek salvation (a salvation which would apply to other men as well as to himself), by dying to self and to the world and dedicating himself to the contemplation of the Ideas.[62] Looking back on his childhood from his full maturity, Sartre explains the religious nature of his attitude to literature as we have found ourselves compelled, in this study, to explain Proust's use of Christian langauge to spread the religion of art: that is, by a displacement of the sacred from Catholicism, which no longer seemed believable, to literature, which could still command faith. In this religious attitude the young Sartre had no difficulty in incorporating (as did Proust) the ideas of faith, predestination, and eternal life in the form of immortal fame. Sartre concludes by saying that the religion of art remained at the back of his mind long after he had lost all temptation to think about God. But now his atheism has triumphed over the religion of art as well as over the Christian religion, although he still continues to write, and he sometimes wonders whether he is not cherishing his old dreams in secret.[63]

If Sartre's attitude were to prevail in the years to come, then *A la Recherche du temps perdu* might well take on the aspect of that deserted temple of a long-forgotten cult which Proust feared it might become. But there is one detail which may give hope to Proust's admirers, even as they envisage this gloomy prospect. Although Sartre makes no allusion in *Les Mots* to any other French classic, except to say what his attitude toward it was when he was a child, he quotes from Proust to make a point about one of his feelings. Speaking of the impulse toward a literary career which he received from his grandfather, he compares himself, wondering whether he is not working to fulfill the wishes of a dead old man in a way which the latter would not fail to condemn, to Swann telling himself that he has been wasting his life for a woman who was not his type.[64] Even though the religion of art may be dead for Sartre (and perhaps deservedly dead, in view of its parasitic dependence on traditional religious feeling to establish its claims), Proust's analyses of character and delineations of emotional experience are still alive for him, and can be used by him as valid examples, as unhesitatingly as if he were referring to a familiar friend. Perhaps the religion of art was too deeply rooted in a particular moment of time, a moment

[62] Ibid., pp. 147–148.
[63] Ibid., pp. 207–212.
[64] Ibid., p. 135.

when Christianity was fading away and other beliefs were fascinating the Western mind, but when religious language still held its force, to survive for long the passing of that moment. But if the religion of art does die, aesthetic agnostics may still read *A la Recherche du temps perdu* and find inspiration in it, as religious agnostics can read *The Divine Comedy* and find inspiration in that, today.

BIBLIOGRAPHY

I. MARCEL PROUST: WORKS

a) *Fiction, Criticism, and Journalism*:

A la Recherche du temps perdu, texte établi et présenté par Pierre Clarac et André Ferré, 3 vols. (Paris: Gallimard, 1954).

Remembrance of Things Past, trans. C. K. Scott Moncrieff, 2 vols. (New York: Random House, 1934).

Chroniques (Paris: Gallimard, 1936).

Contre Sainte-Beuve, suivi de Nouveaux Mélanges (Paris: Gallimard, 1954).

Pastiches et mélanges (Paris: Gallimard, 1958).

Les Plaisirs et les jours (Paris: Calmann Lévy, 1896).

Jean Santeuil, 3 vols. (Paris: Gallimard, 1952).

Textes retrouvés, recueillis et présentés par Philip Kolb et Larkin B. Price, avec une bibliographie des publications de Proust (1892–1967) (Urbana: University of Illinois Press, 1968).

b) *Translations and Prefaces*:

La Bible d'Amiens de John Ruskin, traduction, notes et préface par Marcel Proust (Paris: Mercure de France, 1926).

Propos de peintre de Jacques-Émile Blanche, 3 vols. (Paris: Émile Paul, 1919–28), I, *De David à Degas*, préface par Marcel Proust.

Sésame et les lys: des trésors des rois; des jardins des reines de John Ruskin, traduction, notes et préface par Marcel Proust (Paris: Mercure de France, 1935).

Tendres stocks de Paul Morand, préface par Marcel Proust (Paris: Gallimard, 1921).

c) *Correspondence*:

A un ami (Paris: Amiot-Dumont, 1948).

Autour de soixante lettres de Marcel Proust par Lucien Daudet, Les Cahiers Marcel Proust, V (Paris: Gallimard, 1929).

Choix de lettres, présentées et datées par Philip Kolb (Paris: Plon, 1965).

Correspondance avec sa mère, lettres inédites, présentées et annotées par Philip Kolb (Paris: Plon, 1953).

Correspondance générale de Marcel Proust, publiée par Robert Proust et Paul Brach, 6 vols. (Paris: Plon, 1930–36).

Lettres à André Gide, avec trois lettres et deux textes d'André Gide (Neuchâtel: Ides et Calendes, 1949).

Lettres à Reynaldo Hahn, présentées, datées et annotées par Philippe Kolb; préface d'Émmanuel Berl (Paris: Gallimard, 1956).

Lettres à une amie: recueil de quarante-et-une lettres inédites adressées à Marie Nordlinger, 1889–1908 (Manchester: Éditions du Calame, 1942).

Lettres de Marcel Proust à Bibesco (Lausanne: Guilde du livre, 1949).

Lettres retrouvées, présentées et annotées par Philip Kolb (Paris: Plon, 1966).

Marcel Proust et Jacques Rivière, correspondance (1914–1922) présentée et annotée par Philip Kolb (Paris: Plon, 1955).

II. PROUST STUDIES

Autret, Jean. *L'Influence de Ruskin sur la vie, les idées et l'œuvre de Marcel Proust* (Genève: Droz, 1955).

Barker, Richard Hindry. *Marcel Proust: A Biography* (New York: Criterion Books, 1958).

Beckett, Samuel. *Proust* (New York: Grove Press, 1957).

Bell, Clive. *Proust* (New York: Harcourt Brace, 1929).

Bell, William Stewart. *Proust's Nocturnal Muse* (New York: Columbia University Press, 1962).

Benoist-Méchin, Jacques. *La Musique et l'immortalité dans l'œuvre de Marcel Proust* (Paris: S. Kra, 1926).

Bersani, Leo. *Marcel Proust: The Fictions of Life and of Art* (New York: Oxford University Press, 1965).

Bonnet, Henri. *Alphonse Darlu (1849–1921), le maître de philosophie de Marcel Proust* (Paris: Nizet, 1961).

————. *Le Progrès spirituel dans l'œuvre de Marcel Proust,* 2 vols. (Paris: Vrin, 1946–49).

Brée, Germaine. "La Conception proustienne de 'l'esprit,' " *Cahiers de l'Association Internationale des Études Françaises,* No. 12 (juin, 1960), 199–210.

————. *Du Temps perdu au temps retrouvé: introduction à l'œuvre de Marcel Proust* (Paris: Les Belles Lettres, 1950).

————. *The World of Marcel Proust* (London: Chatto and Windus, 1967).

Cattaui, Georges. *L'Amitié de Proust,* Les Cahiers Marcel Proust, VIII (Paris: Gallimard, 1935).

————. *Marcel Proust,* précédé de *Vie et survie de Marcel Proust* par P. de Boisdeffre (Paris: Éditions Universitaires, 1958).

————. *Marcel Proust: Proust et son temps; Proust et le temps* (Paris: Julliard, 1952).

Celly, Raoul. *Répertoire des thèmes de Marcel Proust,* Les Cahiers Marcel Proust, VII (Paris: Gallimard, 1935).

Champigny, Robert. "Temps et reconnaissance chez Proust et quelques philosophes," *PMLA,* LXXIII (March, 1958), 129–135.

Chernowitz, Maurice Eugene. *Proust and Painting* (New York: International University Press, 1945).

Cocking, John Martin. *Proust* (London: Bowes and Bowes, 1956).

Coleman, Elliott. *The Golden Angel: Papers on Proust* (New York: Coley Taylor, 1954).

Curtius, Ernst Robert. *Marcel Proust*, traduit de l'allemand par Armand Pierhal (Paris: La Revue Nouvelle, 1928).

Daniel, Georges. *Temps et mystification dans "A la Recherche du temps perdu"* (Paris: Nizet, 1963).

De Chantal, René. *Marcel Proust, critique littéraire*, 2 vols. (Montréal: Les Presses de l'Université de Montréal, 1967).

Deleuze, Gilles. *Marcel Proust et les signes* (Paris: Presses Universitaires de France, 1964).

De Ley, Herbert. *Marcel Proust et la duc de Saint-Simon* (Urbana: University of Illinois Press, 1966).

Entretiens sur Marcel Proust, sous la direction de Georges Cattaui et Philip Kolb (Paris, La Haye: Mouton, 1966).

Ferré, André. *Les Années de collège de Marcel Proust* (Paris: Gallimard, 1959).

Fiser, Émeric. *L'Esthétique de Marcel Proust* (Paris: La Revue Française, 1933).

Girard, René, ed. *Proust: A Collection of Critical Essays* (Englewood Cliffs, N.J.: Prentice-Hall, 1962).

Gordon, Pauline (Newman). *Marcel Proust et l'existentialisme* (Paris: Nouvelles Éditions Latines, 1953).

Graham, Victor E. *The Imagery of Proust* (Oxford: Basil Blackwell, 1966).

Green, Frederick Charles. *The Mind of Proust: A Detailed Interpretation of "A la Recherche du temps perdu"* (Cambridge: Cambridge University Press, 1949).

Hier, Florence. *La Musique dans l'œuvre de Marcel Proust* (New York: Columbia University Press, 1933).

Hindus, Milton. *The Proustian Vision* (New York: Columbia University Press, 1954).

———. *A Reader's Guide to Marcel Proust* (New York: Farrar, Straus and Cudahy, 1962).

Hommage à Marcel Proust, Les Cahiers Marcel Proust, I (Paris: Gallimard, 1927).

Houston, John Porter. "Literature and Psychology: the Case of Proust," *L'Esprit Créateur*, V, No. 1 (Spring, 1965), 3–13.

Jaquillard, Pierre. "En Marge de la Recherche du temps perdu," *Bulletin de la Société des Amis de Marcel Proust et des Amis de Combray*, No. 14 (1964), 160–165; No. 15 (1965), 304–327.

———. "Le Grain de moutarde ou l'Esthétique de la grâce," *Études Asiatiques* (1953), 134–152.

Johnson, Pamela Hansford. "Marcel Proust: Illusion and Reality" in *Essays by Divers Hands*, Transactions of the Royal Society of Literature, n.s., XXXII (London, 1963), 58–71.

Kneller, John William. "The Musical Structure of Proust's 'Un Amour de Swann,'" *Yale French Studies*, II, No. 2 (1949), 55–62.

Kolb, Philip. *La Correspondance de Marcel Proust: chronologie et commentaire critique* (Urbana: University of Illinois Press, 1949).

———. "Proust et Ruskin: nouvelles perspectives," *Cahiers de l'Association Internationale des Études Françaises*, No. 12 (juin, 1960), 259–273.

———. "Some Proustian Enigmas," a paper delivered at the seventy-sixth annual meeting of the Modern Language Association, before the Romance section, in Chicago, December 27, 1961.

Lempart, Magda Edith. "La Transposition esthétique de la morale chrétienne dans l'œuvre de Marcel Proust" (diss. University of California at Los Angeles, 1962).

Martin-Deslias, Noël. *Idéalisme de Marcel Proust* (Paris: Nagel, 1952).

Mauriac, Claude. *Proust par lui-même* (Paris: Éditions du Seuil, 1959).

Mauriac, François. *Du Côté de chez Proust* (Paris: Éditions de la Table Ronde, 1947).

Maurois, André. *A la Recherche de Marcel Proust* (Paris: Hachette, 1949).

Mein, Margaret. *Proust's Challenge to Time* (Manchester: Manchester University Press, 1962).

Miller, Milton L. *Nostalgia: A Psychological Study of Marcel Proust* (Boston: Houghton Mifflin, 1956).

Monnin-Hornung, Juliette. *Proust et la peinture* (Genève: Droz, 1951).

Moss, Howard. *The Magic Lantern of Marcel Proust* (London: Faber and Faber, 1963).

Mouton, Jean. *Proust* (Bruges: Desclée De Brouwer, 1968).

Nathan, Jacques. *La Morale de Proust* (Paris: Nizet, 1953).

Painter, George Duncan. *Marcel Proust: A Biography*, 2 vols. (London: Chatto and Windus, 1959–65).

Pierre-Quint, Léon. *Marcel Proust, sa vie, son œuvre* (Paris: Éditions du Sagittaire, 1925).

Piroué, Georges. *La Musique dans la vie, l'œuvre et l'esthétique de Proust* (Paris: Éditions Denoël, 1960).

————. *Par les chemins de Marcel Proust: essai de critique descriptive* Neuchâtel: A la Baconnière, 1955).

Pommier, Jean. *La Mystique de Proust* (Paris: Droz, 1939).

Poulet, Georges. *L'Espace proustien* (Paris: Gallimard, 1963).

Shattuck, Roger. *Proust's Binoculars: A Study of Memory, Time and Recognition in "A la Recherche du temps perdu"* (New York: Random House, 1963).

Spitzer, Leo. "L'Étymologie d'un 'Cri de Paris,'" *Romanic Review*, XXV, No. 3 (October, 1944), 244–250.

Strauss, Walter A. *Proust and Literature* (Cambridge, Mass.: Harvard University Press, 1957).

Trahard, Pierre. *L'Art de Marcel Proust* (Paris: Éditions Dervy, 1953).

Vallée, Claude. *La Féerie de Marcel Proust* (Paris: Fasquelle, 1959).

Vial, André. *Proust: structures d'une conscience et naissance d'une esthétique* (Paris: Julliard, 1963).

Zéphir, Jacques J. *La Personnalité humaine dans l'œuvre de Marcel Proust, essai de psychologie littéraire* (Paris: M. J. Minard, 1959).

III. STUDIES OF LITERATURE

Benda, Julien. *La France byzantine, ou le Triomphe de la littérature pure: Mallarmé, Gide, Proust, Valéry, Alain, Giraudoux, Suarès, les surréalistes; essai d'une psychologie originelle du littérateur* (Paris: Gallimard, 1945).

Butor, Michel. *Essais sur les modernes* (Paris: Gallimard, 1964).

Chisholm, Alan Rowland. *Towards "Hérodiade": A Literary Genealogy* (Melbourne: Melbourne University Press, 1934).

Christy, Arthur. *The Orient in American Transcendentalism: A Study of Emerson, Thoreau and Alcott* (New York: Columbia University Press, 1932).

Fiser, Émeric. *Le Symbole littéraire, essai sur la signification du symbole chez Wagner, Baudelaire, Mallarmé, Bergson et Proust* (Paris: Corti, 1941).

Martino, Pierre. *Parnasse et symbolisme (1850–1900)* (Paris: A. Colin, 1935).

Meyerhoff, Hans. *Time in Literature* (Berkeley and Los Angeles: University of California Press, 1955).

Petitbon, René. *L'Influence de la pensée religieuse indienne dans le romantisme et le parnasse: Jean Lahor* (Paris: Nizet, 1962).

Poulet, Georges. *Études sur le temps humain* (Paris: Plon, 1950).

Ullman, Stephen. *The Image in the Modern French Novel: Gide, Alain-Fournier, Proust, Camus* (Cambridge: Cambridge University Press, 1960).

————. *Style in the French Novel* (Cambridge: Cambridge University Press, 1957).

Wilson, Edmund. *Axel's Castle: A Study in the Imaginative Literature of 1870–1930* (New York: Charles Scribner's Sons, 1931).

IV. STUDIES IN MYSTICISM AND RELIGION

St. Augustine. *Confessions*, translated, with an introduction, by R. S. Pine-Coffin (Harmondsworth: Penguin Books, 1961).

Eliade, Mircea. *Images and Symbols: Studies in Religious Symbolism*, trans. Philip Mairet (New York: Sheed and Ward, 1961).

————. *The Myth of the Eternal Return*, trans. Willard R. Trask, Bollingen Series, XLVI (New York: Pantheon Books, 1954).

————. *Patterns in Comparative Religion*, trans. Rosemary Sheed (New York: Sheed and Ward, 1958).

France, Anatole. *La Vie littéraire*, 3 vols. (Paris: Calmann-Lévy, 1919).

Humphreys, Christmas. *Buddhism* (Harmondsworth: Penguin Books, 1955).

Huxley, Aldous. *The Perennial Philosophy* (London: Chatto and Windus, 1946).

James, William. *The Varieties of Religious Experience: A Study in Human Nature, Being the Gifford Lectures on Natural Religion, Delivered at Edinburgh in 1901–1902* (New York: Longmans, Green and Co., 1915).

Pascal, Blaise. *Pensées et opuscules*, publiés . . . par Léon Brunschvicg (Paris: Hachette, 1951).

Radhakrishnan, Sarvepalli. *Eastern Religions and Western Thought* (New York: Oxford University Press, 1959).

Sen, Kshiti Mohan. *Hinduism* (Baltimore: Penguin Books, 1961).

Taine, Hippolyte. *Nouveaux Essais de critique et d'histoire* (Paris: Hachette, 1909).

Underhill, Evelyn. *Mysticism: A Study in the Nature and Development of Man's Spiritual Consciousness* (New York: E. P. Dutton, 1911).

Zaehner, Robert Charles. *Mysticism, Sacred and Profane: An Inquiry into Some Varieties of Præternatural Experience* (New York: Oxford University Press, 1961).

Zimmer, Heinrich. *Philosophies of India*, ed. Joseph Campbell (New York: Bollingen Foundation, 1951).

V. STUDIES IN PHILOSOPHY AND ART

Collingwood, Robin George. *The Principles of Art* (New York: Oxford University Press, 1958).

Gardiner, Patrick. *Schopenhauer* (Harmondsworth: Penguin Books, 1963).

Langer, Suzanne K. *Problems of Art: Ten Philosophical Lectures* (New York: Charles Scribner's Sons, 1957).

Malraux, André. *La Métamorphose des dieux* (Paris: Gallimard, 1957).

———. *Les Voix du silence* (Paris: Gallimard, 1951).

Maritain, Jacques. *Art et scolastique* (Paris: Rouart, 1935).

———. *La Responsabilité de l'artiste*, traduction de l'anglais par Georges et Christiane Brazzola, revue par l'auteur (Paris: A. Fayard, 1961).

Pool, Phoebe. *Impressionism* (London: Thames and Hudson, 1967).

Sartre, Jean Paul. *L'Etre et le néant, essai d'ontologie phénoménologique* (Paris: Gallimard, 1949).

———. *Les Mots* (Paris: Gallimard, 1964).

Schopenhauer, Arthur. *The Metaphysics of the Love of the Sexes*, in *The Philosophy of Schopenhauer*, edited, with an introduction, by Irwin Edman (New York: Random House, 1956).

———. *The World as Will and Idea*, trans. R. B. Haldane and J. Kemp, 3 vols. (London: Routledge and Kegan Paul, 1883).

Lewis, Wyndham. *Time and Western Man* (London: Chatto and Windus, 1927).

VI. CHARLES LECONTE DE LISLE: WORKS AND STUDIES

a) *Works*:

Œuvres, 4 vols. (Paris: A. Lemerre, 1881).

b) *Studies*:

Putter, Irving. *Leconte de Lisle and His Contemporaries*, University of California Publications in Modern Philology, XXXV, No. 2 (Berkeley and Los Angeles: University of California Press, 1951), pp. 65–107.

———. *The Pessimism of Leconte de Lisle: Source and Evolution*, University of California Publications in Modern Philology, XLII, No. 1 (Berkeley and Los Angeles: University of California Press, 1954), pp. 1–144.

———. *The Pessimism of Leconte de Lisle: The Work and the Time*, University of California Publications in Modern Philology, XLII, No. 2 (Berkeley and Los Angeles: University of California Press, 1961).

VII. JOHN RUSKIN: WORKS AND STUDIES

a) *Works*:

The Art of England and the Pleasures of England: Lectures Given in Oxford in 1883–1885 (London: G. Allen, 1904).

La Bible d'Amiens de John Ruskin, traduction, notes et préface par Marcel Proust (Paris: Mercure de France, 1926).

Giotto and His Works in Padua, Being an Explanatory Notice of the Frescoes in the Arena Chapel (London: G. Allen, 1900).

Modern Painters, 5 vols. (London: G. Allen, 1904).

Sésame et les lys: des trésors des rois; des jardins des reines de John Ruskin, traduction, notes et préface par Marcel Proust (Paris: Mercure de France, 1935).

The Stones of Venice, 3 vols. (London: G. Allen, 1907).

b) *Studies*:

Autret, Jean. *L'Influence de Ruskin sur la vie, les idées et l'œuvre de Marcel Proust* (Genève: Droz, 1955).

Evans, Joan. *John Ruskin* (New York: Oxford University Press, 1954).

Rosenberg, John D. *The Darkening Glass: A Portrait of Ruskin's Genius* (New York: Columbia University Press, 1961).

INDEX

Albertine Simonet: narrator does not want to take her to Venice, 41; telegram apparently from her, 42; narrator's first impression, 49–50; visits Marcouville-l'Orgueilleuse, 51; listens to the narrator discussing Dostoevsky, 57; listens to the narrator discussing Vermeer, 57, 126; Lesbianism, 58, 89, 189; listens to the narrator discussing Tolstoy, 68; prestige, 73; as an art work, 73, 74; behavior, 87; visit to the Trocadéro, 87, 89; rendezvous at the Verdurins' concert, 89; narrator's love, 91, 142, 161; plays Vinteuil, 92; plays the pianola, 97; kept by the narrator, 119; hounded by the narrator, 119; goodnight kiss, 143; need for redemption, 143–144; boasts of friendship with Mlle Vinteuil, 189

Albigensianism, 173

Altruism, 99–100, 124, 128, 184–186

Amiens Cathedral, 168

Appearance, 178. *See also* Truth and illusion

Arabian Nights, 25, 158

Art: Japanese, 61; Buddhist, 182. *See also* Elstir; Impressionists

Artha, 182

Atman, 178–179, 198

Augustine, St.: *Confessions*, 159

Balbec: three trees, 4, 8, 9, 10, 92; involuntary memory, 5, 43, 158; Legrandin's description, 30; Legrandin's sister's residence, 31; imaginary fisher-girl, 37; narrator's longing for, 38–39; narrator's first visit, 42; Elstir pictures, 51, 58–67; prestige, 66; like Vinteuil's septet, 94; narrator with grandmother, 99–100; lack of virtues, 105; narrator meets Mme de Villeparisis, 108; view from hotel window, 137–138; Baron de Charlus watches waiters, 145

Balbec church, 101, 136, 137

Balzac, Honoré de, 29, 113

Baudelaire, Charles, 108, 116, 199 fn, 201; *Correspondances*, 95; *L'Imprévu*, 78; *Le Voyage*, 41

Beausergent, Mme de, 108

Bellini, Gentile, 91, 94

Bergotte: last illness, 7; appreciated by Swann and Bloch, 28; monograph on Racine, 28; visits cathedrals with Gilberte, 28; reveals beauty, 33, 64; has ideas coincide with the narrator's, 34; narrator's, image of Bergotte, 34; confers prestige on Gilberte, 37–38; his style and the narrator's, 44; praises La Berma, 66; heightens narrator's feeling for Albertine, 73; socially

195; the Vedas, 195; Mind-Only, 196; surrender of the will to live, 196; pessimism, 197; nirvana, 197; rebirth, 197

Schubert, Franz Peter, 93

Self, 6, 159, 162, 176, 177, 178–180, 181–182, 188–189, 191, 199

Sévigné, Charles de, 129

Sévigné, Mme de: used as a standard by narrator's grandmother, 20–21, 128–129; literary technique, 65; quoted by narrator's grandmother after her stroke, 100; balance, 108; appreciated by the Baron de Charlus, 108, 129; and Christian values, 128–129

Shakespeare, William, 200

Sherbatoff, Princesse, 112

Simonet, Albertine, *See* Albertine Simonet

Skandhas, 180

Sleep, 178, 188

Society as a snare, 27–28

Sodom, 135, 145

Spectrum, 53

Spirit, 15, 18, 76, 88, 98, 152, 178, 192, 202. *See also* Spirituality

Spirituality, 8, 10, 18, 32, 35, 36, 76, 79, 80, 88, 96–98

Stained glass, 50, 53, 54, 72, 132, 137

Sufism, 173, 174, 176–177

Suffering and artistic production, 114, 118–119

Swann, Charles: and the narrator's mother, 23; quotes Saint-Simon to narrator's grandfather, 25; timid attitude to art, 26, 27, 28, 30; collection of paintings, 26; attitude towards society, 26–27; gives narrator reproductions of Gozzoli and Giotto, 55; "idolatry," 69, 70–71, 81, 92, 142; sees Odette as Botticelli's *Zipporah*, 69, 70–71, 81; response to music, 79–86; love for the *petite phrase*, 79–81; uses the *petite phrase* to foster his love for Odette, 81–82; jealous of Forcheville, 82; tirade against Mme Verdurin and music, 82; re-

fuses to listen to the Vinteuil sonata, 83; goes to Mme de Saint-Euverte's, 83; *petite phrase* reminds him of Odette's love, 84; no longer loves Odette, 86; married to Odette, 86; waning enthusiasm for music, 86; thinks about Odette at Mme de Saint-Euverte's, 89; fails to attain creative spiritual awareness through music, 86, 92; unable to think things through, 92; secretive about his social contacts, 103; kind to Vinteuil and his daughter, 103; encouraged by the Verdurins, 106; rejected by the Verdurins, 107; refuses to gossip, 107; disapproved of by narrator's grandfather for associating with the Verdurins, 108; tells the Guermantes he will be dead in three months, 112; studies Vermeer, 126; referred to by Sartre, 202

Swann, Gilberte. *See* Gilberte Swann

Swann, Odette. *See* Odette Swann

Symbolists, 14, 125, 200

Symbols, 56

Taine, Hippolyte: *Nouveaux Essais de critique et d'histoire*, 199

Tansonville, 1, 103

Tintoretto, 70

Tissot, James, 60

Tolstoy, Count Leo Nikolayevich, 68, 198; *War and Peace*, 68

Travel, 87; and literature, 35–36, 39, 40, 41; and love, 36–37, 37–38, 40, 41, 42, 43

Tristan, 156

Trocadéro, 87, 89, 136

Truth and illusion, 32–36, 49, 50, 54–55, 56, 177, 186, 187–189, 193, 194, 196–197, 198

Turner, Joseph Mallord William, 54, 58; *Bernard Castle*, 59; *The Castle and Regattas at East Cowes*, 59; *The Crook of the Lune*, 59; *Fishermen in the Wind*, 59; *Lulworth Cove*, 59; *The Mouth of the*

DATE DUE

DEMCO 38-297